Jesus and the Nations

Jesus and the Nations

Discipleship and Mission in the Gospel of Matthew

Cedric E. W. Vine

PICKWICK *Publications* · Eugene, Oregon

JESUS AND THE NATIONS
Discipleship and Mission in the Gospel of Matthew

Pickwick Publications
An Imprint of Wipf and Stock Publishers
199 W. 8th Ave., Suite 3
Eugene, OR 97401

www.wipfandstock.com

PAPERBACK ISBN: 978-1-6667-3248-1
HARDCOVER ISBN: 978-1-6667-2625-1
EBOOK ISBN: 978-1-6667-2626-8

Cataloguing-in-Publication data:

Names: Vine, Cedric E. W., author.

Title: Jesus and the nations : discipleship and mission in the Gospel of Matthew / by Cedric E. W. Vine.

Description: Eugene, OR: Pickwick Publications, 2022 | Includes bibliographical references and index.

Identifiers: ISBN 978-1-6667-3248-1 (paperback) | ISBN 978-1-6667-2625-1 (hardcover) | ISBN 978-1-6667-2626-8 (ebook)

Subjects: LCSH: Bible. Matthew—Criticism, interpretation, etc. | Christian life—Biblical teaching. | Missions—Biblical teaching.

Classification: BS2575.2 V5 2022 (print) | BS2575.2 (ebook)

08/09/22

Contents

Preface

THERE ARE THREE REASONS I have written this study on discipleship and mission in the Gospel of Matthew. The first is academic in nature. My doctoral thesis, undertaken at the University of Sheffield, UK, was a critique of one scholarly approach to the Gospel of Matthew in which it is understood to have been written for a very specific audience—a Matthean community, usually located in Antioch or elsewhere in the Roman province of Syria (cf. Matt 4:24).[1] In such readings the Gospel is less a story retelling the events of Jesus's life, death, and resurrection, and more a description of a later community's conflict with wider Judaism sometime in the 80s or 90s CE. I joined a growing number of British and American scholars who have reacted against this way of reading the Gospel by offering my own critique of Matthean community reconstructions. Essentially my thesis attempted to prove a negative, arguing what the Gospel is not about. In this study I aim to build up rather than pull down. I will read the Gospel as intended for an open audience with a particular focus on the themes of discipleship and mission.

The second reason is more personal in nature. I serve in a Christian community in which the Gospel Commission of Matt 28:16–20 plays an important role. It is frequently referred to when defining what it means to be a true follower of Jesus. The central purpose of the disciple is, so the Evangelist tells us, to make other disciples. This is the purpose of the church. Too often, however, the Gospel Commission is explained without

1. Vine, *Audience of Matthew*.

reference to the rest of the Gospel. Other New Testament texts or current missiological theories are instead used to explain the nature of the Commission and how it is to be achieved. I want to read the Gospel Commission in light of the rest of the Gospel.

The third reason for this study relates to the future of the church. In recent decades many parts of the Western world have transitioned from Christian majority to Christian minority societies. For the church to renew itself in such contexts it is necessary to consider afresh New Testament visions of what it means to be a follower of Jesus involved in God's mission. The Gospel of Matthew with its emphasis on discipleship and mission is a great place to start in that it does not presuppose Christendom. It is a narrative that focuses on the nation of Israel and the nations of the Gentiles. This makes it uniquely relevant for post-Christian contexts in which nation states or supranational unions have stepped into the void created by the decline of Christendom. In many other parts of the world, however, the church is growing at a phenomenal rate, forcing the issue of the relationship between the church and state to the fore. In both these contexts, the church needs a vision for the city and nation that extends beyond expanding the four walls of the church. A vision of a transformed society is required, a political theology. The Gospel of Matthew provides us with just such a vision.

Cedric E. W. Vine
September 2021
Andrews University

Abbreviations

AYBRL	Anchor Yale Bible Reference Library
BDAG	Walter Bauer, Frederick W. Danker, W. F. Arndt, and F. W. Gingrich. *Greek-English Lexicon of the New Testament and Other Early Christian Literature*. 3rd ed. Chicago: University of Chicago Press, 2000.
Bib	*Biblica*
BZAW	Beihefte zur Zeitschrift für die alttestamentliche Wissenschaft
BZNW	Beihefte zur Zeitschrift für die neutestamentliche Wissenschaft
CBQ	*Catholic Biblical Quarterly*
CBQMS	Catholic Biblical Quarterly Monograph Series
Charlesworth	*The Old Testament Pseudepigrapha*. Vols. 1 and 2. Edited by James H. Charlesworth. New Haven: Yale University Press, 1983, 1985.
EDEJ	*The Eerdmans Dictionary of Early Judaism*. Edited by John J. Collins and Daniel C. Harlow. Grand Rapids: Eerdmans, 2010.
HALOT	*A Concise Hebrew and Aramaic Lexicon of the Old Testament*. Edited by William L. Holladay. Leiden: Brill, 2000.
IBS	*Irish Biblical Studies*
ICC	International Critical Commentary
JBL	*Journal of Biblical Literature*
JSNT	*Journal for the Study of the New Testament*
JSNTSup	Journal for the Study of the New Testament Supplement Series
JSOTSup	Journal for the Study of the Old Testament Supplement Series
LCL	Loeb Classical Library

Abbreviations

LNTS	Library of New Testament Studies
NICNT	New International Commentary on the New Testament
NETS	*A New English Translation of the Septuagint*. Edited by Albert Pietersma and Benjamin G. Wright. Oxford: Oxford University Press, 2007.
NovTSup	Supplements to Novum Testamentum
NRSV	New Revised Standard Version
NTS	*New Testament Studies*
OCD	*The Oxford Classical Dictionary*. Edited by Simon Hornblower et al. 4th ed. Oxford: Oxford University Press, 2012.
SBL	Society of Biblical Literature
SNTSMS	Society for New Testament Studies Monograph Series
TDNT	*Theological Dictionary of the New Testament*. 10 vols. Edited by Gerhard Kittel and Gerhard Friedrich. Grand Rapids: Eerdmans, 1964–1976.
WUNT	Wissenschaftliche Untersuchungen zum Neuen Testament
VT	*Vetus Testamentum*
WBC	Word Biblical Commentary

Discipleship and Mission in the Gospel of Matthew

Introduction

THIS IS A STUDY on the nature of discipleship and mission in the Gospel of Matthew. Its central observation is that there are five prominent roles in the Gospel of Matthew that are consistently used to define what it means to be a follower of Jesus. Two passages illustrate this phenomenon:

> Whoever welcomes a *prophet* in the name of a *prophet* will receive a *prophet's* reward; and whoever welcomes a *righteous person* in the name of a *righteous person* will receive the reward of *the righteous*; and whoever gives even a cup of cold water to one of *these little ones* in the name of a *disciple*—truly I tell you, none of these will lose their reward." (Matt 10:41–42, italics supplied)[1]

> Therefore I send you *prophets, wise men,* and *scribes,* some of whom you will kill and crucify, and some you will flog in your synagogues and pursue from town to town. (Matt 23:34, italics supplied)

These five roles—prophets, righteous persons, disciples, wise men, and scribes—are found throughout the Gospel. In the Sermon on the Mount, for example, Jesus refers to true and false prophets (5:12; 7:15), the righteous (5:6, 45; cf. 5:20), the wise and the foolish (7:24–27), and scribes (5:20). All five roles feature prominently in the sermon and contribute

---

1. Unless indicated otherwise, scriptural quotations are from the NRSV.

to the framing of what it means to be a follower of Jesus. Matthew 13 explicitly refers to prophets, righteous persons, and scribes (13:17, 52). It also alludes to wise men and discipling (13:11, 52). For the richness of the chapter to be fully appreciated, it must be read in a manner sensitive to each of these different roles. Matthew 24 and 25 similarly refer to true and false prophets (24:11, 15, 24), the righteous and the unrighteous (25:37, 46), the wise and the foolish (25:1–13). These chapters also include a warning of the lawlessness his followers can expect to encounter (24:12), a state exacerbated by scribes who are themselves internally lawless (cf. 23:28). These examples strengthen the impression that the Evangelist has intentionally interspersed references and allusions to each of the five roles throughout his Gospel.

This study is broad in scope and integrative in nature. It addresses the nature of these five roles and how they relate to the person of Jesus and his mission. In essence, I will argue that these five roles are the means by which King Jesus establishes his sovereignty over the nations. These roles function for the Evangelist at the level of the *polis* or nation and offer a counterpoint to, a critique of, contemporary national functionaries equivalent to the Old Testament prophetic critique of the elders, priests, scribes, wise men, and prophets of Israel (e.g., Isa 28:7; Jer 18:18; Ezek 7:26).[2] Not every city or nation is exposed to all five roles. The city of Nineveh repented in response to a prophet, Jonah (Matt 12:41). The queen of the South travelled from the ends of the earth to listen to a wise man, Solomon (12:41). In contrast, Israel is exposed to all five roles, to a climax of revelation that represents a final pre-judgment attempt by God to reassert divine sovereignty over the nation. Here I use the term nation to refer to a large body of people united by a shared history, culture, and geographical location. I will argue that these five roles are not unique to the mission to Israel but rather that they serve as the template for the mission to the nations expounded in the Gospel Commission of Matt 28:16–20.

Approaches to Matthean Discipleship

Understanding discipleship as relating primarily to the *polis* or nation represents a paradigm shift when we consider three prominent approaches to Matthean discipleship. First, a number of scholars have focused on the

2. Cf. Sigal, *Halakhah of Jesus*, 97.

characterization of the Twelve.[3] The advantage of this approach is that it focuses on a clearly defined character group within the Gospel. However, a significant problem from a mission perspective is that the Twelve are decidedly imperfect examples. One minute they demonstrate great faith or insight, the next minute they crumble under pressure. Focusing on the Twelve still leaves the reader seeking a positive ideal for mission. Such readings are typically ahistorical, apolitical, and church-focused and reduce the goal of mission to making disciples rather than, as stated in the Gospel Commission, the making of "disciples of all nations" (Matt 28:19). The God-to-nation dynamic is typically ignored.

A second approach is reflected in the work of those scholars who focus on one of the five roles I have identified.[4] Such studies are often extremely valuable in helping us understand elements of Matthean discipleship. The main weakness of such studies is that they usually concentrate on just one or two of these roles. Some focus on the followers of Jesus as prophets, others on them as wise men or sages, and still others on them as disciples or scribes. My purpose is twofold: (1) to synthesise the insights of such studies in order to present a wholistic and integrative ideal identity that recognizes each role of prophet, righteous person, disciple, wise man, and scribe; and (2) to suggest how these various roles relate to each other as a theological-missional vision. This mission is, as we shall see, highly political in nature.

A third approach has been the widespread scholarly focus on the Gospel as the product of a late first-century Matthean community, usually located on the basis of the reference to Syria in Matt 4:24 either in Antioch or somewhere in or north of Galilee.[5] The Matthean community is an imag-

---

3. E.g., Edwards, *Matthew's Narrative Portrait*, 1–18; Wilkins, *Concept of the Disciple*, 126–72.

4. On the prophet, see Knowles, *Jeremiah in Matthew's Gospel*; Turner, *Israel's Last Prophet*. On righteous and innocent persons, Przybylski, *Righteousness*, 111; Hamilton, *Death of Jesus*. On disciples, Boxall, *Discovering Matthew*, 91–105; Kinney, *Hellenistic Dimensions*. On wisdom and wise men, Suggs, *Wisdom*; Burnett, *Testament*; Deutsch, *Hidden Wisdom*; and, *Lady Wisdom*. On scribes, Cope, *Matthew*; Orton, *Understanding Scribe*; Stendahl, *School of St. Matthew*; Duling, "Matthew as Marginal Scribe"; and, *Marginal Scribe*; Goulder, *Midrash*.

5. See, for example, Gnilka, *Das Matthäusevangelium*, 513–15; Overman, *Matthew's Gospel*, 150–61; Saldarini, *Matthew's Christian-Jewish Community*, 84–122; Sim, *Christian Judaism*, 31–62; Waetjen, *Matthew's Theology*, 11–16. Konradt accepts the possibility of an ethnically mixed community that is "open and targeted to outsiders, that included members of varying levels of commitment, a clientele for the Gospel who are interested in mission to both Jews and Gentiles" (*Israel*, 359).

ined community, inferred from the Gospel, in which the Evangelist served and to which he addressed his Gospel. Scholars who adopt this approach typically provide allegorical readings of the Gospel in which, for example, the Peter of the Gospel is interpreted as a representation of a later leader of the Matthean community, the other disciples are taken as a representation of the rest of the community, and the Pharisees represent those within post-70 CE Judaism who opposed the community. The Gospel is primarily read as a window into later church history rather than as an account of the life and teachings of Jesus of Nazareth. The Evangelist's goal is typically suggested to be the definition and maintenance of the boundaries of his Jewish-Christian community in contradistinction to formative Judaism.

The advantage of this approach is that it seeks to define clearly the first audience of the Gospel. It takes history seriously. Such reconstructions have been challenged, however, by a number of scholars, most notably Richard Bauckham.[6] He criticized community readings for treating the Gospels as though they were epistles, as though, like Paul's epistles, they were written with the aim of intentionally reflecting and addressing a local community setting. He also argued against the idea that early Christians were divided into isolated communities, presenting plausible evidence that early Christians travelled and interacted extensively over wide geographical distances. On this basis, he concluded that early Christians understood themselves to be part of a movement rather than isolated and competing communities and that the Evangelists presumed an open audience for their works, that the Gospels were intended for *all* Christians. I too have added to the debate in *The Audience of Matthew* in which I developed Bauckham's thesis by offering a critique of the literary and historical assumptions that lie behind many Matthean community reconstructions.[7] I concluded that, while I could not prove beyond doubt an intention on the part of the Evangelist to address *all* Christians, the Gospel of Matthew is written in such a manner that suits such a reading. When he included the Gospel Commission in his gospel, he must have understood the enormity of the task ahead and the likelihood that it would take more than one generation to accomplish. If so, the Evangelist anticipated future generations of readers and produced a text without an impending use-by-date.

6. Bauckham, "For Whom Were the Gospels Written?," 9–22. See also Allison, "Was There a 'Lukan Community'?," 62–64; Stanton, *New People*, 45–46; "Revisiting Matthew's Communities," 11–12; Holmberg, *Sociology and the New Testament*, 124–25; Barton, "Can We Identify the Gospel Audiences?," 178.

7. Vine, *Audience of Matthew*, 9–10.

Texts Constructing Communities

Here an observation made by Adele Reinhartz with respect to the Fourth Gospel is particularly appropriate. While she affirms that communities may create texts, she raises the more likely possibility that texts create communities. She argues that the Fourth Gospel is less a description of the Johannine community's situation and more an attempt to "construct a new and idealized identity for its audience."[8] This is reflected in the Fourth Evangelist's extensive use of persuasive language which includes both a *rhetoric of affiliation*, motifs that serve to exhort the reader to believe and be born into a new family, the family of God, and a *rhetoric of disaffiliation*, motifs that encourage disassociation from those that reject Jesus as the Messiah, God's Son.[9] For Reinhartz, the Johannine community hypothesis's main failure is to explain why a "gospel intended for those who have already suffered for their faith" would "engage in such a pervasive rhetorical campaign to encourage belief in the first place."[10]

Such a critique may be applied to the First Gospel in that a *rhetoric of affiliation* is also clearly present. Matthew includes, for example, an appeal for laborers to join the harvest (Matt 9:37–38): "The harvest is plentiful, but the laborers are few; therefore, ask the Lord of the harvest to send out laborers into his harvest." This appeal, which extends beyond the Twelve to the reader, whether first century or later, may be taken less as a description of an existing Matthean community and rather as an appeal to create a community of mission-minded followers of Jesus. The Gospel Commission anticipates that the contents of the Gospel will be used to teach future gentile readers and to involve them in this mission. Repeated references to the five roles identified above are part of this rhetoric, creating, to appropriate the words of Reinhartz, "a new and idealized identity for its audience."[11] This mixed group of prophets, righteous persons, disciples, wise men, and scribes represents what we might term Matthew's discipleship ideal or, in the words of Gerhard Barth, "the essence of being a disciple."[12] The task we face is to unravel a deliberately tangled ball of wool made up of different

---

8. Reinhartz, *Cast Out of the Covenant*, xxvii. Reinhartz views the Gospel's intended audience not as "a church filled with members of an already-existing Johannine community, but in a crowded agora in an urban Greek-speaking center such as Ephesus" (131).

9. Reinhartz, *Cast Out of the Covenant*, xxii.

10. Reinhartz, *Cast Out of the Covenant*, 124.

11. Reinhartz, *Cast Out of the Covenant*, xxvii.

12. Barth, "Matthew's Understanding," 105.

colored yarns. We must seek to understand each role in its own historical terms while trying to understand how they relate to each other. This will reveal the Evangelist's theology of mission.

The Evangelist intentionally omits any account of the Twelve implementing the mission of Jesus (cf. Mark 6:12–13 with Matt 11:1). As a result, the discipleship ideal stands above the subplot of the Twelve and the question as to who will adopt and implement this idealized identity is left open. The effect is to invite readers, whether defined as those who first received the Gospel in the first century CE or those of later generations, to adopt the ideal in their own missions to the nations. As such, I will assume an open or at least a partially transparent text intended to create a missional community.[13] The Gospel will, of course, be read as a first-century text, in a manner sensitive to its original historical-theological setting. When I refer to "the reader," I refer to a nonspecific sympathetic first-century reader. However, the relatively open nature of the Gospel's implied reader or authorial audience suggests that the Evangelist has given later readers permission, even those far removed from his original context, to identify implications for their own missiological praxis.[14]

Seeking the Idealized Disciple

The Gospel participates in the Greco-Roman genre of *bios*, albeit narrated with a heavily Jewish apocalyptic accent.[15] One of the main purposes of this genre was to offer readers an example to imitate. In the ancient world students learned through comprehending a teacher's words and imitating his deeds. In Hellenistic religions and philosophical schools, imitation or *mimesis* supplemented oral discourse as the primary method of teaching.[16] The student or disciple learned through hearing his teacher's words and imitating his deeds. The combined group of prophets, righteous persons, disciples, wise men and scribes of Matt 10:41–42 and 23:34 reflect Jesus's own identity as prophet, righteous person, teacher, wise man and teacher

13. On the distinction between historicizing readings (emphasizing the Twelve as historical characters) and transparent readings (the Matthean disciples are a generic representation of all followers of Jesus or a narrative portrayal of a late first-century Matthean community), see Luz, *Disciples*, 115–42.

14. Cf. Waetjen, *Matthew's Theology*, xiv–xv.

15. Burridge, *What are the Gospels?*, 53–77, 233–43.

16. Malherbe, *Moral Exhortation*, 34–40, 59–66; Barrow, *Education*, 18–19.

of the law. Imitation of Jesus is the key. When Jesus warned the scribes and Pharisees that he would send them prophets, wise men and scribes, he was, in effect, extending his own mission through the future activities of his followers. He is their template for mission.

Space precludes an in-depth consideration of how Jesus fulfilled these roles. Instead, we may note that he regularly prophesied (Matt 17:12, 22; 20:17–19; 26:1–2, 24, 45; 24:1—25:46) and was recognized as a prophet by the crowds (16:14; 21:11, 46; 68). He undertook actions that fulfilled "all righteousness" (3:15) and extensively promoted righteousness in his teachings (e.g., 5:6, 10, 20). He self-identified as a teacher (10:24–25; 19:11; 23:10), frequently taught (4:23; 7:28; 9:35), and was recognized as a teacher by others (8:19; 9:11; 12:38; 17:24; 22:16, 24, 36). He is presented as *the* Teacher in a manner similar to both wisdom and Solomon (cf. Matt 7:28; 23:8; 26:18), and his healings and exorcisms are presented as the manifestation of wisdom (cf. "works of the Christ" in 11:2 with the works of wisdom in 11:19). While not explicitly identified as a scribe, he is asked for and gives his opinion on a range of legal matters such as table fellowship (9:11), fasting (9:15), divorce (19:3), and Sabbath observance (12:1–8, 10).[17] He makes a judgment on the payment of the temple tax in 17:24–27 and provides a midrashic explanation of Ps 110:1 in Matt 22:44.

My approach is thus to posit a discipleship ideal that is found at the intersection between Jesus's own identity and his various statements relating to the purpose, identity, and mission of the different discipleship roles to which he repeatedly refers. That said, there is one role found throughout the Gospel that is missing from this list of discipleship roles, one role not yet applied to the followers of Jesus. This is the role of sovereign or king. The reason for this is that the purpose of mission is to establish the authority of King Jesus over the nations (Matt 28:16–20). In this sense, mission is intensely national in its focus. The nations are to be subsumed into his kingdom. He alone is to be their king.[18]

Each chapter of this study will focus on one of the five roles from a broadly biblical theology perspective. Attention will be given to prominent themes and motifs and to the various intertextual devices employed by the Evangelist to evoke or allude to earlier canonical traditions. Such devices

17. Keith presents strong arguments against any characterization of Jesus as a scribe (*Scribal Elite*, 111–21). The Matthean Jesus is more than a scribal interpreter of Torah. He is presented as a source of authority equal to Moses and the prophets (cf. Matt 17:5).

18. Contrast this with Luke 22:29 in which Jesus confers upon the disciples a kingdom.

include explicit statements, inexplicit citations or borrowing, similar circumstances, key words or phrases, similar narrative structures, and word order.[19] As well as seeking authorial intention, we must also consider the partner in the communication process, the reader or, more likely in a first-century context, the auditor. Christopher Stanley has argued in relation to Paul's audiences, and the same principle applies to the first audiences of Matthew, that we must distinguish between an *informed audience*, a *competent audience*, and a *minimal audience*, each of which would have had a different aural experience of any intertextual devices within the primary text.[20] Noncanonical traditions will thus be considered in that they prove helpful in determining the capacity of first-century auditors to recognize the Evangelist's use of such devices. The greater the capacity of a first-century auditor to pick up on intertextual allusions, the more plausible will be our proposal relating to the Evangelist's intended meaning. First, let me set out some basic parameters that will guide our study.

A Typology of Mission

Discipleship must be understood in the context of mission and mission in the context of political theology. The ending of the Gospel indicates that King Jesus, the Danielic Son of Man, has been given all authority under heaven and earth and the purpose of his followers is to establish his authority over all the nations (Matt 28:18–20; cf. Dan 7:13–14). Authority is not the same as power or force and this difference lies behind the choice of the mechanism by which divine sovereignty is to be established—mission. This mission is undertaken by his followers to the extent that they adopt the discipleship ideal.

Four missions are presented in the Gospel of Matthew. The first mission is to the "lost sheep of the house of Israel" scattered throughout the cities and villages of Galilee (Matt 4:15; 10:6; 15:24). This is the general focus of chapters 4–13. The second mission, an extension of the first, is to the Jerusalem-based shepherds of Israel (chapters 17–27). The third mission is a post-crucifixion mission to Israel, as anticipated by the prophets, wise men and scribes Jesus promises to send to the leaders of Israel in 23:34. The fourth and final mission is to all the nations (28:16–20).

19. This list is taken from Allison, *New Moses*, 19–20. See also Hays's influential seven tests for determining citations, allusions, and echoes in scripture (*Letters of Paul*, 29–32).

20. Stanley, *Arguing with Scripture*, 62–71.

What is the nature of this final mission and how is it to accomplished? To answer this question we will consider the nature of the first two missions. The missions to Galilee and Jerusalem offer a template for the mission to the nations. This approach is somewhat unusual in that those scholars who focus on reconstructing a Matthean community tend to prioritize the first two missions and argue that Matthew is primarily concerned with Jewish issues. Others prioritize references to gentiles and the Gospel Commission and argue for an exclusive focus on a universalistic gentile mission.[21] The correspondence between the mission to the nations and the missions to Galilee and Jerusalem is, however, made explicit in Jesus's command to the disciples to teach the nations everything that he had commanded them (28:20), the setting for his instruction being the first two missions to Israel.

The different missions presented in the Gospel vary in nature. These differences become apparent when we analyze them in view of Martin Goodman's four types of mission in antiquity; informative mission, educational mission, apologetic mission, and proselytizing mission.[22] First, the informative mission. There is much evidence that there were those in the ancient world who sought to share a general message with others without requiring the recipients to convert. Their goal was to tell people something rather than change beliefs or behavior. Secondly, the educational mission. This involved trying to change the recipients by making them more moral or contented. Such a mission did not require them to convert or to acknowledge that such changes were part of the belief system espoused by those calling for change. Much of the Old and New Testaments are of this nature. Thirdly, the apologetic mission. Some in the ancient world sought the recognition of their god's status without requiring their auditors to devote themselves to the deity. Their goal was to protect their worship practices and belief system. Josephus's defences of Judaism fit into this category. Finally, the proselytizing mission. This type of mission incorporates elements from the informative, educational, and apologetic mission types and involved members of a group encouraging outsiders to join their group. This would typically require a change in lifestyle and belief system. Examples include the forced conversion of conquered peoples by the Hasmoneans and the conversion of the king of Adiabene and his household to Judaism

---

21. Strecker argues for a gentile Christian author who uses earlier Jewish-Christian sources (*Der Weg*, 15–35). Cf. Levine, *Social and Ethnic Dimensions*, 3; Kampen, *Matthew*, 184–202.

22. Goodman, *Mission and Conversion*, 3–5.

(*Ant.* 20.34–48.24). These four mission types are ideal types. In practice it is often hard to distinguish between them because those involved in mission frequently have unclear or mixed motives.

When we apply these four mission types to the Gospel, we find a mixed picture. Initial impressions would suggest that the missions to Galilee and Jerusalem are of an inward and educational nature, one in which Jesus tries to move the sheep and shepherds of Israel to a more faithful disposition toward God. In this reading, Jesus was seeking to reform rather than convert. In contrast, the mission to the nations is of a more proselytizing nature, inviting the nations to join those who already acknowledge the God of Israel and his messiah.

There is much to be said for such a reading and it has been persuasively applied to the Gospel.[23] It is one which, in general terms, I accept. Nevertheless, it needs nuancing. The Gospel's plot throws up a number of challenging questions: Is the nature of Jesus's mission to Israel consistent or does it change as the plot develops? Where do Jesus's appeals to fellow Jews to leave everything and follow him fit within this scheme? Is he calling them to become members of a new group, and if so, is it still within Judaism? Does a Jew deemed to be in a state of idolatry need reforming or converting? How do we categorise chance encounters between Jesus and gentiles? The Canaanite woman's encounter with Jesus, for example, was not the result of an intentional proselytizing mission to gentiles (Matt 15:21–28). Such questions caution us against driving an overly blunt conceptual wedge between the various missions. The fact that the teachings of Jesus in the first two missions provide the material for the proselytizing mission to the nations means that the nature and tenor of the earlier missions leak over into the final mission.[24] The logic of the Gospel is that the mission of Jesus to the nation of Israel provides the template, despite differences in missional circumstances, for the mission of his followers to the nations.

Political Theology and the Gospel

Our understanding of mission is intimately related to our understanding of political theology. One introductory text defines political theology as the search for "the best form of government by asking about God, rather than

23. Runesson, *Divine Wrath*, 374–78.

24. Wilkins describes the Gospel as a "manual of discipleship" for those implementing the Gospel Commission (*Concept of Discipleship*, 162).

about man."[25] It is a search for God's ideal for the nation. A more focused definition is provided by Johannes Baptist Metz, a leading European political theologian, who believes that the purpose of political theology is

> to make contemporary theologians aware that a trial is pending between the eschatological message of Jesus and the socio-political reality. . . . It is impossible to privatize the eschatological promises of biblical tradition: liberty, peace, justice, reconciliation. Again and again they force us to assume our responsibilities towards society.[26]

Christian belief is not to be privatized in that its eschatological claims implicate wider society. Oliver O'Donovan, another prominent advocate of political theology, observes that New Testament terms such as "king," "kingdom," "judge," "deliver," "servants," "saints," "glory," "overcome," "redeemed," and even "son" and "pray," are inherently political.[27] Building upon this observation, he suggests that "theology needs more than scattered political images; it needs a full political conceptuality."[28] Without such a conceptuality, the gospel is neutered and leaves people "enslaved where they ought to be set free from sin—their own and others."[29] Faith is reduced to piety, an ethics of interior motivation. Should the Gospel be read in such a manner as advocated by O'Donovan? Yes, in that it clearly includes many of the political terms he identifies. In addition, the Gospel (1) presents the highly political story of a king reasserting his sovereignty over his nation and its leaders, and (2) anticipates the extension of this sovereignty over other nations through the mission of his followers. It climaxes with the judgment of the nations. The Gospel is a political text.

Contrasting the Gospel with later political theologies helps highlight, despite being a somewhat anachronistic exercise, the nature of the Evangelist's political vision for the nations. Political theology has historically sought to negotiate the tension between the two kingdoms of the church and the state. For the first three centuries of the Christian era the church was subject to the state, a non-Christian state which sporadically persecuted and oppressed the church. However, with the rise to power of Emperor Constantine in 312 CE, church and state were fused into one. John

---

25. Kirwan, *Political Theology*, 92.

26. Metz, *Theology of the World*, 113–14.

27. O'Donovan, *Desire of the Nations*, 1.

28. O'Donovan, *Desire of the Nations*, 2.

29. O'Donovan, *Desire of the Nations*, 3.

Howard Yoder describes how this development fundamentally changed Christianity:

> Before Constantine, one knew as a fact of everyday experience that there was a believing Christian community but one had to "take it on faith" that God was governing history. After Constantine, one had to believe without seeing that there was a community of believers, within the larger nominally Christian mass, but one knew for a fact that God was in control of history.[30]

In such a system, nominal Christians represented the majority of the population and true believers were identified as members of the *ecclesia invisibilis*, the "invisible church." Ethics served to strengthen the state and mission involved extending the empire's borders. It involved crusade. This state of affairs ended with the sacking of Christian Rome in 410 CE, an event which was both a political and theological crisis in that God's visible kingdom on earth had now been defeated. Augustine responded to pagan criticism of defeated Christian Rome by arguing in *The City of God* that the Roman empire should not be confused with the kingdom of God. They are two separate entities. Instead of a church-state union, there are two kingdoms (or cities). We are to seek God's heavenly city, the New Jerusalem, while commingling with the earthly city, the "city of Babylon," seeking the peace of Babylon while not seeking to usurp Babylon (*Civ.* 19:26; cf. Jer 29:7). A separate church and state are to coexist in creative tension rather than in either a fusion of the two or in antagonistic isolation one from the other. Only such a relationship between the two will permit the church to hold the state to account when it takes on beast-like qualities. Only such a church, separate from the state, can survive the perpetual rise and fall of nation states.

The subsequent rise of Christendom in the West resulted in a return to the domination of the state by the church as epitomized in Pope Gregory VII (ca. 1025–85 CE) and his assertion of spiritual authority over the secular powers. Unfortunately, this theocratic fusion of church and state eliminated many of the checks and balances required to hold either the church or the state in check. The Reformation challenged this fusion and advocated the separation of the two kingdoms. The magisterial reformers of Luther and Calvin accepted the necessity of the temporal authorities, the magistrates, with Luther in particular, heavily influenced by Augustine, maintaining the need for the civil and the religious kingdoms to work in close cooperation to promote the goals of the gospel. Over time, however,

---

30. Yoder, *Priestly Kingdom*, 137.

this cooperation, influenced by the rise of the Enlightenment, resulted, according to Jürgen Moltmann, in the exclusion of spiritual matters from the temporal kingdom and in a bourgeois, privatized, and nonpolitical form of Christianity characterized by pious introspection that ultimately failed with the rise of Hitler to hold the temporal kingdom to account.[31] By allowing itself to be excluded from the public sphere, the spiritual kingdom lost its ability to hold in check a temporal kingdom that had turned evil. In contrast to the magisterial reformation, the radical reformation advocated that the church adopt a more distant and critical stance toward the state. As with the magisterial reformation, this often resulted in the withdrawal of the church from the public space and the increasing secularization of the temporal kingdom.

Our own view as to the ideal church-state relationship will shape how we understand discipleship and mission in the Gospel. Those who promote the union of church and state will tend to interpret Matthean discipleship in institutional terms. Disciples are to serve the interests of the state. The danger with such an approach is that when the state adopts leviathan-like characteristics, disciples often fail to offer a prophetic critique because of their close association with the state. In contrast, those who prefer to keep church and state separate face the danger of a restricted understanding of discipleship and mission, reading discipleship in the Gospel as an activity undertaken primarily by the church and for the church, with little consideration given as to how it might relate to the nation. Discipleship and mission will be framed in apolitical and private terms. Christopher Rowland suggests that this has been the approach of much modern biblical exegesis, in part "because of the hegemony of German biblical scholarship, pervaded with Lutheran Two Kingdoms theology, which has tended to underline the 'nonpolitical' character of the Christian gospel."[32]

Matthew's Political Theology?

I would suggest that the Gospel of Matthew may be read in a manner that challenges both approaches. It is not political in the sense of preferencing a "right wing," "centrist" or "left wing" political stance. Nor does it advocate a particular political structure or organizational configuration that the village, city, or nation must adopt. It does not define a particular relationship

31. Moltmann, "Covenant or Leviathan?," 39.
32. Rowland, "Scripture," 158.

between the two kingdoms, whether it be a fusion or separation of church and state. Political structures have historically proved to be very fluid, and the Gospel allows for such fluidity. It allows for a variety of national political structures. Instead of advocating a particular relationship between church and state, the Evangelist envisages an adaptive process in which a small cadre of individuals adopt different discipleship roles and work within existing national structures to establish divine sovereignty. Historically, these roles were embedded within the sociopolitical structures of first-century Israel and, when combined, offered a coherent political theology that is anticipatory rather than final in nature. At no point in the Gospel are we presented with an example of a nation that has fully accepted or implemented divine sovereignty; Israel rejects Jesus and his followers, and the gentile nations have yet to be approached.

The Evangelist's vision may be summarized as follows. The prophet confronts the nation, warning of divine judgment while offering hope of renewal. The presence of the righteous person offers the means of postponing judgment in the same manner that the presence of ten righteous persons would have postponed the destruction of Sodom and Gomorrah (Gen 18:20–33). A breathing space is provided, judgment is delayed. Change for the good may thus be affected. The disciple/teacher provides the means of deepening the initial response of the nation through education. It ensures nominal followers become committed followers. Wise men serve as leaders of the nation, reflecting the national roles played in the Old Testament by wise men such as Joseph, Solomon, and Daniel. Scribes ensure that the legal traditions necessary for the nation's spiritual health are preserved and adhered to. If these various roles are accepted, the nation is transformed for the better and the kingship of Jesus is affirmed. The empire of God's kingdom is expanded.

In crude terms, this is a vision in which a theocratic movement seeks to transform nations from within, whether first-century Israel in the case of the Gospel's original audience or the national settings of later gentile recipients. The strength of this theology is that it does not advocate a particular relationship between church and state, or, in a first-century context, between the followers of Jesus and Israel. It leaves the question open. It presents a process rather than a final state. The various discipleship roles represent different postures that followers of Jesus may adopt toward the nation that range from a more distant stance (e.g., condemning prophet) to a closer stance (e.g., wise man and scribe). A more distant stance avoids the pitfalls of the union of church and state while a closer stance avoids the dangers of the two kingdoms approach such as the disengagement of the church from the state or the state's exclusion of the church from the public sphere. The sovereignty of Jesus is to be extended to all parts of the nation, or in Matthean terms, from the home to the council, from the lowly laborer to the king and governor, from the sheep to the shepherds.

2

The Prophet

Calling the Nation to God

Introduction

THE PROPHET IS THE catalyst that starts the process of national transformation. This is signaled early in the Gospel through the precursory prophetic ministry of John the Baptist and the opening to Jesus's public ministry expressed in his prophetic call to repent (Matt 3:1–12; 4:17). The priority of the prophetic role is further emphasized in the references to the different discipleship roles in 10:40–42 and 23:34, both of which start with prophets:[1]

> Whoever welcomes a prophet in the name of a prophet will receive a prophet's reward; and whoever welcomes a righteous person in the name of a righteous person will receive the reward of the righteous; and whoever gives even a cup of cold water to one of these little ones in the name of a disciple—truly I tell you, none of these will lose their reward. (Matt 10:41–42)

> Therefore I send you prophets, sages, and scribes . . . (Matt 23:34)

Whatever else the missions to the lost sheep of the House of Israel and the shepherds in Jerusalem might entail, they both involve prophets. Early in the mission to Galilee, Jesus invites his audience to interpret their experience within the trajectory of the earlier prophets of Israel: "Blessed are you when people revile you and persecute you . . . for in the same way they persecuted the prophets who were before you" (5:11–12). The reader is

1. The term "prophet" is used thirty-seven times in Matthew, six times in Mark, and twenty-nine times in Luke. Clearly this is an important term for the Evangelists.

invited, nay, encouraged, to draw parallels between his or her own experience and that of the prophets. Which prophets, we may ask? Unlike recent scholarship, Jesus does not distinguish between different types of prophets, whether they be cultic, clerical, sapiential, popular, leadership, action or oracular. While such distinctions may be helpful from a historian's perspective, they were not uppermost in the thinking of the Evangelist. Instead, we find that the prophetic identify of Jesus and his followers is placed in continuity with Israel's prophets as a whole.[2]

Prophets are not just necessary at the beginning of the process of transforming the nation. For a balanced political theology there is an ongoing need for prophets in that they act as dissenting voices within God's kingdom and ensure that those in political authority do not make an image of God out of themselves.[3] They constitute a rejection of political absolutism.

In this chapter I will argue that we encounter in Matthew an intentional sequence of prophetic motifs that chart what may be described as a divine dance between God and the city or nation. In this dance, the respective partners step toward or away from each other in choreographed moves which either end in embrace or rejection. The prophet is the interface between these two dance partners: (1) the calls to repent in Matt 3:2 and 4:17 are an invitation from God to a distant nation to draw near to him; (2) the deeds of power in Matt 8 and 9 testify that God himself has drawn near with the intention to save and transform the nation; (3) woe and judgment oracles in Matt 11:20–24 and 23:13–39 warn that God, as a result of the nation's rejection of him, will once more draw near, this time not to save but to judge; and (4) following the rejection of the divine invitation, the parables of Matt 13 polarize the nation, jolting a faithful remnant from their complacency while further hardening the already hardened hearts of the majority. These motifs chart a journey in which the prophet delivers a twofold message, first, focusing on salvation, and then, following the rejection of this message, on judgment.

The Divine Dance and the Role of the Prophet

The Old Testament story of Israel's dance with the presence of God is the context for understanding the role of prophets within the Gospel. A basic principle we find in the Old Testament is that when Israel steps back from

---

2. Matt 1:22; 2:5, 15, 23; 5:17; 7:12; 11:13; 13:17, 35; 21:4; 22:40; 26:56.

3. O'Donovan, *Desire of the Nations*, 65.

God, God steps back from Israel. When Israel returns to God, God returns to Israel. This back-and-forth movement is explicitly articulated in the prophetic message of Azariah son of Oded to Asa, king of Judah, in which he sets out a series of actions and responses that typify the nation's relationship with God:

> The spirit of God came upon Azariah son of Oded. He went out to meet Asa and said to him, "Hear me, Asa, and all Judah and Benjamin: The LORD is with you, while you are with him. If you seek him, he will be found by you, but if you abandon him, he will abandon you. For a long time Israel was without the true God, and without a teaching priest, and without law; but when in their distress they turned to the LORD, the God of Israel, and sought him, he was found by them." (2 Chr 15:1–4)

The message of Azariah, described as a prophecy in 15:8, articulates a certain dynamic played out in Israel and Judah's history in which the nation, typically led by its king, either (1) abandons God, resulting in him abandoning them, or (2) seeks God, leading to him drawing close to them. These dynamics are made explicit to the reader through numerous references to "seeking," coming "back to the Lord," and "abandoning."[4] We also find affirmations that "God is with us" (13:12), he is "with" certain individuals (17:3), or that he has been "found" (15:4). These various descriptors of movement and location serve to emphasize the foundational principle articulated by Azariah that "the LORD is with you, while you are with him" (15:2). His presence is neither guaranteed nor under the control of Israel. The nation steps back from God, he steps back from them. The result is an environment particular to that spiritual moment in which God has reduced in some sense his presence. When this occurred with Judah, he "sent them prophets among them to bring them back to the LORD" (24:19).[5] When the nation seeks God, he permits himself to be found and his presence is experienced in a more immediate manner.

Before we consider this dynamic in more detail, permit me a moment to emphasize the great value this dynamic has for explaining the experience of many Christians in the West. Many Western societies have stepped back from formal Christianity and eschewed any role for God in the public square. The dynamic outlined above would suggest that God reciprocates such a move by stepping back from such nations. The result is a widening

---

4. E.g., 2 Chr 11:16; 12:1, 14; 13:10; 14:7; 15:12, 15; 17:4; 19:4; 20:3, 14; 24:20.

5. On the sending of prophets, Westermann, *Basic Forms*, 100–115.

gap between God and the nation. In a very real sense, God reduces his presence within the nation. This helps polarize the situation further in that those who reject God now live in an environment that confirms their choice. They live in a world in which God is absent, not because he does not exist, but because he has removed himself just as Jesus removed himself from the cities of Galilee when they rejected him.

Nonetheless, God does not leave himself without a witness. In the Gospel, Jesus's absence from the cities is mitigated when he sends out the disciples as his representatives, his presence in the cities: "Whoever welcomes you, welcomes me, and whoever welcomes me welcomes the one who sent me" (Matt 10:40). Those sent, whether they be prophets, righteous persons or disciples (10:41–42), function as emissaries to the divine presence, but in an environment in which the divine presence has been reduced. Christians in the West may well be living in an environment in which God's presence is increasingly absent because he respects the corporate choices of cities and nations. This is not the worst of it. In the Gospel we find that the vacuum created by God's withdrawal is filled with the debilitating and hostile presence of Satan and his demons. Spiritual survival in such a hostile situation requires the adoption of the prophetic mindset.[6]

The dynamic of the nation's movement away from God followed by his withdrawal and the sending of warnings and invitations is found in the Old Testament Prophets. Isaiah, for example, describes a situation in which the nation has stepped back from God, requiring that it return to him through repentance ("return," *šwb*, Isa 1:27). To repent is to return.[7] There is a danger, however, that the nation might return to God in body only and not in spirit—an empty act of repentance: "Because these people draw near with their mouths and honor me with their lips, while their hearts are far from me, and their worship of me is a human commandment learned by rote; so I will again do amazing things with this people, shocking and amazing" (Isa 29:13–14). Israel dances as a zombie, physically near while their hearts are far from God. In such a situation, God sends this near-but-distant nation to be where their hearts are, into exile. This is not, however, the end of the dance. Oracles of salvation look forward to a time when a remnant shall return physically to Zion, the hope being that they will also return their

---

6. On the mental anguish of Jeremiah resulting from the distance between God and the nation, see Jer 4:19; 6:11; 8:21; 9:1; 17:14–18; 20:7–10. See also O'Donovan, *Desire of the Nations*, 76–79.

7. Metz helpfully notes that when God approaches man, the "distance and difference from him are not wiped out . . . , but created and made visible" (*Theology of the World*, 28).

hearts to the Lord (cf. Isa 35:10; 44:22; 51:11). One final event is required to restore the dance. The glory of Yahweh which had departed his people will return, once more drawing near (Isa 40:3–5, 9–10).

The prophet stands between these two dance partners as a mediating presence through whom God communicates. These communications are usually given when Israel is far from its dance partner, often when it is idolatrously dancing with other gods. Instructions may involve positive oracles of salvation: "Return to me and I will save you" (e.g., Isa 41:8–13). These hope-giving, affirmative appeals are often counter-balanced by more serious warnings of judgment: "If you do not return to me, I will return to you in judgment" (e.g., 2 Kgs 1:3, 4; Isa 29:1–16). The nature of the appeal often changed in response to Israel's intransigence. First, the prophets would deliver their sermons in, as suggested by Greg Beale, a "rational and sermonic way, exhorting the audience about their sin and reminding them about their past history in which God had judged their fathers because of the same kind of selfish disobedience."[8] The response of Israel to such invitations was usually rejection. They closed their ears and were as unresponsive to God's mediated voice as the idols were to which they directed their attention. As a result of such hostile responses, the prophets would adopt a different tone. They would use symbolic action and parable to arrest the attention of Israel. This change in mode of warning was only effective with those, usually described as a remnant, who still retained spiritual insight. The hoped-for effect was to jolt Israel out of its spiritual complacency. To those who eyes were blind like the idols they worshipped, the symbolic parables were intended as a judgment to blind them even further. We find all these prophetic forms of communication in the Gospel.

The divine dance is more complex in the Gospel than that which I have just outlined for the reason that Jesus is both a prophet and the very presence of Yahweh. Jesus, as the presence of Yahweh, is a moving presence who draws near to the cities and villages of Galilee in Matthew 4 to 13, draws back in chapters 14 to 16, and then, from chapters 17 on, makes his way to Jerusalem, where he is rejected. The presence of Yahweh comes close, but also withdraws. His presence may sometimes be present, sometimes absent. Yahweh-as-Jesus is, however, even when physically close to his host community, at the same time the medium of divine communication that occurs when his people are distant from him and he is distant from them. He is near and present and yet communicates in the mode of distance. The most

8. Beale, *We Become*, 244.

compelling explanation of this tension is that even though Yahweh-as-Jesus draws close, first to Galilee and then to Jerusalem, their hearts remain far from him, requiring him to function as a prophet. As a prophet, he communicates to a people whom he describes, quoting Isa 29:13, as honoring "me with their lips, but their hearts are far from me; in vain do they worship me, teaching human precepts as doctrines" (Matt 15:8–9).

The Return of Yahweh

The Old Testament prophets predicted the departure of Yahweh's Shekinah from the temple and his subsequent return to save his people.[9] The start of Jesus's ministry is clearly presented in such terms, as the return of Yahweh:[10]

> This is the one of whom the prophet Isaiah spoke when he said,
> "The voice of one crying out in the wilderness:
> 'Prepare the way of the Lord,
>   make his paths straight.'"
> *phōnē boōntos en tē erēmō;*
> *hetoimasate tēn hodon kyriou,*
>   *eutheias poieite tas tribous autou.* (Matt 3:3)

As in Mark 1:3, John the Baptist is presented as fulfilling LXX Isa 40:3. Of particular significance is the adaptation of the parallelism in the LXX. This will be made clearer if we quote LXX Isa 40:3 in full:

> A voice of one crying out in the wilderness:
> "Prepare the way of the Lord; make straight the paths of our God."
> *phōnē boōntos en tē erēmō*
> *Hetoimasate tēn hodon kyriou, eutheias poieite tas tribous tou theou hēmōn.*
> (LXX Isa 40:3, NETS)

In the LXX, the "way of the Lord" is followed by "the paths of our God," a clear instance of parallelism. Parallelism is common throughout the Old Testament and involves two lines of approximate length (called "cola") in which the grammar, syntax, and meaning reinforce one another. In Matt 3:3, as in Mark 1:3, the second line (colon) has been altered from "make straight the paths of our God" (so LXX) to "make his paths straight." In

---

9. E.g., Isa 40:1–5; 52:8; Ezek 8:4; 10:4–5, 18–19; 11:22–23; 43:2–5; 44:4.

10. The arguments put forward by Marcus for the Markan way of the Lord as the return of Yahweh also apply to Matthew (*Way of the Lord*, 12–47). See also Davies, *Setting*, 30–32.

context, the change to *his* paths refers to the way of Jesus and indicates a willingness on the part of both Evangelists to identify Jesus with Yahweh.[11]

How John is to prepare the way is not made explicit. His clothing of camel's hair with a leather belt marks him out as a prophet.[12] A more specific association may be made with Elijah the Tishbite who, according to 2 Kgs 1:8, was a hairy man (or one who wore a garment of haircloth), and who wore a leather belt around his waist.[13] For Matthew, John is the predicted Elijah figure of Mal 4:5, preparing the way for the coming of Yahweh (Matt 11:14; 17:12). Accordingly, the presence of Yahweh is now manifested in the physical presence of Jesus among the cities of Galilee and in Jerusalem. His presence is, as we have already observed in our discussion of the Gospel's plot, a mobile presence. As outlined above, in chapters 4 to 9 his presence dwells among the cities of Galilee. In chapters 11 and 12, the cities respond with hostility to Yahweh-as-Jesus and he prepares to withdraw. This occurs in chapters 14 to 16, after which, he begins his long road to Jerusalem. The final chapters of the Gospel tell of Jerusalem's rejection of his presence.

The Prophetic Invitation: Repent!

The prophetic invitation to repent conveys to Israel that it is currently distant from its dance partner. In contrast to the prophets, sages did not typically view it as their role to call the people to repentance.[14] The call to repent is specific to the prophet.[15] The Evangelist portrays both John and Jesus as opening their public ministry with this characteristically prophetic invitation (Matt 3:2; 4:17). John's call to repent, *metanoeite* (Matt 3:2), has often been explained etymologically as referring to a change of one's mind. It was certainly used in this manner in classical Greek.[16] It is also used this way in the LXX.[17] This definition, however, while it should not be downplayed or ignored, is too narrow when it comes to the Gospel. Certainly, a change of mind is envisioned. The Evangelist's use of *metanoeō* has, however, been influenced by the Hebrew verbs *nḥm* ("to

---

11. Davies and Allison, *Matthew 1–7*, 293.

12. Cf. Zech 13:4; Heb 11:37; 1 Clem. 17:1.

13. For supporting sources, Davies and Allison, *Matthew 1–7*, 295.

14. Urbach, *Sages*, 463.

15. For repentance as a requirement of gentiles, Runesson, *Divine Wrath*, 397.

16. E.g., Xen., *Hell.* 1.7.19. Cf. Behm and Würthwein, "μετανοέω," *TDNT*, 4:976–77.

17. E.g., LXX 1 Kgs 15:29.

become remorseful") and *šwb* ("to turn around, repent").[18] The latter is what we find in Old Testament prophetic calls for the nation to turn away from their idols and return to God:

> Turn back (*šûḇû*) to him whom you have deeply betrayed, O people of Israel. (Isa 31:6; cf. 19:22; 30:15; 44:22; 55:7)

> Go, and proclaim these words toward the north, and say: "Return (*šûḇâ*), faithless Israel, says the LORD. I will not look on you in anger, for I am merciful, says the LORD; I will not be angry forever." (Jer 3:12; cf. 3:14, 22; 4:1; 8:5)

> Therefore say to the house of Israel, "Thus says the Lord GOD: Repent (*šûḇû*) and turn away from your idols; and turn away your faces from all your abominations." (Ezek 14:6)

The call of the prophet is an invitation to a wandering dance partner to return to the dance. While *šwb* "return" is normally translated in the LXX using a variant of *epistrephō*, it is also, although considerably less frequently, translated using *metanoeō* (cf. Isa 46:8). Often the two terms are closely associated, as in Joel 2:13, implying that the two acts, changing one's mind and returning, are part of the same process by which the nation returns to its God. In the Gospel, the grounds for this invitation to return is the nearness of the kingdom of heaven ("for the kingdom of heaven has come near," Matt 3:2). John's call to return is made in light of the approaching presence of God: repent-return to God, because he is returning to you. Jesus's prophetic call, while reflecting that of John the Baptist, occurs at a different stage in the dance in that the return of Yahweh is no longer a future event, as from the perspective of John (4:17). The Return has now taken place in the coming of Jesus. Returning to Yahweh is required of the nation to ensure that his return is restorative rather than punitive.[19]

The repentance motif is found in a number of other instances in the first half of the Gospel.[20] John the Baptist warns the Pharisees and Sadducees to "produce fruit," a Hebrew idiom for doing good works, "worthy

---

18. Behm and Würthwein, "μετανοέω," *TDNT*, 4:999; Davies and Allison, *Matthew 1–7*, 306.

19. Wright, *Victory*, 246–58. Runesson emphasizes the role of repentance in removing the defilement of sin, thereby allowing a holy God to dwell among his people (*Divine Wrath*, 195).

20. On the repentance motif in the Gospels, see Meyer, *Aims of Jesus*, 123.

of repentance" (*axion tēs metanoias*, 3:8).[21] The call for fruit reflects a wider awareness that evidence of repentance was often necessary due to the possibility that repentance could be undertaken with an attitude of insincerity.[22] In Matt 3:11, John describes his baptism as being *eis metanoian* "for repentance." The relationship between baptism and repentance is somewhat ambiguous. Baptism may be undertaken as a result of repentance or it may be the critical act that leads to repentance.[23] In 11:20, Jesus begins to reproach the cities of Galilee in which he performed his deeds of power because "they did not repent" (*ou metenoēsan*). The call for the cities and villages of Galilee to repent, buttressed by the strongest of warnings, is ultimately rejected, resulting in the withdrawal of Jesus in chapters 14 to 16 into the countryside and surrounding regions. The divine dance partner's invitation has been rejected and so he honors the wishes of his dance partner and once more steps back, away from the dance. I should qualify this last point with the observation that the crowds who follow Jesus into the countryside originate from the cities of Galilee, thereby signaling to the reader that rejection of the prophetic proclamation is by no means universal. Many respond positively, resulting, as in the Old Testament, in the deferral of judgment.[24]

Repentance is not the only means of establishing a positive encounter with the divine presence. As we will see in our next chapter on the role of righteous persons, when the nations extend hospitality to the followers of Jesus, they are counted as righteous (25:31–46). This also ensures favorable judgment. Each method of securing a positive outcome is based on different motifs and is complementary to the other.

The idea that repentance may be supplemented by other means of expiation is not unique to the Gospel. There is in John the Baptist's call for the Pharisees and Sadducees to bear fruit worthy of repentance, a recognition that repentance may be insincere, requiring evidence of its sincerity (Matt 3:8). In Acts 2:38, baptism is required in addition to repentance: "Peter said to them, 'Repent, and be baptized every one of you in the name of Jesus Christ so that your sins may be forgiven; and you will receive the gift of the Holy Spirit.'" We find in rabbinic literature from the Tannaitic period (10–200 CE) the concept that repentance, while held in high esteem, only

21. Davies and Allison, *Matthew 1–7*, 305.

22. Urbach, *Sages*, 462–71.

23. Davies and Allison, *Matthew 1–7*, 312; Luz, *Matthew 1–7*, 138.

24. Runesson, *Divine Wrath*, 112–30.

atones for light transgressions.[25] Iniquities of a more serious nature could only be expiated by repentance augmented by additional methods of expiation. These might include participating in special days, the giving of charity, reliance on God's promises as in the case of Moses in the wilderness, or through sin offerings (cf. the distinction between unintentional and intentional sins in Lev 4–6).[26]

Evidence of the Divine Presence: Deeds of Power

It is not enough for the prophet to denounce. He or she must also cast a vision of renewal. Oliver O'Donovan writes that "the prophet needs a point of view from which it is possible to criticize without criticism becoming a mere form, empty of substance. The prophet is not allowed the luxury of perpetual subversion. After Ahab, Elijah must anoint some Hazael, some Jehu."[27]

Evidence of the renewal associated with the return of Yahweh is found in the nine healing and nature miracles of chapters 8–9.[28] The significance of these miracles is explained twofold. First, when John the Baptist questions whether Jesus is "the one who is to come," Jesus responds by telling his disciples to report to him what they hear and see: "the blind receive their sight, the lame walk, the lepers are cleansed, the deaf hear, the dead are raised, and the poor have good news brought to them" (Matt 11:5). Jesus is alluding here to a number of passages in Isaiah, the primary passage being Isa 35:5–6 in which such deeds, complemented by a tumultuous rejoicing and renewal of nature, are evidence that the glory of Yahweh has returned to his people:[29]

> The wilderness and the dry land shall be glad,
>> the desert shall rejoice and blossom;
>>> like the crocus
> it shall blossom abundantly,
>> and rejoice with joy and singing.

---

25. Urbach, *Sages*, 465–71. Runesson, *Divine Wrath*, 57–59.

26. See also the difference between sins unto death and sins not unto death in 1 John 5:16–17.

27. O'Donovan, *Desire of the Nations*, 12.

28. On the tripartite structure (three groups of three miracles) of Matt 8–9, see Allison, *New Moses*, 209–10.

29. Cf. Isa 26:19; 29:18; 42:7, 18; 61:1. Davies and Allison, *Matthew 8–18*, 242.

The glory of Lebanon shall be given to it,
    the majesty of Carmel and Sharon.
They shall see *the glory of the LORD*,
    the majesty of our God.

Strengthen the weak hands,
    and make firm the feeble knees.
Say to those who are of a fearful heart,
    "Be strong, do not fear!
Here is your God.
    He will come with vengeance,
with terrible recompense.
    He will come and save you."

Then the eyes of the blind shall be opened,
    and the ears of the deaf unstopped,
then the lame shall leap like a deer,
    and the tongue of the speechless sing for joy.
For waters shall break forth in the wilderness,
    and streams in the desert;
the burning sand shall become a pool,
    and the thirsty ground springs of water;
the haunt of jackals shall become a swamp,
    the grass shall become reeds and rushes. (Isa 35:1–7, italics supplied)

The opening of the eyes of the blind in Isaiah is fulfilled in the healing of the two blind men in Matt 9:27–31. The unstopping of the ears of the deaf and the restoration of speech is realized in the healing of the mute and deaf demoniac of 9:32–34. The healing of the lame occurs with the healing of a paralytic in 9:2–8. In his response to John the Baptist, Jesus has increased the categories of restoration of Isa 35:5–6 to include the cleansing of lepers, the raising of the dead, and the proclamation of good news to the poor. The result is a list that both reminds the reader of Isaiah while at the same time summarizing Jesus's own deeds in Matt 8:1—9:38.[30]

A second explanation of the miracles of chapters 8–9, while not an explanation *per se*, is found in Jesus's description of them as "deeds of power" (*hai dynameis*, Matt 11:20, 21, 23; 13:58).[31] In the Old Testament the power of God is the personal manifestation of his presence in specific situations

---

30. Davies and Allison, *Matthew 8–18*, 242; Watts, *New Exodus*, 241–52.

31. On Jesus's miracles as an expression of divine authority, Gerhardsson, *Mighty Acts*, 45–48.

rather than an impersonal force to be manipulated by magical means.[32] The primary revelation of Yahweh's presence was his deliverance of Israel from bondage in Egypt, a revelation of both his strength and his power (*tēn ischyn sou kai tēn dynamin sou*, LXX Deut 3:24).[33] In Josh 4:23–24, a divine motive is provided for this revelation of power. It was "so that all the nations of the earth may know that the power of the Lord is mighty and in order that you [i.e., Israel] may worship the Lord your God for all time." An enhanced divine reputation and an enduring doxological response are to result.[34] Often a prophet was the means by which the divine power was revealed:

> And there has not again arisen a prophet in Israel like Moses whom the Lord knew face-to-face, with all the signs and wonders, whom the Lord sent to do them in the land of Egypt, against Pharaoh and his attendants and his entire land and the great wonders and the strong hand which Moses exhibited before all Israel. (LXX Deut 34:10–12, NETS; cf. "wonders and signs" in *Ant.* 20.167–68)

In Matt 13:54–58, the performance of deeds of power is explicitly linked to Jesus's prophetic identity and his proclamation in their synagogues:

> He came to his hometown and began to teach the people in their synagogue, so that they were astounded and said, "Where did this man get this wisdom and these deeds of power?" . . . And they took offense at him. But Jesus said to them, "Prophets are not without honor except in their own country and in their own house." And he did not do many deeds of power there, because of their unbelief. (Matt 13:54, 57–58)

When Jesus taught in their synagogue, he was not undertaking the equivalent of modern-day revival meetings. Synagogues were places of both Torah proclamation *and* local administration, the Torah being the legal basis by which the community was to be governed.[35] He was, in effect, extending

32. Grundmann, "δύναμαι/δύναμις," *TDNT*, 2:290–94.

33. Cf. Exod 15:6, 13; 32:11; Deut 9:26, 29; 26:8; 1 Macc. 4:9–11; 3 Macc. 2:6.

34. For doxological responses to divine power, see 1 Chr 29:10–12; Pss 21:13; 59:16.

35. On public Torah reading in the synagogue, see Runesson, *Origins of the Synagogue*, 193–232. Runesson distinguishes between semi-public voluntary association synagogues (cf. the "synagogue of the freedmen," Acts 6:9) and public local assemblies which had "formal authority structures, but no universal ideology" (379–80). Ryan accepts the distinction between public and association synagogues and argues that the synagogues visited by Jesus in the Gospels were public synagogues, which he describes as "communal local-official institutions" (*Role of the Synagogue*, 25–34, 77). See also Keith, *Jesus' Literacy*, 124–46; Kampen, *Matthew*, 146–49.

his jurisdiction over the administrative organs of the nation, exerting his sovereignty over Israel's political and religious life.

Are those involved in the mission to the nations expected to perform such deeds of power? There is, after all, no call to perform such deeds in the Gospel Commission (28:18–20). If we define such deeds as evidence of the manifestation of the divine presence through powerful deeds, then the answer is no. The divine presence, while manifested indirectly through his emissaries (10:40–42; 28:20), is no longer directly present. His presence will only be fully manifested at the coming of the Son of Man (24:29–31, 39, 44; 25:31), or, as variously stated, when "the master arrives" (24:46, 50), "the bridegroom comes" (25:6, 10), or when, after a long time, "the master returns from his journey" (25:19).[36]

Israel's Situation: Physically Postexilic but Spiritually Preexilic

In what state does Yahweh-as-Jesus encounter Israel upon his return? Answering this question is important because it develops the ability of the reader of the Gospel to determine the state of his or her own nation. N. T. Wright has strongly argued that a principle characteristic of late Second Temple Judaism was a deep yearning for the end of exile.[37] This position has been nuanced by a number of scholars.[38] I too, will offer a response.

While it goes without saying that the setting of the Gospel is historically a post-captivity setting in that those in Babylonian exile had been permitted to return to Jerusalem (see Nehemiah's reference to those "who escaped the captivity," Neh 1:2; cf. Ezra 1:1–4), the Evangelist portrays the cities of Galilee and Jerusalem as being in a preexilic spiritual state facing impending judgment along the lines of the Babylonian exile. Israel is physically postexilic but spiritually preexilic.[39] This reflects Old Testament

---

36. In Matt 28:20, Jesus tells his disciples that he will always be with them, to the end of the age. Davies and Allison read this as a reference to divine assistance rather than divine presence. Davies and Allison, *Matthew 19–28*, 687.

37. Wright, *People of God*, 268–72, 299–301; and, *Victory*, 202–9. Cf. Zvi and Levin, eds, *Concept of Exile*.

38. E.g., Piotrowski, *Matthew's New David*; Scott, *Exile*. Evans suggests that Jews believed themselves to be in bondage rather than in exile ("Jesus," 77–100).

39. Cf. this with Josephus's characterization of Israel's return from exile as a recovery and rebirth of the land of their fathers (*anaktēsin kai palingenesian tēs patridos, Ant.* 11.66)

traditions which predicted that the preexilic idolatrous state of Israel would continue well into exile.[40]

> The LORD will scatter you among the peoples; only a few of you will be left among the nations where the LORD will lead you. There you will serve other gods made by human hands, objects of wood and stone that neither see, nor hear, nor eat, nor smell. (Deut 4:27–28; cf. 28:64–65; 29:4, 17–18)

The Deuteronomist offers the same solution to Israel's plight as that later put forward by Jesus:

> From there you will seek the LORD your God, and you will find him if you search after him with all your heart and soul. (Deut 4:29; cf. Jer 29:13)

> Ask, and it will be given to you; search, and you will find; knock, and the door will be opened for you. For everyone who asks, receives, and everyone who searches finds, and for everyone who knocks, the door will be opened. (Matt 7:7)

For Matthew, Jesus's call to Israel to "seek" and "find" indicates that he believed that Israel, despite being "after the deportation" (Matt 1:12; cf. 1:11, 17),[41] continued in its preexilic idolatrous state.[42] Yahweh, embodied in Jesus, has thus returned to save his people not just from external powers, but from their own sinful condition (1:21). This negative appraisal of the spiritual state of Israel was by no means unique to Jesus or the Evangelist. Mark Adam Elliott has convincingly argued in his comprehensive work on the theme of remnant in Second Temple Judaism that many groups in Israel considered themselves to be a pure and holy remnant, sharply distinguishing themselves from what they perceived to be the idolatrous majority.[43]

A further indication that Israel has returned from captivity in body but not in spirit is in the Evangelist's portrayal of Israel as being in a state of idolatry (cf. Matt 15:8–9; cf. Isa 29:13). Greg Beale has drawn our attention to the spiritual lesson that you become like that which you worship. In our dance analogy, if you dance with another partner, God will allow you to take on your partner's characteristics. This may well explain why we have

40. Beale, *We Become*, 71–76.

41. Evans, "Jesus and the Continuing Exile," 99.

42. Compare this with Wright's view that Israel's problem was its adoption of violence against Rome and a failure to live up to its scriptural vocation (*Victory*, 324–25).

43. Elliott, *Survivors of Israel*.

so many references in the Gospel to the blind, the deaf, and the lame, corporate symptoms of Israel's underlying spiritual state. Beale argues, starting with Isa 6, that when Israel allowed deaf and blind idols to flourish, they soon lost the ability to "hear" and "see" the message of the prophets: "These worshipers [of idols] became as spiritually void and lifeless as the idols they committed themselves to."[44] This principle is explicitly stated in the following passages from the Psalms:

> Our God is in the heavens;
>> he does whatever he pleases.
> Their idols are silver and gold,
>> the work of human hands.
> They have mouths, but do not speak;
>> eyes, but do not see.
> They have ears, but do not hear;
>> noses, but do not smell.
> They have hands, but do not feel;
>> feet, but do not walk;
>> they make no sound in their throats.
> *Those who make them are like them;*
>> *so are all who trust in them.* (Ps 115:3–8, italics supplied)

> The idols of the nations are silver and gold,
>> the work of human hands.
> They have mouths, but they do not speak;
>> they have eyes, but they do not see;
> they have ears, but they do not hear,
>> and there is no breath in their mouths.
> *Those who make them*
>> *and all who trust them*
>> *shall become like them.* (Ps 135:15–18, italics supplied)

The prophet Isaiah describes his nation as having "forsaken the Lord" (Isa 1:4; 2:6) and "despised the Holy One of Israel" (1:4). They have filled their land with idols and worship the work of their hands (2:8). In Isaiah 6, the prophet is commissioned to stop the ears of those who already refuse to listen, and to shut the eyes of those unwilling to see:

> And he said, "Go and say to this people:
>> 'Keep listening, but do not comprehend;
>> keep looking, but do not understand.'

---

44. Beale, *We Become*, 16, 36–70. See also Beale, "Isaiah 6:9–13," 257–78.

> Make the mind of this people dull,
>> and stop their ears,
>> and shut their eyes,
> so that they may not look with their eyes,
>> and listen with their ears,
> and comprehend with their minds,
>> and turn and be healed." (Isa 6:9–10; cf. Jer 10:1–16)

Part of God's judgment involves making an idolatrous nation like the gods it worships.[45] The Matthean Jesus quotes this very passage to explain why he speaks in parables to the crowds from the cities and villages of Galilee (Matt 13:14–15). By quoting Isaiah in this manner, he equated his own generation with the preexilic idolatrous generation of Isaiah.[46]

Idolatrous Israel and the Presence of Satan

This leads us to question whether the inhabitants of Galilee and Jerusalem in the time of Jesus worshipped idols. Consideration of other sources will help us address this question. Although referring to a time period somewhat earlier to the Gospel, the author of 1 Maccabees testifies to the willingness of many in Israel to profane the Sabbath, to sacrifice to idols, and to erect a "desolating sacrilege on the altar of burnt offering" (1 Macc. 1:41–42, 54–55).[47] In *Mart. Isa.* 2:7, dated to the first century CE, a pseudepigraphal Isaiah withdraws from Jerusalem in response to those in the "service of Satan." Clearly other Jewish authors contemplated the possibility of Israel's idolatry.

When it comes to the Gospel, however, our initial reaction might be to deny such practices in view of the absence of explicit references to idolatry. Beale cautions against such a response:

> Though words for *idol* and *false god* hardly appear in the Gospels, this does not mean that there is no concept of idolatry there. Rather, though Israel's reliance on idols in Jesus's day did not take

---

45. The blindness of Israel, suggests Beale, reflects the blindness of the idols they worship, a principle most explicitly portrayed in Isa 43:8, 10–13; 44:18 (*We Become*, 42–45).

46. Hays, *Gospels*, 129–30. In Matt 13:13b, Matthew replaces Mark's *hina* with a *hoti*. Matthew's Jesus does not speak in parables *in order that* the crowds not understand but *because* they do not understand. Konradt, *Israel*, 250–52.

47. See also the warnings against idolatry in Wis 14:8—15:19; *Jub.* 22:16–18. CD IV.13–21 describes Belial as running unbridled throughout Israel and ensnaring Israel in the traps of fornication, wealth, and defilement of the sanctuary. This is in fulfillment of Isa 24:17. Klawans, "Idolatry, Incest, and Impurity," 410–13.

the form of bowing down to images, nevertheless, they did put their trust in something else besides God, bringing judgment on themselves, as it had come on earlier generations of Israel. Consequently, they were still idol worshipers in essence, though the outward form of it was expressed differently.[48]

Support for this position is found in Jesus's appeal to Old Testament passages, particularly from Isaiah, which in their original setting addressed the issue of idolatry.[49] Beale is less clear in defining the object of this implied idolatrous worship. He draws on the work of Rikki Watts to suggest that it is the worship of the "idol of tradition," which he further expands as "human-made, stale, empty tradition."[50] The evidence for this position, however, is sparse and would suggest that Beale has conflated the effect of idolatry (i.e., empty tradition) with the object of idolatry, the worship of other gods.

In support of Beale's wider argument, however, we may argue that the Gospel portrays a situation in which idolatry is to be expected. The third temptation in the wilderness involves Satan offering Jesus all the kingdoms of the world if he will fall down and worship him (Matt 4:9).[51] If we are to understand the temptation narrative as part of a wider reenactment of Israel's conquest of the promised land in which Jesus's baptism equates to his namesake Joshua's crossing of the Jordan (Josh 3:1–17), then the implication is that in moving from the Jordan into the wilderness, Jesus is entering the equivalent of Canaanite territory. For the Evangelist, it is land under the control of Satan. In the three temptations, Satan emerges as a counterfeit deity and patron. By the third temptation, in which, as Yahweh offered Moses the kingdoms of Canaan, Satan offers Jesus the kingdoms of

48. Beale, *We Become*, 162–63. Sandelin suggests that the reference to the abomination of desolation (Matt 24:15; Mark 13:14), Jesus's citation of the *shema* (Matt 22:37; Mark 12:28–34), his injunction to hallow the name of Our Father (Matt 6:9), and his description of his generation as "evil and adulterous" (12:38–42; 16:1–4), all hint at idolatry ("Jesus-Tradition," 412–20).

49. E.g., Isa 6:9–10 in Matt 13:13–15; Mark 4:12; Luke 8:10; John 12:39–40; Isa 29:9–10, 13 in Matt 15:7–9; Mark 7:6–13. Beale, *We Become*, 163–83.

50. Beale, *We Become*, 176. See also Watts, *New Exodus*, 190–99, 238–52.

51. Leim draws our attention to the parallel between the magi falling down and worshipping Jesus in Matt 2:11 and Satan's request that Jesus fall down and worship him in 4:9 (*Matthew's Theological Grammar*, 4–14). For Leim, the statement in 4:10 that one should "worship the Lord your God and serve only him" (cf. Deut 6:13) requires us "to relearn how to say θεός" (p. 14) in light of those instances in the Gospel where homage or worship is directed to Jesus (cf. *proskyneō* in Matt 2:2, 8, 11; 8:2; 9:18; 14:33; 15:25; 20:20; 28:17; cf. 18:26).

the world, Satan has usurped the role of the God of the exodus. To push the parallel even further, Judea now needs to be cleared primarily not of the forces of Imperial Rome, but rather, and somewhat shockingly when contrasted with the typical messianic movements presented to us by Josephus, of the first-century CE equivalent of the Canaanite gods and their places of worship (cf. Deut 12:1–12).[52] Jesus, quoting repeatedly from Deuteronomy in his responses to Satan, is the new Deuteronomic Joshua reconquering the promised land, a land polluted by a foreign deity dressed in the stolen garb of the God of the exodus.[53]

Satan is an ever-present threat to Israel in the Gospel. Jesus frames his ministry as entering the house (i.e., Israel) of a strong man (i.e., Satan), and tying him up in order to plunder his property (Matt 12:29). This plundering process involves freeing those under Satanic and demonic control (cf. 12:22–23). Satan will resist this. In the parable of the sower, the seed that lands on the path is snatched away by "the evil one" (*ho ponēros*, 13:19). In this context, his followers are to pray for deliverance "from the evil one" (*apo tou ponērou*, 6:13).

The Evangelist hints at the form Israel's idolatry might take. In Matt 6:24, Jesus warns that no one can serve two masters: "You cannot serve God and mammon." Efforts to link mammon with a Syrian deity or a particular demon remain unconvincing.[54] Jesus's reference to mammon is instead a personification of wealth. Nevertheless, the use of the term "to serve" evokes the widespread Old Testament association of idolatry with the service of other gods (e.g., "to serve Baal," Judg 10:6, 10, 13). Brian Rosner has argued convincingly that Jesus's injunction against serving mammon is part of a wider Jewish (and New Testament) belief that greed was a form of idolatry ("greed, which is idolatry," Col 3:5; cf. Eph 5:5). Rosner sets out a political model of idolatry which may well apply to the Gospel. In the Old Testament, Israel entered into alliances with other nations against the wishes of Yahweh, thereby acknowledging the sovereignty of their gods: "Jeremiah and Ezekiel denounce Israel's treaties with Assyria and Egypt in terms that add up to nothing less than the charge of idolatry, even though the literal worship of other gods is nowhere in view."[55] Isaiah condemns his people for welcoming diviners from the east, soothsayers like the Philistines, and for

---

52. E.g., Josephus, *Ant.* 17.273–81.

53. Leim, *Matthew's Theological Grammar*, 73–77.

54. Davies and Allison, *Matthew 1–7*, 643–45; Rosner, *Greed*, 18–19.

55. Rosner, "Concept of Idolatry," 25. See also *Greed*, 143–48.

"clasping hands with foreigners" (Isa 2:6). The Gospel portrays the leaders of Israel manipulating the Roman authorities and, it may be implied, Rome's gods, to achieve their own ends—the removal of Jesus.

Another important argument of Beale is that those who worship idols, share the fate of idols, i.e., being burned to the point of destruction. This principle may be clearly discerned in the Gospel. References by Jesus to being thrown into Gehenna evoke the valley of the sons of Hinnon (2 Kgs 23:10; Neh 11:30; Jer 19:2).[56] The valley was southwest of Jerusalem and joined the Kidron valley which lay to the southeast of the city. Prior to the exile, the valley became a center of idol worship (2 Chr 28:3; cf. 33:6; Jer 32:35). In 2 Kings 23:1–25, we find a description of Josiah's reforms, which included the defiling of the altar in Gehinnon by scattering human bones throughout the valley to ensure that it could not be used again for idolatrous worship.[57] We may conclude that in referencing Gehenna, part of Jesus's intention was to evoke for his audiences the threat of punishment traditionally associated with idolatry. A further possible illusion to the punishment of idolatry may be implied in John the Baptist's words to the Pharisees and Sadducees: "Even now the axe is lying at the root of the trees; every tree therefore that does not bear good fruit is cut down and thrown into the fire" (Matt 3:10). In the Old Testament Prophets, cultic and idolatrous trees, often representing an idolatrous Israel, were to be cut down and burned with unquenchable fire (e.g., Isa 1:29–31; 6:13).[58]

Oracles of Doom

When a city or nation rejects the invitation to repent and the manifestation of the divine presence, reproach is the prophet's next message: "Then [Jesus] began to reproach (*oneidizein*) the cities in which most of his deeds of power had been done, because they did not repent" (Matt 11:20). In the Gospel, this reproach takes the form of an oracle of doom.[59] In Matt 11, there are two such oracles, the first addressed to Chorazin and Bethsaida

---

56. Cf. Matt 5:22, 29–30; 10:28; 18:9; 23:15, 33.

57. So too, 2 Chr 34:1–7.

58. Beale, *We Become*, 52–59.

59. Cf. Isa 5:11–17, 18–23; 29:15–21; 33:1; Mic 2:1–5; Hab 2:9–11. Davies and Allison, *Matthew 8–18*, 265.

(vv. 21–22) and the second to Capernaum (vv. 23–24). Both follow the same pattern:[60]

A. Address (vv. 21a, 23a): "Woe to you . . ."

B. Indictment (hypothetical condition, hypothetical response; 21b–c; 23b–c): "If the deeds of power had been done in . . . , they would have repented long ago"

C. Verdict (comparison of fate with other cities; vv. 22, 24): "It will be more tolerable on the day of judgment for . . . than for you"

Similar oracles are delivered to Jerusalem in Matt 23:

A. Address (vv. 13a, 15a, 16a, 23a, 25a, 27a, 29a): "Woe to you scribes and Pharisees"

B. Indictment (vv. 13b–14; 15b–c; 16b–19; 23b–24; 25b; 27b–28; 29b–33): "For you . . ."

C. Verdict (vv. 37–39): "Jerusalem, Jerusalem . . . Your house is left to you, desolate"

Both the mission to the cities of Galilee and the mission to Jerusalem include such oracles, illustrating their importance in the Evangelist's conception of mission. The purpose of these oracles, introduced with the interjection "woe," is to communicate pain and displeasure, threat and warning. It is a warning delivered with great sadness, as illustrated by the lament of Matt 23:37–39 that judgment is about to occur. Assuming a willingness to deliver such a message, the reader must first decide whether the city has rejected the prophetic call to repent. As we shall see in our next chapter, the idealized prophet does not make this decision alone. He or she should take into account how the city responds to those followers of Jesus who are righteous persons, determining whether or not they have been accepted by the community.

The consequence of delivering an oracle of doom is a sharp rise in hostility between the community and the prophet. The oracles of doom in Matt 11:20–24 lead to a Sabbath filled with hostile confrontations in chapters 12 and 13. These conflicts include the legal dispute over the plucking of grain on the Sabbath (12:1–8), the healing in the synagogue of the man with the withered hand (12:9–14), the accusation by the Pharisees that Jesus casts out demons by Beelzebul (12:22–32), and the request by the

60. I have expanded the pattern of Davies and Allison, *Matthew 8–18*, 265.

scribes and Pharisees for a sign (12:38–42). Finally, in 12:14, the Pharisees conspire against Jesus, how to destroy him.

On the Use of Parables: "Let He Who Has Ears, Hear"

Despite intense conflict, it is not yet time for the prophet to withdraw. One more task remains. The idealized prophet is to harden even further the hearts of those in rebellion. Where this is most clearly seen is in Jesus's use of parables in chapter 13. In popular perception, parables are not normally associated with prophetic condemnation.[61] However, parables have a dual function in that they harden the hearts of the idolatrous and cause a sinful remnant to reassess their spiritual state and to deepen their levels of commitment. I return to Beale's explanation of how this process works.[62]

In the Old Testament, the prophets first delivered warnings in a reasoned and sermonic manner, warning that unless the nation repented of its idolatry, divine judgment would ensue. When these warnings failed to move their audience, the prophets took up a different form of warning, using symbolic actions and mashals (mšl, Gk parabolē) to grab the nation's attention.[63] This change in medium unfortunately rarely worked due to the nation's lack of spiritual insight. Instead, such parables normally caused already hardened hearts to harden further. In our dance analogy, when a nation dances with another partner and rejects God's invitation to return to him, he deepens the nation's commitment to the partner of their choice. As discussed above, this dynamic is most clearly expressed in Isa 6:9–10.[64] This Isaianic warning follows a parable about a vineyard in Isa 5:1–7, suggesting that the parabolic aspect of Isaiah's message is closely linked with the hardening commission of Isa 6:9–10.

A similar pattern is found in Ezekiel. In LXX Ezek 3:27, we find "hearing" language similar to that found in Isa 6:9–10 ("he who hears, let him hear"). What immediately follows is the prophet's first parable. Similarly, "seeing" and "hearing" language is found in LXX Ezek 12:2 (they "have eyes to see and do not see and ears to hear, but do not hear") and is followed in 12:3–16 by the prophet's first parabolic act. Elsewhere in Ezekiel, parables

---

61. See, for example, Hauge's suggestion that they reflect Greco-Roman fables ("Fabulous Parables," 89–106).

62. Beale, *We Become*, 244–48.

63. On the prophetic parable, see Westermann, *Basic Forms*, 201–2.

64. Gnilka, *Das Matthäusevangelium*, 483–84.

are frequently used to confront a rebellious nation. A good example is the "pot parable" in Ezek 24:1–14 in which the prophet speaks a parable of judgment against the rebellious house of Israel concerning the impending siege by Babylon. The parable compares a corroded caldron to Jerusalem and various pieces of meat placed in the caldron to its inhabitants undergoing divine judgment in response to their shedding of blood.[65] Often such parables are found in contexts in which idolatry features prominently (e.g., Ezek 11:18, 21; 12:16, 24; 14:1–7).[66] Their purpose is to blind those who, though they outwardly confess loyalty to God, are in fact dancing with another partner. In contrast to this hardening effect, the shock effect of a parable on a believing but sinful remnant may result in repentance. A good example is found in David's reaction to the prophet Nathan's parable following his adultery with Bathsheba and murder of Uriah the Hittite (2 Sam 12:12–16). In this instance, David is moved to repentance.

This same parable dynamic is played out in the Gospel. This is signaled in Jesus's appeal, "Let anyone with ears listen!" (Matt 13:43), a clear echo of the "hearing" motif of Ezekiel and other Old Testament prophets. To retrace our steps, Jesus's forcefully stated appeal to the cities of Galilee to repent is sadly rejected (4:17, 23; 11:20–24). In response, Jesus switches from direct speech to parabolic speech. The disciples then ask Jesus why he speaks to the crowds in parables. His response is that they, the disciples, have been given to know the secrets of the kingdom of heaven, but to the crowds it has not been given, for "to those who have, more will be given, and they will have an abundance; but from those who have nothing, even what they have will be taken away" (13:12). The purpose of Jesus's parables is to polarize further an already polarized audience.[67] Jesus explains his rationale in 13:13 by paraphrasing Isa 6:9 (because "seeing they do not perceive, and hearing they do not listen, nor do they understand").[68] Because of this generation's state of spiritual lethargy, whatever is said to them will make little difference beyond confirming their spiritual choices. Jesus then quotes LXX Isa 6:9–10 in full, explicitly equating his own generation with that of the preexilic generation of Isaiah's day:[69]

---

65. Cf. Ezek 12:23; 17:2; 18:2; 20:49; 21:5.

66. Beale, *We Become*, 245–46.

67. Against this reading, Runesson believes the parables were to aid the understanding of the crowds, to make the obscure clear (*Divine Wrath*, 277–91).

68. Davies and Allison, *Matthew 8–18*, 392.

69. Isa 6:9–10 is paraphrased in Matt 13:13 and then, in its LXX form, quoted in full

> With them indeed is fulfilled the prophecy of Isaiah that says:
> "You will indeed listen, but never understand,
>   and you will indeed look, but never perceive.
> For this people's heart has grown dull,
>   and their ears are hard of hearing,
>   and they have shut their eyes;
>   so that they might not look with their eyes,
>   and listen with their ears,
>   and understand with their heart and turn—
>   and I would heal them." (Matt 13:14–15)

The implication of Jesus's appeal to Isa 6:9–10 is that his use of parables is to blind the spiritually blind and deafen the spiritually deaf, making them even more like the idols they worship. In contrast, the effect of the parables on the seeing and hearing disciples is the enhancement of their sight and hearing: "But blessed are your eyes, for they see, and your ears, for they hear" (13:16). The use of parables is thus intended to confirm one's choice of dance partner. In the case of the blind and the deaf, it is God confirming their desire to remain in a state of idolatry. The Evangelist subsequently confirms the prophetic nature of the parables when he states that "without a parable [Jesus] told [the crowds] nothing" (13:34). This was to fulfill, according to the Evangelist, what had been spoken by the Old Testament prophet, at which point he merges Jesus's persona with that of the prophet with the declaration, "I will open my mouth to speak in parables, I will proclaim what has been hidden from the foundation of the world" (Matt 13:35; cf. Ps 78:2).

Withdrawal from the Cities of Galilee in Matthew 14 to 16

The intervening chapters between the mission to Galilee and the mission to Jerusalem model divine withdrawal.[70] The rejection of Jesus by the cities of Galilee results in him putting into effect his own instructions to the disciples to "shake off the dust from your feet as you leave that house or town" (10:14). In chapters 14 to 16, Jesus withdraws from the cities of Galilee and instead spends his time in a "deserted place by himself" (14:13); on a mountain "by himself" (14:23); in Gennesaret (14:34); in the district of

---

in 13:14–15. This has led a number of scholars to conclude that 13:14–15 is an early post-Matthean interpolation. Cf. Davies and Allison, *Matthew 8–18*, 393–94; Hannan, *Nature and Demands*, 106–7; Konradt, *Israel*, 250–51.

70. Cf. *anachōreō* in Matt 12:15; 14:13; 15:21.

Tyre and Sidon (15:21); along the sea of Galilee and on a mountain (15:29); in the region of Magadan (15:39); in the district of Caesarea Philippi (16:13); and on a high mountain (17:1).[71] The emphasis is on regions and districts rather than cities. It would press the evidence too far to describe this as a proto-gentile mission. Nonetheless, the mission to the nations is anticipated in this section of the Gospel.

Geographical associations are reversed throughout the Gospel, but this is especially apparent in Jesus's retreat from the cities of Galilee. Earlier in the Gospel, Egypt, normally a place where God's people face persecution, offers sanctuary to Joseph, the child, and his mother (2:13–15). In this central section of the Gospel, we encounter stories redolent with exodus imagery; the feedings of the 5,000 and 4,000 both remind the reader of the provision of manna in the wilderness (cf. Exod 16:1–36//Matt 14:13–21; 15:32–39).[72] Such allusions suggest a new exodus, not from Egypt, but, dramatically, from the cities and villages of Galilee.[73] Jesus's avoidance of the cities and villages of Galilee results in him rejecting his disciples' suggestion during the feeding of the 5,000 that he send the crowds away from their deserted place into the villages to buy food for themselves (14:15). Clearly the disciples have failed to determine the true spiritual state of the surrounding cities and villages. They are places to escape from rather than places of safety to which to retire.

We also find in these intervening chapters between the mission to Galilee and the mission to Jerusalem a shift away from the public deeds of power of chapters 8 and 9, many of which were performed in villages, synagogues, or homes (cf. 8:5, 14, 34; 9:10, 18, 28). Their purpose was to demonstrate the kingdom's presence and move the cities of Galilee toward repentance. When Jesus performs miracles in this middle section of the Gospel, however, it is far from the glare of the Galilean authorities, as in the feedings of the 5,000 and 4,000 (14:13–21; 15:32–39). In 15:21–28, Jesus heals the daughter of a Canaanite woman, her Canaanite identity being another exodus-conquest allusion, in the district of Tyre and Sidon, again, far from the cities of Galilee.[74] Her faith contrasts with "the lost sheep of the house of Israel" (v. 24) and demonstrates the willingness of other

---

71. Jeremias, *Jesus' Promise*, 31.

72. I accept the 4,000 as Jewish. See Loader, *Jesus' Attitude*, 212; Cousland, "Feeding," 1–23.

73. See Charette, *Recompense*, 54–60.

74. Vine, "Repatriating the Canaanite Woman," 7–32.

nations to respond even to partial revelation. When Jesus finally returns to Capernaum, he undertakes a private miracle when he provides a coin in the mouth of a fish for Peter to pay the temple tax (17:24–27). This mid-section concludes with Jesus beginning to teach his disciples that he must go to Jerusalem where he would undergo "great suffering at the hands of the elders and chief priests and scribes, and be killed, and on the third day be raised" (16:21).

We may surmise as to the pastoral purpose of this withdrawal narrative. At a minimum it prepares readers for their own wilderness sojourn, their own time as wanderers, outsiders, and the excluded. It engenders a willingness in readers, when necessary, to break existing social ties and loyalties in the knowledge that they, like those faithful Hebrews who left Egypt with Moses, will survive their wilderness sojourn.

Implications

The prophets of the Old Testament predicted (1) the imminent destruction of Jerusalem due to its idolatry, (2) the future judgment of the nations, and (3), national restoration by means of a faithful remnant. The Evangelist operates within this basic framework. He predicts the judgment of idolatrous Israel and, at the *parousia*, the judgment of the nations. A remnant, represented by those sent by Jesus on his various missions, become the nucleus of a renewed Israel obedient to God's original intention for Israel to be a light to the nations.

Reading the Gospel in light of this framework shapes the reader's attitude toward the *parousia*. The emphasis in a number of New Testament texts is on the need to hasten the *parousia* (cf. 2 Pet 3:12; Rev 6:9–11; 22:20). This not, however, the primary emphasis of the Gospel. Instead, the Evangelist presents the *parousia* as a terror inspiring day of judgment (cf. Matt 8:12; 13:42, 50; 22:13; 24:51; 25:30). It is a day of weeping and gnashing of teeth, not something you would wish on your worst enemy. Instead of looking forward to the *parousia*, readers are invited to stand in the shoes of Jeremiah, Jonah, and other Old Testament prophets, and warn the nations of judgment in the hope that, as a result of their repentance, it may be postponed.[75]

---

75. Contrast the prayers for the peace of the nations in 1 Clem. 60–61 and Tertullian, *Apol.* 30.

How does the Gospel shape its readers into prophets? One way is through its consistent focus on cities and nations.[76] The Evangelist is, above all, focused on God's dance with cities and nations. Forming or maintaining a separate Christian community is of secondary importance. The focus throughout the Gospel on Galilee and Jerusalem encourages the reader to adopt a similar prophetic attitude in which the focus of one's spiritual experience is less on one's interior life or the life of the community of Jesus-followers and instead on the relationship between God and the city, region, or nation. It is the dance between the nation and God which takes priority over any personal agendas of the prophet. A failure to incorporate the idealized prophetic outlook into the discipleship ideal will result in Jesus-communities that are inward-looking, self-focused, and isolated from the *polis*. The prophet defines the problem which other discipleship roles address. No prophet—no problem. No problem—no purpose. And the problem is the state of the nation.

In this context, Matthew's idealized prophet receives his or her message direct from God: "When they hand you over, do not worry about how you are to speak or what you are to say; for what you are to say will be given to you at that time; for it is not you who speak, but the Spirit of your Father speaking through you" (Matt 10:19–20). This provides comfort to the prophet in that he or she is no longer required to second guess the message God desires the nations to hear. The divine message is not determined by the personal considerations of the prophet but rather by the ongoing dance between God and the nation. The message is contingent, contextual. The prophet is required to relinquish control of the message, allowing God to judge the tempo of the dance. Within this dance, the prophet will often personally experience the inhabiting presence of God while at the same time being required to operate in a national context in which the dance is going badly, a demonically dominated context from which God may well have withdrawn. This is the pain of the prophetic experience—loss of control and marginalization of personal needs. It is a high stakes mission in which the prophet contributes to a rise in tension which may ultimately result in his or her own persecution and death (5:11–12; 23:29–31).

---

76. Waetjen, *Matthew's Theology*, 10.

3

The Righteous Person

Being Righteous to Save Others

Introduction

IF THE ROLE OF the prophet is to call a nation distant from God back into a
close relationship with him, the role of the righteous person is to provide a
focal point whereby the nation's attitude to God is made explicit. How the
nation responds to the righteous person, known as a *Saddîq*, determines
its fate. A positive response results in the delaying of judgment. Hostile
treatment of the *Saddîq* precipitates judgment. The *Saddîqim* focalize the
promise to Abraham: "I will bless those who bless you, and the one who
curses you I will curse; and in you all the families of the earth shall be
blessed" (Gen 12:3). They are a polarizing presence that pressures the nation into choosing between acting with gracious charity or with unjustified
violence. In political theology terms, righteous persons are the bellwether
by which God determines whether the community accepts his authority.

The identity of the righteous person is applied throughout the Gospel
to the followers of Jesus:

> Blessed are those who hunger and thirst for righteousness, for they
> will be filled. (Matt 5:6)

> Blessed are those who are persecuted for righteousness' sake, for
> theirs is the kingdom of heaven. (Matt 5:10)

> . . . and whoever welcomes a righteous person in the name of a
> righteous person will receive the reward of the righteous . . . (Matt
> 10:41)

In Matt 1:19, Joseph, the husband of Mary, is described as being a righteous person (*dikaios ōn*). The fact that Joseph is presented as a *Saddîq* before Jesus enters the scene affirms that Israel has already been exposed to righteous persons in the same way that there were prophets who also came before him (see 23:29). In describing Joseph in such terms, the Evangelist is alluding to a tradition well established by the first century CE, that of the *Saddîq*, the righteous person.[1] This tradition identified Noah as the first *Saddîq* based upon the description of him in Gen 6:9 as a "righteous man" (MT: *ṣaddîq*; LXX: *dikaios*), perfect (MT: *tāmîm*; LXX: *teleios*) in his generation: (cf. 7:1). In describing Noah in such terms, he is likened to Yahweh who is righteous.

In the Old Testament, the righteousness of God refers to God conforming to his holy nature.[2] The counterpart of divine righteousness is human righteousness, which is viewed as conformity to the will of God.[3] His will is primarily expressed in the Torah and in wisdom traditions. The application of Torah results in righteous judgments and those who keep the Torah are deemed righteous.[4] In terms of wisdom, those that fear the Lord and seek and speak wisdom are also deemed righteous.[5] Throughout our sources, whether Torah or wisdom traditions, the righteous are contrasted with the wicked.[6] Space does not allow for an in-depth consideration of the concept of the righteous person. Instead, we will limit our discussion to two important Old Testament passages.[7]

The first passage is found in Ezek 18 and provides us with a detailed law-based definition of the righteous person:

> If a man is righteous and does what is lawful and right—if he does
> not eat upon the mountains or lift up his eyes to the idols of the
> house of Israel, does not defile his neighbor's wife or approach a
> woman during her menstrual period, does not oppress anyone,
> but restores to the debtor his pledge, commits no robbery, gives
> his bread to the hungry and covers the naked with a garment, does
> not take advance or accrued interest, withholds his hand from

1. E.g., Philo, *Congr.* 90.
2. Isa 45:21; Ps 71:15–24; Hos 10:12; Mic 6:5; 7:9.
3. Gen 18:19; Deut 6:25; Isa 5:16; Ps 1:4–6.
4. Deut 16:18–20; 25:1; Ezek 18:5.
5. Ps 19:9; 34:9, 11, 15–19; Prov 8:8; 9:9; 10:11, 20–21, 31. See also Sir 9:16.
6. Gen 18:23; Prov 3:33.
7. See also Ps 15.

> iniquity, executes true justice between contending parties, follows
> my statutes, and is careful to observe my ordinances, acting faith-
> fully—such a one is righteous; he shall surely live, says the Lord
> GOD. (Ezek 18:5–9)

There is a strong legal flavor to this passage. Walther Zimmerli suggests that this definition of the righteous person may well, despite few verbal points of contact, follow the general order of the Decalogue.[8] The first pair of clauses—eating on a mountain, lifting up your eyes (v. 6a)—relate to right worship. The second pair of clauses—defiling your neighbor's wife, approaching a woman during her menstrual period (v. 6b)—relate to ritual regulations. The final three groups of couplets and triplets in vv. 7–8a relate to social life. This ten-point definition concludes in v. 9 with a general appeal to follow the statues and ordinances of the Lord God. The *Saddîq* is one who acts righteously toward both God and his fellow man in a manner that honors the principles of the Torah. Of particular importance for our discussion, the righteous person "gives his bread to the hungry and covers the naked with a garment," a characteristic of the righteous taken up by Jesus in Matt 25:35–46.

The second passage is Isaiah 58 which identifies an additional quality of the *Saddîq*—the keeping of the Sabbath. Chapter 58 addresses the nation as a whole, asking why it is that Yahweh does not respond to its fasts and entreaties. The answer is that it has failed to act righteously by fasting and praying for its own interests (58:2–3). Its entreaties need to reflect the interests of Yahweh:

> Is not this the fast that I choose:
>> to loose the bonds of injustice,
>> to undo the thongs of the yoke,
>> to let the oppressed go free,
>> and to break every yoke?
> Is it not to share your bread with the hungry,
>> and bring the homeless poor into your house;
> when you see the naked, to cover them,
>> and not to hide yourself from your own kin? (Isa 58:6–7)

As in the definition of the *Saddîq* in Ezek 18:5–9, the emphasis is on the need to eliminate social injustices through the sharing of bread with the hungry, bringing the homeless poor into their houses, clothing the naked, and helping their own kin (58:7, 10). Graham Stanton notes that this list is

---

8. Zimmerli, *Ezekiel 1*, 378.

the closest in the Old Testament to the behavior of the righteous in Matt 25:31–46.[9]

The Sabbath is closely associated with justice.[10] Judith Gärtner has argued that in Isaiah a restored Israel is called to belong to the creator God of the world.[11] This belonging is to be expressed through the keeping of the covenant and Sabbath observance. Sabbath observance, suggests Gärtner, extends beyond Israel and is a sign of universal righteousness in a "new heavens" and "new earth" (Isa 66:22). This includes the nations, regarding whom, declares Yahweh, "from new moon to new moon, and from Sabbath to Sabbath . . . will come to worship in my presence" (66:23).[12] The nation is called to refrain from trampling the Sabbath. We return to Isa 58:

> If you refrain from trampling the sabbath,
>> from pursuing your own interests on my holy day;
> if you call the sabbath a delight
>> and the holy day of the LORD honorable;
> if you honor it, not going your own ways,
>> serving your own interests, or pursuing your own affairs;
> then you shall take delight in the LORD,
>> and I will make you ride upon the heights of the earth;
> I will feed you with the heritage of your ancestor Jacob,
>> for the mouth of the LORD has spoken. (Isa 58:13–14)

This call to honor the Sabbath is a further component of what it means to act righteously and should not be viewed as secondary to the earlier call to social justice. As well as affirming the creator God, the seventh-day Sabbath was a weekly celebration of Israel's deliverance from slavery in Egypt and, as such, was a time when all, regardless of social or economic status, might enjoy rest from their labors (cf. Deut 5:12–15).

In later Tannaitic (first and second centuries CE) and Amoraic (third to six centuries CE) rabbinic traditions there emerged legends of the *Saddîqim*. These were believed to exist in every generation and included a range of Old Testament characters such as Noah, Isaac, and Moses. It was believed that their existence was a precondition for the existence of the world.[13] The sages inferred this from Prov 10:25, "But the righteous

---

9. Stanton, *New People*, 218.

10. Gärtner, "Keep Justice!," 98.

11. Gärtner, "Keep Justice!," 86–99.

12. Gärtner, "Keep Justice!," 92–99.

13. Urbach, *Sages*, 487.

are the foundation of the world."[14] Various sages sought to put a figure to the number of righteous persons required for the continued existence of the world. Some argued that one alone was necessary. Others argued for thirty, thirty-six or forty-five.[15] They pointed to the story of the destruction of Sodom and Gomorrah as evidence that the presence of the righteous can defer judgment.[16] It is this point we will take up in our next section in which I will argue that the righteous persons Jesus sends into the villages and cities of Galilee have the potential to delay judgment.

Throughout these various traditions there is an emphasis on the *Saddiqim* as those who implement the law and seek wisdom. Their actions are righteous. While they may not be sinless, they shun sin and undertake acts of charity, reflecting the fullness of the divine character.[17] They keep the Sabbath. Their righteousness is a rebuke to the wicked, who respond with persecution (e.g., Wis 2:17–22). This results in judgment in favor of the righteous and against the wicked. There is increasing recognition that Matthew's use of righteousness is nearer to this paradigm rather than to any concept of imputed righteousness. This is not to argue that for the Evangelist salvation is not a free gift from God (cf. Matt 1:21; 26:28). It is simply to recognize that, as asserted by Benno Przybylski, "Matthew expresses this idea without reference to the concept of righteousness."[18] It is to the role the righteous play in either delaying and precipitating judgment that we now turn.

Delaying Judgment through the Presence of the Righteous

The prophetic call to repentance is one way of deferring judgment. However, the righteous person's presence also contributes to the delaying of judgment. Several interrelated motifs support this suggestion.

Righteous Persons and the Saving of Sodom and Gomorrah

Two references by Jesus to Sodom (and Gomorrah) in Matt 10:15 and 11:23–24 indicate that the cities served as an important paradigm in his

14. *Mekhilta de-R. Ishmael, Shîra*, 1. See also Gen. Rabba, 30.1, cited in Urbach, *Sages*, 487n1.

15. See b. Sanh. 97b, b. Sukkah 45b. Urbach, *Sages*, 488–89.

16. For sources, Urbach, *Sages*, 489.

17. Runesson, *Divine Wrath*, 85.

18. Przybylski, *Righteousness*, 107.

understanding of his mission to the cities of Galilee.[19] Warren Carter suggests that partial citations or allusions were used in ancient literature to evoke for an audience a well-known larger text:

> An audience elaborates the gaps or indeterminacies of a text to build a consistent understanding not by supplying whatever content it likes but by utilizing the tradition it shares with the author. The common traditions provide the audience with a frame of reference, the "perceptual grid," for its interpretive work.[20]

When Jesus alludes to Sodom and Gomorrah, Matthew expects his readers to bring the larger Genesis narrative and its echoes in later traditions to the interpretative table.[21] Further allusions in the Gospel reinforce this picture. Jesus's command for his Judea-based followers to "flee to the mountains" without going "down to take what is in the house" or returning from the field to get a coat (Matt 24:17–18) echoes the command to Lot to "flee to the hills" without looking back (Gen 19:17). The destruction of Sodom serves as a type for the destruction of Jerusalem in the same way that Noah's global flood serves as a type for the Son of Man's global judgment of the nations ("as the days of Noah were," Matt 24:37). The Lukan Jesus makes the link to Sodom explicit with the injunction to "remember Lot's wife" (Luke 17:32; cf. v. 29). Once the holy ones have left Judea, righteous in their concern that their flight may not fall on the Sabbath (Matt 24:20; cf. Isa 58:13–14), God will bring judgment upon the remaining wicked. Parallels to the destruction of Sodom strongly suggest themselves.

In support of this reading, W. D. Davies and Dale Allison argue that Lot's prototypical flight from wickedness "became, in Jewish eschatology, a type of the eschatological flight from wickedness in the final days."[22] In picking up on such allusions, modern commentators are simply following earlier interpretations.[23] Eusebius, for example, writing anywhere between 311 and 324 CE, associates the destruction of Jerusalem in 70 CE with the

---

19. Cf. Luke 17:26–32.

20. Carter, "Evoking Isaiah," 506. This suggestion is based upon John Foley's work on traditional referentiality (*Immanent Art*, 1–60).

21. For Jerusalem as Sodom and Gomorrah, see Isa 1:8–9; 3:9; Jer 23:14; *Mart. Ascen. Isa.* 10; T. Levi 14:6.

22. Davies and Allison, *Matthew 19–28*, 347–48. Examples they cite include Amos 2:15–16; Zech 14:5; Ps Sol. 17:16–17, 25; Matt 3:7; Rev 12:6; *Liv. Pro.* 2:15; *Mart. Ascen. Isa.* 4:13 and *Apoc. El.* 4:21.

23. E.g., Epiphanius the Latin, *Interp. Evangel.* 33.

desertion from the capital of all holy men, whom he identifies as those who believed on Christ (*Hist. eccl.* 3.5.3).

When we turn to the Old Testament account of the destruction of Sodom and Gomorrah we find that the two motifs of *hospitality* and *righteous persons* play a key role in determining the timing of judgment. In Gen 18:1–8, Abraham extends hospitality to three strangers who approach his tent. Abraham implores them not to pass by and instead offers them generous hospitality in the form of water to wash their feet and a place to rest. He then provides them with a lavish feast of bread made from choice flour, a calf—a rare delicacy, and curds and milk. Abraham personally serves his guests and stands nearby, ready to attend to their needs. After the meal, the guests turn toward Sodom (18:16). At this point, Yahweh decides not to hide from Abraham what he is about to do to Sodom and Gomorrah. The reason for this disclosure is because Abraham is the repository of the promise that through him, all nations will be blessed, and because his children are to keep the eternal values of "righteousness and justice" that constitute the "way of the Lord" (18:19). The Lord informs Abraham that he must respond to the outcry of the oppressed that has arisen against Sodom and Gomorrah by judging the gravity of their sin (18:20–21). In the Old Testament, an outcry to the Lord usually occurs when justice and righteousness is denied, whether, for example, to God's people in slavery in Egypt (Exod 3:7), or to the widow and orphan in Exod 22:21–23.

The men then depart toward Sodom, upon which Abraham enters into an extended dialogue with Yahweh by demanding whether he will sweep away the righteous with the wicked (Gen 18:23). Abraham's conviction is that God must act with justice: "Shall not the Judge of all the earth do what is just" (18:25). He cannot destroy the righteous with the unrighteous. The Lord concedes and agrees to forgive Sodom "for the sake of fifty righteous," if they can be found in the city (18:26). Abraham then negotiates the number down from fifty to forty-five, forty-five to forty, forty to thirty, thirty to twenty, and finally, from twenty to ten righteous persons (18:27–32). The principle is thereby established that the Lord will not destroy the city as a result of the presence of righteous persons.

This principle derived from the Sodom story that Yahweh would desist from judgment for the sake of the righteous led to the development within rabbinic traditions of a more general belief that the presence of righteous persons within the world postpones divine judgment.[24] These traditions,

---

24. *Gen. Rab.* 44.3. See also Prov 11:10.

some likely contemporary to Matthew, did not develop in a vacuum but were part of wider matrix of ideas that developed in Second Temple legends relating to the righteous. It was believed by some Tannaim, for example, that God did not destroy Israel after the golden calf incident because Moses could name, as in the Sodom story, ten righteous persons (*Exod Rab.* 44.7). These included the three Patriarchs plus himself, Aaron, Eleazar, Ithamar, Phinehas, Joshua, and Caleb.

I share this example simply as evidence of the likelihood that the Evangelist held to the principle that for the sake of the righteous, judgment would be delayed. This understanding is most recognizably present in the parable of the wheat and the tares in which the Son of Man leaves the tares in the field because if they were to be uprooted, the wheat would be damaged, identified as the righteous in Matt 13:43. For the sake of the wheat—the righteous, the tares are left in place.

We return to the story of Sodom. After the conversation between Yahweh and Abraham, the two men, now revealed to be angels, meet Lot at the city gateway. Lot, as Abraham previously, offers them hospitality in the form of lodging, the washing of their feet, and a feast (Gen 19:1-2).[25] But before the angels lie down for the night, the men of the city, described as "both young and old," an indication that not a single decent individual could be found among them, surround the house and demand that Lot's guests be brought out that "they might know them" (19:3-5). Lot seeks to uphold his duty of hospitality to the two strangers by offering instead his two betrothed daughters, who "have not known a man," to the mob (19:8). The two angels intervene, striking the mob with blindness and delivering Lot and his daughters from Sodom (Gen 19:9-23). Yahweh then rained down sulphur and fire on Sodom and Gomorrah, presumably now justified as a result of the absence of any righteous persons in the two cities (19:24-25).

We find in the Gospel a number of important motifs common to the Genesis account; explicit references to Sodom and Gomorrah and the motifs of hospitality, righteous persons, and flight from judgment.[26] It thus seems reasonable to conclude that the righteous followers of Jesus function theologically in a manner similar to the righteous persons who, had they been present in Sodom, would have deferred judgment.

---

25. Clement understood Lot to have been saved because of his hospitality and godliness (1 Clem. 11).

26. Cf. the deliverance of the righteous Noah and Lot in 2 Pet 2:4-10.

We should note that the Evangelist does not indicate the number of righteous persons necessary to postpone judgment. Instead, he presents us with a two-stage process whereby the number of righteous persons may be increased within the community. First, the righteous followers of Jesus are to remain in those cities of Galilee that extend to them a hospitable welcome. In a very direct sense, this increases the number of righteous persons in the city, by introducing them from outside. Second, the disciples are sent to the cities of Galilee in a manner that invites hospitality and righteous behavior on the part of the inhabitants of the cities. Jesus sends his followers with minimal provisions and resources. They cannot survive on their own. They need help. When the inhabitants of the cities offer them help, they fulfil Ezekiel's definition of a righteous person: "If a man is righteous . . . [he] gives his bread to the hungry and covers the naked with a garment," Ezek 18:5, 7. They are thus counted as righteous persons.

Righteous Persons in Search of a Home

As noted above, the first way of increasing the number of righteous persons within a city is for them to enter from outside the community. This is what we find when Jesus sends the Twelve, idealized in Matt 10:41 as righteous persons, to the lost sheep of the house of Israel (cf. 10:6).[27] He requires that when they enter a city, village or house, they determine, as did the angels in Sodom, the nature of the reception extended them:

> Whatever town or village you enter, find out who in it is worthy [axios], and stay there until you leave. As you enter the house, greet it. If the house is worthy, let your peace come upon it; but if it is not worthy, let your peace return to you. If anyone will not welcome you or listen to your words, shake off the dust from your feet as you leave that house or town. Truly I tell you, it will be more tolerable for the land of Sodom and Gomorrah on the day of judgment than for that town. (Matt 10:11–15)

When entering a city or town, they are not to stay just anywhere.[28] Rather, they are to carefully choose where they stay. The righteous person's presence should not be imposed on a city. They are instead to be embraced and

27. Luz takes the reference to gentiles in Matt 10:18 and generic statements throughout 10:5–42 as indicators that the chapter represents a "basic manifesto" for the church (*Matthean Manifesto*, 144–49).

28. Davies and Allison, *Matthew 8–18*, 174.

welcomed. Jesus outlines two steps the disciples are to take to determine whether this is the case. First, they are to enquire as to whom is worthy (10:11). This raises the question as to what it means to be worthy. What particular reputation are they to look for? The second step Jesus commands is that they locate the house of the worthy person and determine for themselves the truth of his or her reputation. If they find that the house, i.e., the head of the household, is indeed worthy (10:13), they are to remain there. In contrast, the failure to welcome may be understood as an indication of what it means to be unworthy. If they find out that the owner of the house, despite the views of the town, fails to extend a welcome, they are to depart, publicly manifesting this rejection by shaking the dust off their feet as they "leave that house or town" (10:14). The presence of righteous envoys of Jesus must be with the active consent of households within the city.

The city must demonstrate its willingness to accept the righteous followers of Jesus as his envoys. Margaret Mitchell has drawn our attention to pervasive envoy traditions in the Greco-Roman world suggesting that the cultural assumption behind such texts as Matt 10:40–42 ("Whoever welcomes you welcomes me . . .") is "that the one who is sent should be treated according to the status of the one by whom he was sent, not the status he individually holds."[29] To extend hospitality to a follower of Jesus is to accept him or her as Jesus's envoy.[30] To accept Jesus into your home is to accept Jesus as an envoy of the Father ("and whoever welcomes me welcomes the one who sent me," 10:40). It is to accept, although indirectly, the presence of the Father into your community.

Extending Charity to Disciples in Need

The strong emphasis in Matt 10:11–15 and 40–42 on the need for the community to extend a welcome to the followers of Jesus is coupled with Jesus sending them out with minimal provisions. They are forbidden from taking gold, silver or copper, a bag for their journey, or two tunics, sandals or a staff (Matt 10:10). The reason for this is that "laborers deserve their food" (10:11). Their physical survival depends upon the community extending

---

29. Mitchell, "New Testament Envoys," 647.

30. We may draw a parallel with the righteous Jesus's own practice of accepting hospitality from sinners. Numerous references in the Gospel attest to a strong tradition that Jesus ate and drank with tax collectors and sinners (e.g., Matt 9:10; 11:19). Meyer, *Aims of Jesus*, 158–62.

hospitality to them. They are, we might say, to have the mindset and experience of the homeless wanderer, the mindset of Abraham.

In the case of Matt 10, the physical needs of the disciple are exacerbated or exaggerated by Jesus's prohibition against taking extra provisions. They are made artificially poor, deliberately dependent upon their community. This motif is reinforced in the story of the rich man who is told by Jesus that if he wants to be perfect, he must, while keeping the commandments, also sell all his possessions, give them to the poor, and follow him (19:16, 21).

In contrast, in Matt 25 there is no artificiality to the suffering of those followers of Jesus involved in the mission to the nations. They are described in the parable of the sheep and goats in Matt 25:31–46 as the hungry, the thirsty, strangers, the naked and sick, those in prison. There is no indication that this is a self-imposed status. All indications point to a direct link between the wars, famines, earthquakes, and the hostile reaction of the nations to the followers of Jesus in chapter 24 and the description of them in chapter 25 as "the least of these who are members of my family," those in need of food, clothing, visitation, and charity from the community (24:6–9; 25:40).[31] The ill-treated followers of Jesus of chapter 24 are treated with charity and compassion by some within the nations, thereby conferring upon their helpers the important status of righteous persons (*hoi dikaioi*, 25:37). Those that help are, in fact, exhibiting the behavior of the righteous person of Ezek 18:5–9, who, among many things, "gives his bread to the hungry and covers the naked with a garment" (v. 7).[32]

Consequences result from the community's response to the needy envoys of Jesus. First, the extension of hospitality results in the disciple reciprocating this warm welcome by greeting the house and conferring upon it his "peace" (Matt 10:13; cf. Luke 10:5). Conferring peace is far more than a casual greeting. In ancient Judaism the concept of *shalom* has strong eschatological associations. The messianic or new age will be an age of deep peace.[33] In contrast, a failure to welcome the messengers of Jesus will result in them brushing the dust off their feet, a public declaration, according to

---

31. Gray identifies a general trend among interpreters to ignore the parabolic elements of the passage (*Least of My Brothers*, 352).

32. On the relationship between charity and salvation, see Ulmer and Ulmer, *Righteous Giving*, 47; Garrison, *Redemptive Almsgiving*, 10, cf. 60–62; Downs, *Alms*, 10. Cf. Tob 4:7–11; 12:8–9; Sir 29:11–13; 40:24.

33. Cf. Mic 5:5; Isa 52:7; *Sib. Or.* 2:29.

Davies and Allison, "of the breaking off of communion and the forfeiting of responsibility."[34]

Serious national consequences are implied in the parable of the sheep and goats. Daniel Harrington draws our attention to the separate judgments for Jews and gentiles in Jewish traditions.[35] Israel is judged on the basis of its faithfulness to the covenant, the gentiles are judged according to their treatment of Israel (cf. 2 Bar. 72:4–6). For Harrington, this provides the Jewish background to Matt 25:31–46. What is new in the parable is that the gentiles are no longer judged according to their treatment of Israel but rather according to their treatment of the followers of Jesus, who, like Abraham, are wandering among the nations, strangers in need of hospitality.[36] If gentiles extend charity to Jesus's righteous followers, they too will be counted as righteous (25:37). Through such acts they have in fact extended charity not only to the followers of Jesus, but to Jesus himself. On judgment day, the Son of Man will say to those at his right hand, "Come, you that are blessed by my Father, inherit the kingdom prepared for you from the foundation of the world; for I was hungry and you gave me food, I was thirsty and you gave me something to drink, I was a stranger and you welcomed me, I was naked and you gave me clothing, I was sick and you took care of me, I was in prison and you visited me" (25:34–37). As in chapter 10, the relationship between God and the community is focalized in its response to his followers. A failure to extend charity to members of the king's family results in judgment: "Truly I tell you, just as you did not do it to one of the least of these, you did not do it to me" (25:45). This group will depart from the king and enter into eternal punishment (25:46).

In summary, repeated references in the Gospel to Sodom (and Gomorrah) would suggest that one purpose of those sent out among the cities and villages of Galilee is to increase, whether directly or indirectly, the number of righteous persons within the community. It is to preserve the world from judgment through a salting process. As presumed in the Sodom account, the presence of righteous persons delays judgment, most clearly expressed in the Gospel in the role played by the righteous wheat

---

34. Davies and Allison, *Matthew 8–18*, 178.

35. Ezek 39:21; Joel 3; Obad 15; 1 En. 91:14; Pss. Sol. 17:29; 4 Ezra 13:33–39; 2 Bar. 72, cited in Harrington, *Matthew*, 359.

36. Gallagher, "Blessing on the Move," 151. Sympathetic readers may either associate themselves with the sheep who help others or with the "least of these my brethren" who receive help from the sheep. For the plausibility of both readings, see Heil, "Double Meaning," 3–14.

in delaying the collection of the weeds in the parable of the wheat and the tares (*hoi dikaioi*, Matt 13:43). In addition, Jesus sends out his followers with minimal resources, requiring them to seek help from the wider community. As in Ezekiel 18, those that extend charity to destitute followers of Jesus are counted as righteous, most clearly demonstrated in the Gospel in the status of the righteous sheep in the parable of the sheep and the goats (Matt 25:31–46). The number of righteous persons within the community is thereby multiplied.

Precipitating Judgment: Righteous Persons and the Shedding of Innocent Blood

If judgment may be delayed by increasing the number of righteous persons within the community, it may also be precipitated by community persecution of the righteous. Before we consider how this works, it is first necessary that we consider the use by Jesus of the epithet "this generation" to describe his immediate audience (*hē genea hautē*, cf. LXX Gen 7:1).

"This Evil and Adulterous Generation"

Evald Lövestam has traced extensive Jewish traditions relating to particular generations known for their wickedness. These include the generation of Enoch, a generation particularly associated with idol worship, and the generations of the flood, the dispersion at the tower of Babel, Sodom and Gomorrah, and the wilderness.[37] Such generations failed to stand the scrutiny of judgment and are excluded from the world to come as a result of their wicked and sinful state. Their exclusion is sealed in the case of the generations of the flood, Sodom, and the wilderness, through their destruction. The only ones to survive such generations are the righteous—Noah being a case in point, a *Saddîq* who survived the judgment of his generation. The rabbis disagreed as to whether Noah was righteous "in an absolute sense or only in comparison with his unrighteous contemporaries."[38] They also disagreed as to the initial cause of each generation's wickedness. In the case of the generation of the flood, some sources trace it back to the

---

37. On the association of the generation of Enoch with idolatry, see Gen 4:26 according to Tg. Neof. More generally, see m. Sanh. 10:3.

38. Lövestam, *Jesus*, 13.

murder of Cain, others to the "sons of God" and their relationships with the "daughters of men" in Gen 6:1–2. This same generational framework is applied by Josephus to justify the destruction of Jerusalem:

> I believe that, had the Romans delayed to punish these reprobates, either the earth would have opened and swallowed up the city [i.e., like Korah and company in Num 16:32], or it would have been swept away by a flood, or have tasted anew the thunderbolts of the land of Sodom. For it produced a *generation* far more godless than the victims of those visitations, seeing that these men's frenzy involved the whole people in their ruin. (*J.W.* 5.566 [Thackeray, LCL, italics supplied])

Josephus justifies the destruction of Jerusalem by associating his godless generation with the wicked generations of the flood, Sodom, and the wilderness—further evidence that such beliefs were widely held when the Evangelist wrote his Gospel.

The Evangelist's theology reflects this concept of particularly wicked generations. Jesus's increasingly antagonistic relationship with the cities of Galilee and inhabitants of Jerusalem results in him addressing them over and over again as "this generation":

> But to what will I compare this generation? It is like children sitting in the marketplaces and calling to one another . . . (Matt 11:16)

> But he answered them, "An evil and adulterous generation asks for a sign, but no sign will be given to it except the sign of the prophet Jonah." (Matt 12:39)

> "The people of Nineveh will rise up at the judgment with this generation and condemn it, because they repented at the proclamation of Jonah, and see, something greater than Jonah is here! The queen of the South will rise up at the judgment with this generation and condemn it, because she came from the ends of the earth to listen to the wisdom of Solomon, and see, something greater than Solomon is here!" (Matt 12:41–42)

> "Then it goes and brings along seven other spirits more evil than itself, and they enter and live there; and the last state of that person is worse than the first. So will it be also with this evil generation." (Matt 12:45)

> "An evil and adulterous generation asks for a sign, but no sign will be given to it except the sign of Jonah." Then he left them and went away. (Matt 16:4)

Jesus answered, "You faithless and perverse generation, how much longer must I be with you? How much longer must I put up with you? Bring him here to me." (Matt 17:17)

"Truly I tell you, all this will come upon this generation." (Matt 23:36)

"Truly I tell you, this generation will not pass away until all these things have taken place." (Matt 24:34)

These instances portray the inhabitants of the cities of Galilee and of Jerusalem as an evil and spiritually adulterous generation that is in danger of precipitating divine judgment through their rejection of Jesus. Their spiritual condition reflects a build-up of sin over the generations, as foreshadowed in the genealogy of Matt 1:2–17. They are "descendants of those who murdered the prophets" (23:31) and are about to "fill up the measure of their ancestors" (23:32). Jesus compares Galilee and Jerusalem with the generation of Sodom (10:15; 11:23–24) and the generation of the final judgment of the nations with the generation of the flood (24:37–38). These comparisons are appropriate; the destruction of the city Sodom prefigures the destruction of the city Jerusalem, the worldwide destruction of all the unrighteous at the flood prefigures the destruction of all the unrighteous at the *parousia*. Jesus also, according to Lövestam, compares in Matt 12:38 and 16:1 those who tested him by demanding a sign with the generation of the wilderness who rejected Yahweh's signs and instead made their own demands of him (Exod 17:2; Num 11:4–15, 22; Pss 78:17–20, 32; 106:13–14).[39] They are like the exodus generation.

The theme of "this generation" is closely related to the death of Jesus (cf. Matt 23:35). From one point of view Jesus's death is not for the benefit of "this generation" but rather is caused by "this generation." This is the standard reading among most Matthean scholars.[40] His death results in their judgment. Some scholars believe that this judgment is final, that it includes all of Israel,[41] others that it is limited to "this generation" or to a particular section of Israel.[42] Either way, and ambiguity may be inten-

---

39. Lövestam, *Jesus*, 22.

40. Bonnard, *Matthieu*, 398; Hamilton, "His Blood Be upon Us," 83–85; and, *Death of Jesus*, 5–7.

41. Key to this position is the reading of *pas ho laos* (Matt 27:25) as reflecting LXX usage with respect to Israel as God's chosen people. E.g., Marguerat, *Le Jugement*, 374–77; Gundry, *Matthew*, 565; Hamilton, *Death of Jesus*, 187.

42. For a limited judgment specific to the generation of Jesus or a segment of Israel,

tional on the part of the Evangelist, the murder of Jesus contributes to the destruction of Jerusalem, as evidenced by the cry of the Jerusalem crowds that "his blood be upon us and upon our children" (27:25).

Other scholars have reacted against this traditional interpretation by arguing that the crowd's plea in Matt 27:25 is highly ironic.[43] Timothy Cargal, for example, argues that in accepting Jesus's blood upon themselves, they are, he suggests, unwittingly providing the means for their own salvation and fulfilling the words of the angel in 1:21 that Jesus would save his people from their sins. Others have rejected such a reading on the basis that it ignores the ominous overtones of the people's cry.[44] Instead, they argue, the people's cry is tragically ironic for a different reason, in that they were unwittingly contributing to the fall of Jerusalem. The reason why judgment flows from their willingness to take upon themselves the blood of Jesus lies in the Old Testament concept of the shedding of innocent blood.[45]

Innocent Blood in the Old Testament

Why in particular does the shedding of innocent or righteous blood result in judgment? One highly plausible explanation is that the shedding of innocent or righteous blood is considered in the Torah to be one of the most serious of sins. It defiles the land. In Numbers, we read, "You shall not pollute the land in which you live; for blood pollutes the land, and no expiation can be made for the land, for the blood that is shed in it, except by the blood of the one who shed it" (Num 35:33). The shedding of innocent blood is a sin that cannot be expiated or cleansed through the normal sacrificial system (cf. Deut 21:1–9; 2 Sam 21:1). Purgation is necessary. Idolatry and sexual sin also defile the land, making it uninhabitable by both God and Israel (cf. Lev 18:24–25; Ezek 36:16–18). As a result, the land will eventually vomit out its inhabitants.

---

see Davies and Allison, *Matthew 19–28*, 592; Luz, *Matthew 21–28*, 501–3; Runesson, *Divine Wrath*, 293–303.

43. Cargal, "His Blood Be upon Us," 101–12; Heil, "Blood of Jesus in Matthew," 124; *Death and Resurrection*, 75–76; Turner, *Israel's Last Prophet*, 253–66. Hays suggests that Matthew himself "may be oblivious to the ironic ambiguity of the crowd's grim assumption of responsibility for Jesus's blood on their heads" (*Gospels*, 136).

44. Davies and Allison, *Matthew 19–28*, 591–92.

45. Hamilton, *Death of Jesus*, 10.

In the case of bloodguilt, it results in the end of mercy and the precipitation of judgment, which, in the case of Israel, involved the destruction of Jerusalem. In Ezek 8:17–18, for example, God acts in wrath, without pity. Judgment begins at the sanctuary, the place where one would least expect bloodguilt (9:5–6). The land and people have been stained in blood and so the people are vomited out of the land (22:15). For Ezekiel, the destruction of Jerusalem and the subsequent exile in Babylon occurred because the sins of the people could no longer be expiated. Pollution requires expiation.

The Shedding of Innocent Blood in the Gospel

Catherine Sider Hamilton has proposed in an important study on the death of Jesus in Matthew that the Old Testament concept of innocent blood helps explain the link between the rejection of Jesus and the judgment of Israel. Her focus is Matt 23:35, which is worth quoting in its immediate context:

> Therefore I send you prophets, wise men, and scribes, some of whom you will kill and crucify, and some you will flog in your synagogues and pursue from town to town, so that upon you may come all the righteous blood [*haima dikaion*] shed on earth, from the blood of righteous Abel to the blood of Zechariah son of Barachiah, whom you murdered between the sanctuary and the altar. Truly I tell you, all this will come upon this generation. (Matt 23:34–36; cf. Luke 11:50)

Jesus refers to two deaths, those of Abel and Zechariah son of Barachiah. Why these two deaths in particular? The death of Abel occurs in the first book of the Old Testament—Genesis, and the death of Zechariah occurs in the last book of the Old Testament according to the Hebrew canonical order—2 Chronicles.[46] Thus Abel to Zechariah serves as a merism for all innocent blood. The shedding of innocent blood is described by the Evangelist as the shedding of "righteous blood" (*haima dikaion*), illustrated by the murder of the righteous Abel (Matt 23:35). The association of the death of the righteous with the shedding of innocent blood is widely attested in

---

46. We should note the discrepancy between Matthew's "Zechariah son of Barachiah" (23:35) and the "Zechariah son of the priest Jehoiada" of 2 Chr 24:20. One option is to assume that Matthew is referring to the "prophet Zechariah son of Berechiah son of Iddo" (Zech 1:1), although there is little to indicate he died the death of a martyr. Based on the narrative parallels between Matt 23:35 and 2 Chr 24:20–22, Davies and Allison propose that the Evangelist is alluding to the Zechariah of 2 Chr 24 although they concede that he has conflated his identity with that of the canonical prophet (*Matthew 19–28*, 318–19).

the Old Testament. The psalmist, for example, describes the wicked in these terms: "They will hunt down the soul of a righteous one (*dikaiou*), and innocent blood (*haima athōon*) they condemn" (LXX Ps 94:21). Such traditions shape the theology of the Gospel. Importantly, both deaths involve a cry for justice. The blood(s) of the righteous Abel "cries out" to the Lord from the ground (Gen 4:10). A similar call was made by Zechariah as he fell under the blows of those stoning him: "May the LORD see and avenge" (2 Chr 24:22).

Of particular interest for Hamilton is the Evangelist's portrayal of the deaths of Abel and Zechariah in extra-canonical traditions. There is a strong association in Jewish traditions between the death of Abel as innocent blood which pollutes the land and its purgation through the flood (see esp. 1 En. 6–11).[47] These traditions, argues Hamilton, have influenced Matthew in his move from the murder of Abel in Matt 23:35 to applying flood imagery to the *parousia* just a few verses later: "For as the days of Noah were, so will be the coming of the Son of Man. For as in those days before the flood they were eating and drinking, marrying and giving in marriage, until the day Noah entered the ark, and they knew nothing until the flood came and swept them all away, so too will be the coming of the Son of Man" (Matt 24:37–39).[48]

Zechariah's death is particularly important due to its close association with the temple and exile. Hamilton traces the development of traditions relating to the innocent blood of Zechariah and persuasively demonstrates they were reasonably well known when the Evangelist wrote his Gospel. In the Old Testament, Zechariah the priest-prophet is stoned to death as a result of his prophetic denunciation:

> Then the spirit of God took possession of Zechariah son of the priest Jehoiada; he stood above the people and said to them, "Thus says God: Why do you transgress the commandments of the Lord, so that you cannot prosper? Because you have forsaken the Lord, he has also forsaken you." But they conspired against him, and by command of the king they stoned him to death in the court of the house of the Lord. King Joash did not remember the kindness that Jehoiada, Zechariah's father, had shown him, but killed his son. As he was dying, he said, "May the Lord see and avenge!" (2 Chr 24:20–22)

47. For traditions dependent upon 1 En. 6–11, see Hamilton, *Death of Jesus*, 47–129, 161–75. Cf. Hamilton, "Blood and Secrets," 132–34.

48. Hamilton, *Death of Jesus*, 167–69; and, "Blood and Secrets," 105–11.

What stands out is the call of the dying Zechariah for the Lord to see what is happening to him and to judge accordingly. In a number of Jewish traditions, the death of innocent Zechariah leads to judgment, realized in the destruction of Jerusalem and exile to Babylon.[49]

One such tradition, an early second-century CE legend most likely based upon earlier traditions from the first century, is attributed to an old man from Jerusalem (cf. *b. Git.* 57b). As in Matthew, the death of Zechariah is reflected upon in relation to the destruction of Jerusalem. The legend tells how Nebuzaradan, captain of the Babylonian guard, attacks and destroys Jerusalem. While in the temple, he sees the blood of Zechariah seething and bubbling and asks what it is. He is told that it is the "blood of the bullocks, sheep, and rams that we offer on the altar" (*y. Ta'an.* 69a). He immediately sacrifices such animals to stop the blood seething, but to no avail. In anger, he tortures some of the inhabitants of Jerusalem, leading to their confession that, "It is the blood of a priest, prophet, and judge, who prophesied against us concerning everything that you are now doing to us, and we rose up against him and killed him" (69b). Nebuzaradan attempts again to quiet Zechariah's blood by slaughtering 80,000 young priests on it, but still it continues to bubble up; in the Babylonian version 940,000 men, women and children are slaughtered. In anger, he cries out to the blood, "What do you want? Should we destroy your entire nation on your account?" At this point the Lord is filled with compassion and says, "How if this one, who is a mere mortal and cruel (i.e., Nebuzaradan), is filled with mercy for my children . . . [should I have mercy on them]!" (69b).[50] Forthwith, the Lord gave a sign to Zechariah's blood, and it was swallowed up by the ground. This tradition represents a considerable development from 2 Chr 24 in that the blood of Zechariah now has a living quality that personifies the ongoing absence of justice with respect to his murder.

In *Lives of the Prophets*, a Jewish text written in the first quarter of the first century CE, we find a significant development of 2 Chr 24:

> Zechariah was from Jerusalem, son of Jehoiada the priest, and Joash the king of Judah killed him near the altar, and the house of David poured out his blood in front of the *Ailam*; and the priests

---

49. See Blank, "Death of Zechariah," 327–46; Hamilton, "His Blood Be upon Us," 86n9; and, *Death of Jesus*, 130–80.

50. The Babylonian version is found in *b. Git.* 57b. A further account is found in *b. Sanh.* 96b. For discussion, Blank, "Death of Zechariah," 338–45; Hamilton, *Death of Jesus*, 132–33.

took him and buried him with his father. From that time visible portents occurred in the Temple, and the priests were not able to see a vision of angels of God or to give oracles from the *Dabeir*, or to inquire by the Ephod, or to answer the people through Urim as formerly. (*Liv. Pro.* 23:1–2 [Charlesworth])

In 2 Chronicles, Zechariah is stoned. There is no mention of his blood. The author of *Lives of the Prophets* adds the ideas that Zechariah was killed near the altar, that his blood was poured out in front of the altar, and that judgment resulted against the temple and the priests.[51] Matthew reflects such traditions when he refers to the blood of Zechariah and to his murder as taking place "between the sanctuary and the altar" (Matt 23:35). The temple becomes the object of judgment in that its function is severely restricted (cf. *J.W.* 5.288–301).

In each of these sources, severe consequences flow from the murder of Zechariah. His blood defiles the land and demands purgation.[52] In the Jerusalem Talmud, 80,000 young priests are killed in judgment (*y. Taʾan.* 69b); in the Babylonian version, 940,000 men, women, and children are killed (*b. Giṭ.* 57b); in *Liv. Pro.* 23:1, the temple is judged. Similarly, in Matt 23, the scribes and Pharisees will murder some of those Jesus will send to them, thereby bringing judgment "upon this generation" (23:36). The shedding of innocent blood pollutes the land and judgment is the means by which it may be cleansed.[53] Jesus proceeds by prophesying the destruction of Jerusalem, the city that "kills the prophets and stones those sent to it" (cf. 23:37–39). Two verses later, in 24:2, he states that "not one stone will be left upon another; all will be thrown down." This clearly reflects the paradigm of the legends. Hamilton states:

> All the versions tie Zechariah's blood to the defeat of Jerusalem: the story is, in one way or another, a meditation on the reasons for that defeat. "Woe to the bloody city!" *Lamentations Rabbah* and tractate *Taanit* of the Jerusalem Talmud exclaim: Jerusalem is defeated because her blood is in the midst of her. The proof? The boiling blood of Zechariah. *Leviticus Rabbah* and *Ecclesiastes*

---

51. Hamilton, *Death of Jesus*, 135.

52. On pollution and the fate of the land, see Hamilton, "His Blood Be upon Us," 99; and, *Death of Jesus*, 136–47; Runesson, "Purity, Holiness," 163; *Divine Wrath*, 56. For the link between pollution and purging in Josephus, see Mason, "Pollution and Purification," 181–207.

53. Josephus, *J.W.* 4.201, 388; 5.381, 402; 6.126–27.

Rabbah tie the story to the text, "I saw . . . in the place of righteousness that wickedness was there" (Eccl 3:16).[54]

The destruction of Jerusalem is thereby related to the history of the people
of Israel and the justice of God. As Hamilton observes, story serves theod-
icy.[55] The suffering of Israel is neither random nor arbitrary. It results from
righteous judgment.

Zechariah traditions endured well into the time of the Church Fathers.
Theophilus describes Zechariah as "the last of the prophets" (*Theoph.* 23).
Tertullian argues that the righteous have always been subject to martyrdom
and cites as examples the prophets: "David is persecuted; Elias put to flight;
Jeremiah stoned; Esaias cut asunder; Zacharias butchered between the altar
and the temple, imparting to the hard stones lasting marks of his blood"
(*Scorp.* 8). According to Jerome, "simpler folk point out that the red stones
in the temple were reddened by the blood of Zechariah" (*Comm. Matt.* 23
[*PL* 26.181a]).[56] As in Second Temple literature and Matthew's Gospel, Israel's fate results from its long history of persecution of those sent by God.

The Death of Jesus as a Righteous Person

Hamilton's paradigm is particularly helpful when it comes to understanding
the death of Jesus in the Gospel. For Judas, Pilate, and the people, Jesus's death
involves the shedding of innocent blood. Judas confesses, "I have sinned
by betraying innocent blood (*haima athōon*)" (27:4). The chief priests and
elders respond, "What is that to us, see to it yourself." Judas returns his blood
money to the chief priests and elders, "Throwing down the pieces of silver
in the temple," thereby defiling the temple with innocent blood (27:5).[57] The
chief priests and elders react by using the blood money to purchase the Field
of Blood (27:8). This was to fulfill what had been spoken through the prophet
Jeremiah (27:9, other authorities read Zechariah or Isaiah). The shedding of
innocent blood is an important motif for Jeremiah, who condemns Israel for
such acts (*haimatōn athōon*, LXX Jer 19:4; cf. 26:15). For him, the shedding

---

54. Hamilton, "His Blood Be upon Us," 89.

55. Hamilton, "His Blood Be upon Us," 89.

56. Hamilton, "His Blood Be upon Us," 87n10. These references are hers.

57. On the defilement of the temple in Qumran and rabbinic literature, see Klawans,
Purity, Sacrifice, 131–83.

of innocent blood, the blood of the righteous, results in divine judgment and the loss of the kingdom (e.g., 19:9).

When Pilate concedes to the crucifixion of Jesus, he washes his hands and declares his innocence of "this man's blood" (*athōos eimi apo tou haimatos toutou*, Matt 27:24). This evokes the ritual of hand washing and the killing of a heifer as expiation for innocent blood shed by an unknown assailant (cf. Deut 21:1–9). Pilate's actions occur after his wife declares Jesus to be a righteous person (*tō dikaiō ekeinō* "that righteous man," Matt 27:19). The crowds, identified as "the whole people," express their willingness to take the blood of Jesus upon themselves and their children (27:24–25). The issue at stake is who will take the bloodguilt. In taking upon themselves the blood of Jesus, the crowd reverses the ceremony of expiation. For Hamilton, this is where irony is to be found; through an ironic inversion of "Deuteronomy's ancient expiation ceremony," they have "chosen bloodguilt rather than absolution."[58]

These explicit references to innocent blood and the death of Jesus as a righteous person are further reinforced through extensive allusions to Pss 22 and 69 in which an innocent person, although not explicitly named a righteous person, suffers "without cause" (69:4) at the hands of the wicked:

Matthean allusions to the Persecution of the Innocent in Pss 22 and 69

Jesus is crucified (Matt 27:35; cf. his hands and feet are pierced in LXX Ps 21:17)

His clothes are divided by the casting of lots (Matt 27:35; LXX Ps 21:19)

He is offered wine mixed with gall and sour wine to drink (Matt 27:34, 48; cf. "vinegar" in LXX Ps 68:22)

He suffers reproaches and insults (Matt 27:39, 41; LXX Pss 21:8; 68:8, 10, 20–21)

His attitude to the temple contributes to his suffering (Matt 27:40; LXX Ps 68:10)

The crowds mock him for committing his cause to the Lord (Matt 27:43; LXX Ps 21:9)

He cries out, "My God, my God, why have your forsaken me?" (Matt 27:46; MT Ps 22:2)

---

58. Hamilton, "His Blood Be upon Us," 98.

It is clear from these allusions that Jesus dies the death of an innocent person, or, in the words of Robert Gundry, as a "model of a persecuted righteous person," a *Saddîq* who trusts in the Lord even unto death.[59] Being complicit in the death of Jesus, both Israel's leaders and its people contribute to judgment by affirming their association with earlier generations who murdered the prophets and shed innocent and righteous blood.

We may briefly note another factor that leads to judgment. Matthew identifies the desecration of the temple as leading to judgment: "So when you see the desolating sacrilege standing in the holy place, as was spoken of by the prophet Daniel (let the reader understand), then those in Judea must flee to the mountains" (24:15–16).[60] It would seem that national judgment results from multiple causes—the murder of Jesus, the shedding of the innocent blood of the righteous, the persecution of the prophets, and the extreme ritual defilement resulting from the overthrow of the regular temple services by a hostile force (cf. the desolating sacrilege of Dan 9:27; 11:31; 12:11).

The Death of Jesus and the Judgment of Jerusalem

This emphasis on the relationship between defilement and judgment leads us to affirm that the death of Jesus is not, however surprising this may seem to some readers, the only reason for the judgment of Jerusalem. This point is often overlooked in the discussion on bloodguilt and judgment. Some commentators limit the destruction of Jerusalem to God's response to the murder of Jesus.[61] This reading diminishes, however, the significance of those future deaths of the righteous anticipated by Jesus in Matt 23:34–36. I quote the passage once more to emphasize the point:

> Therefore I send you prophets, sages, and scribes, some of whom you will kill and crucify, and some you will flog in your synagogues and pursue from town to town, so that upon you may come all the *righteous* blood shed on earth, from the blood of *righteous* Abel to the blood of Zechariah son of Barachiah, whom you murdered

---

59. Gundry, *Matthew*, 566. So too, Hays, *Gospels*, 161–62.

60. Runesson, "Purity, Holiness," 150.

61. Hamilton, *Death of Jesus*, 14, 23–24, 32, 35–36, 153, 182, 204, 223. On p. 232, Hamilton implies a link between the destruction of Jerusalem and the deaths of the prophets, sages, and scribes (and, of course, of Zechariah and Jesus).

between the sanctuary and the altar. Truly I tell you, all this will come upon this generation. (Matt 23:34–36, italics supplied)

For the Evangelist, the judgment of Jerusalem will occur not just in response to the death of Jesus but when the authorities kill and crucify some of those subsequently sent to them (23:34). Some they will flog in their synagogues and pursue from town to town, thereby spreading pollution throughout the land. The purpose of their deaths is "so that" (*hopōs*) *all* the righteous blood shed on earth, starting with the death of the *Saddîq* Abel to that of Zechariah, will come upon this generation. The deaths of Jesus's followers—his prophets, wise men, and scribes, as with his death, is the shedding, by association, of innocent blood and contributes to the further pollution and defilement of the land, thereby triggering judgment. There is no indication that their blood serves to expiate bloodguilt. Rather, it increases bloodguilt. Rather than the shedding of more innocent blood, it is judgment alone that expiates defiled land.

Who are the righteous prophets, sages, and scribes that Jesus will send? One possibility is they include the many "holy ones" who emerged from their tombs immediately upon the death of Jesus in Matt 27:52 (cf. Isa 26:19; Ezek 37:1–14). Jens Herzer, developing a suggestion of Joachim Gnilka, emphasizes the link between the open tombs and the many holy ones of Matt 27:53, and the tombs and decorated graves of the murdered prophets and righteous persons referred to earlier in 23:29–33: "In Matt 27, as well as in Matt 23, the saints, that is, the righteous, are already dead and their tombs play a significant role."[62] If this is the case, and it seems a plausible suggestion, then due to their renewed warnings and their preserving righteous presence, the city may once again enjoy the status of "holy city."[63] Judgment may yet be avoided, however unlikely this may be. Their presence, following the death of the righteous Jesus, ensures that at no point is Jerusalem left without the preserving presence of the righteous.

Finally, we should highlight two complementary explanations of the death of Jesus we find in the Gospel. From the point of view of those involved in the murder of Jesus, it is the shedding of innocent blood that leads to judgment. Alternatively, however, when Jesus is alone with his disciples, all good first-century Jews, he explains his death in quite different terms. In

---

62. Herzer, "Riddle," 153. Cf. Gnilka, *Das Matthäusevangelium*, 447.

63. Jerusalem is described as a holy city in Matt 4:5, in which the presence of Jesus is presumed. In 5:35, Jerusalem is "the city of the great king." For more discussion, see Runesson, "Purity, Holiness," 148–53.

a private discussion of the nature of true kingship in Matt 20:20–28, Jesus explains that his followers are to imitate the Son of Man, who came "not to be served but to serve, and to give his life a ransom for many" (20:28). In the intimate setting of the pre-crucifixion Passover meal, Jesus describes the Passover cup as "my blood of the covenant, which is poured out for many for the forgiveness of sins" (26:28). In such private settings, the emphasis is not on the shedding of innocent blood, but rather on the renewal of the covenant for "the many" of Israel through the blood of Jesus.[64] For those in Israel hostile to Jesus, his death counts as murder that defiles and demands judgment. For his followers, however fallible they may be, it is the means for a renewed covenantal relationship between them and God. It is in this second sense, as the blood of the covenant, that the death of Jesus is clearly distinguishable from the deaths of his followers. His blood is both innocent blood and the blood of the covenant. Their blood is only innocent blood.

Implications

Several important implications flow from this analysis of the *Saddîq* element of the Evangelist's discipleship ideal. First, I have proposed that the response to the disciples as righteous persons is critical in determining the fate of the city and the nation. Three responses are presented. (1) When a community extends hospitality to an in-need righteous person, it acts righteously and defers judgment in the same way that Sodom and Gomorrah would have been spared judgment through the presence of ten righteous persons. Judgment is delayed. (2) Withholding hospitality may not result in immediate judgment. Instead, it results in a hiatus. The cities of Galilee found themselves in this situation in that they rejected Jesus but did not take his life. The consequence of this response is that future judgment will be more severe. They will fare worse than Sodom and Gomorrah. (3) Persecution of righteous persons through the shedding of innocent blood leads directly to judgment. The death of righteous prophets, wise men, and scribes adds to the cry of previously shed innocent blood for judgment, a judgment which now occurs not just because of the murder of Jesus, but also because of his martyred followers. Judgment is hastened.

The reader is not told how many righteous persons need to be welcomed by the community to delay judgment. Fifty? Forty-five? Forty? Thirty? Twenty? Ten? (cf. Gen 18:24–33). Neither is the reader told how many

---

64. "The many" is likely an allusion to LXX Isa 53:12.

have to die to precipitate judgment. The reader lives with this ambiguity. The power of this narrative lies not in providing readers with the means to predict the timing of judgment. Rather, its power lies in attributing incredible significance to both their missional successes and their sufferings. Their successes delay judgment. Their sufferings speed it up. The emphasis the Evangelist places on the value of martyrdom may well be necessary to prepare the sympathetic reader with the mindset for mission: "If I die, my life is not wasted. It contributes to the blood crying out to God and will hasten his return."

Second, righteous persons are to strive to be righteous not for the purpose of achieving personal salvation but for the purpose of saving their communities from judgment.[65] The result is an emphasis on righteousness which avoids falling into the trap of self-serving legalism. Righteous persons honor and keep the law of God in order to save others from judgment. They also adopt an attitude of generosity toward their communities in that, rather than seeking to hasten their personal vindication on judgment day, they seek to delay the judgment of the community. The well-being of the community is more important than their own well-being.

Third, the *Saddîq* was expected in the Old Testament and subsequent traditions to reveal the two sides of God's character—his justice and holiness through keeping and implementing his statutes and commandments, and his compassion through practicing charity. The *Saddîq* embodies both holiness and gracious generosity. I have said little in this chapter on the nature of Matthean law-keeping. We will address this issue in chapter 6 when we consider the role of the scribe.

When it comes to charity, righteous persons are themselves to avoid giving alms for ulterior motives and are to show unfettered generosity to others (Matt 5:38–42; 6:2–4). The unexpected move, however, is that Jesus places less of an emphasis on the obligation of his followers to help others and more on the righteous person's own need for help from the community. Followers of Jesus are called to travel light and to request hospitality. They will encounter times of extreme deprivation, hunger, thirst, nakedness, and imprisonment (10:9–10; 19:21; 24:15–20). In this state they offer communities an opportunity to show righteous compassion. They approach their communities not from a position of strength or self-sufficiency. Rather, they approach in weakness, in need of help. Jesus's mission is undertaken from a deliberate posture of weakness, removing the ability to plead a lack of resources.

---

65. Cf. Rom 3:21; 9:30—10:13; Gal 2:15–21.

4

The Disciple-Teacher

Guarding Against a Nominally Observant Populace

Introduction

THE TERM MATHĒTĒS IS used seventy-three times throughout the Gospel in relation to the followers of Jesus, John the Baptist (Matt 9:14), and the Pharisees (22:16) and is understood in general terms to refer to "one who engages in learning through instruction from another, [a] *pupil, apprentice*," and in a more technical sense to "one who is rather constantly associated with someone who has a pedagogical reputation or a particular set of views, [a] *disciple, adherent*."[1] Its cognates *mathēteia* ("lesson," "instruction") and *mathēteuō* ("to be a pupil" or "to teach") further testify to the educational connotations of the term.[2] The followers of Jesus are, according to the Gospel Commission, to disciple and teach others (*mathēteusate, didaskontes*, Matt 28:19, 20). It is clear that the Evangelist's discipleship ideal includes a strong educational component.

My focus in this chapter is a little different from that of the previous two chapters in which I stressed the Old Testament background to various motifs found in the Gospel. There is, of course, a strong Old Testament tradition that God will teach his ways to his people and the nations (e.g., Isa 48:17; 51:4; 54:13).[3] In this chapter, however, rather than focusing on the

---

1. BDAG, 609–10.

2. For *mathēteuō*, see Matt 13:52; 27:57; and 28:19.

3. While there is a relative absence of discipleship terminology in the Old Testament, this does not mean that the concept is not present. Wilkins (*Concept of Disciple*, 91) convincingly demonstrates that the master-disciple relationship is strongly represented in

Old Testament background to teaching motifs found in the Gospel, we shall instead consider the Gospel in light of pedagogical practices contemporary to the Evangelist. We will focus on the memorization of the teacher's words and the imitation of his deeds.

If the role of the prophet is to call the community back to God and that of the righteous person is to nudge it toward righteous behavior, the role of the student-teacher, and these roles are really two sides of the same coin, is to preserve the teachings of the master teacher. At the national level, such teachers guard against the development of a nominally observant populace who pay lip service to God. They seek to ensure that external confession is matched by internal commitment, that those professing religious commitment practice what they preach (cf. Matt 6:22–23; 23:3). Before we turn to the Gospel, we first need to clarify the nature of first-century Jewish education.

Jewish Educational Practices

We have little direct evidence of the nature of Jewish schools from the early first century CE.[4] Our sources are mostly from the Tannaitic (first and second centuries CE) and Amoraic (third to six centuries CE) periods. As elsewhere in the ancient world, there was no state-run system of education. Instead, parents were largely responsible for the education of their children.[5] The limitation of this approach was that it relied on parents being present. Awareness of this limitation may well have been one of the contributing factors that led to the appointment of schoolteachers in Jerusalem as a result of an ordinance proposed by high priest Joshua b. Gamela around 64 CE (*b. Bat.* 21a). Various Amoraic traditions testify to there being around 480 synagogues in Jerusalem at the time of Vespasian's assault on Jerusalem, each with a "schoolhouse and a house of learning, a schoolhouse for Scripture and a house of learning for Mishnah" (*y. Meg.* 3.1; cf. *b. Ketub.* 105a). While it is difficult to verify such traditions, we can nevertheless surmise that in the first century CE there were private schools

---

"the nature of the prophetic ministry, the writing prophets, the scribes, and the wisdom tradition."

4. On Second Temple education, see Hezser, *Jewish Literacy*, 39–109; Carr, *Tablet of the Heart*, 111–72, 201–14; Keith, *Pericope Adulterae*, 53–117.

5. Hezser, *Jewish Literacy*, 59.

throughout Jerusalem and likely throughout the rest of Palestine. This does not mean, of course, that everyone received an education.

Despite strong reactions against perceived Hellenization, Jewish schools in general reflected the Hellenistic system. In Hellenistic education, students were first taught at elementary school to read and recite texts from memory by a teacher of letters (*grammatistes*). Students were then taught at the next school level by a grammarian (*grammatikos*), who continued the process of teaching classical texts, this time with direct interpretation which followed set rules. The third level, rhetor-sophistos schools, continued the practice of memorization of set texts. At this level, students, usually limited to the sons of the elite, memorized definitions and principles of rhetoric, model compositions, and great portions from the works of leading authors. This third level was complemented by the various schools of philosophy. These schools followed the same pedagogical principles as lower-level education in that students were expected to memorize and comment on the most important writings of the philosophers. Imitation of worthy role models was the goal. The first-century CE Jewish system of education broadly reflected these educational levels.

In the Jewish system, the first level of education was the *bet sefer* "house of the book," at which boys were taught to read the Torah. Boys would start schooling between the ages of five to seven and would be taught by men knowledgeable in the Scriptures. These were typically priests and Levites, often referred to as *soferim* "scribes," who were of lower rank than the rabbis. The goal of the *bet sefer* was to teach boys to be able to read fluently rather than to interpret the text.

Memorization played a key role in early years' Jewish education. Jerome, for example, claimed that the Palestinian Jews of his day knew Moses and the Prophets by heart.[6] Supporting evidence for this claim is found in the Talmud in which the rabbis do not provide any scriptural references as it is assumed that every teacher and student knows where the text may be found. When a scholar shows indecision with the written Torah, he is recommended to return to elementary school (*b. Sanh.* 33b). One result of memorization was that traditional wordings of the text were preserved in the memory of both teacher and student. This acted as a restraint on the introduction of textual variants. At this level of education, students were not expected to interpret the Torah. Instead, they were discouraged from

---

6. Jerome, *Comm. in Ep. ad Tit.* 3.9. See Gerhardsson, *Memory and Manuscript*, 64; Scheck, *St. Jerome's Commentaries*, 342.

interpreting it. Texts were learned passage by passage. According to a haggadah in Eka R. 1.31, a man who wanted to be taught requested another fellow to "teach me to read a column, teach me to repeat a section."[7] We can quite easily imagine a similar process by which the Gospel was memorized, pericope by pericope.

Upon graduating from the *bet sefer*, the best students progressed to the *bet hamidrash*, the "house of study." Our sources are again very sketchy. At this level of education, students would continue memorizing the written Torah and begin memorizing through rote repetition the oral Torah. Students were taught through two methods. The first was the midrashic method which involved reading through the Torah while providing a running interpretation. In this method, the text set the agenda and interpretation was extremely conservative.[8] Parallel to this method was the mishnaic method in which the contents of the oral Torah were studied independently of the written Torah. In this approach, material was organized topically, as reflected in the various sections of the Mishnah. Students were also taught techniques of interpretation, application, and dialectics.

The third level of education was the rabbinic college attended by only the most gifted of students. Its purpose was to deepen knowledge of and the ability to interpret both the written and the oral Torah. This required a continued emphasis on memorization. An important difference between this level and the *bet hamidrash* was that the teacher would add a more detailed commentary of the text. The text was also the basis for detailed discussion. Leading rabbis would meet periodically to give instruction at this level.[9] At such gatherings they would model legal rulings and interpretation of the text.

In this educational setting the Gospel is a story about a first-century Jewish teacher recruiting and educating a group of mature students to our equivalent of higher education. What is surprising, however, is that Jesus's students are not chosen on the basis of their parents' ability to pay or their academic abilities, as in the Greco-Roman and Jewish systems.[10] Rather, the Twelve are a diverse collection of individuals who would normally never gain access to higher education. Tellingly, the Evangelist does not inform

7. Eka rabbati, Midrash on Lamentations, quoted in Gerhardsson, *Memory and Manuscript*, 114.

8. Gerhardsson, *Memory and Manuscript*, 90.

9. Gerhardsson, *Memory and Manuscript*, 91.

10. This needs qualifying by Hezser's observation that in late antiquity most rabbis and their students "seem to have stemmed from the working middle strata of society, while only a few of them were wealthy" ("Torah versus Homer," 20).

his reader on what basis the Twelve were chosen. This sends the message that in the "school of Jesus," access to higher education has been blown wide open to everyone. While the Gospel portrays an adult educational scenario, this does not rule out the use of the Gospel with children. Adult literature was used throughout the ancient world to instruct children. There was little to no literature specifically for children.

Low Literacy Levels in Roman Palestine?

The picture painted above has been critiqued by Catherine Hezser who is highly skeptical of the portrayal in Amoraic traditions of an extensive pre-70 CE network of private educational institutions.[11] Instead, building on the earlier work of William Harris, she estimates low levels of school attendance in Roman Palestine and a literacy rate anywhere below the Roman average, estimated by Harris to be 10 to 15 percent (here defined as the ability to read in at least one language and to write more than one's signature).[12] Part of her rationale for this judgment is her belief that rural parts of the Empire had lower levels of literacy to urban areas and Palestine was more rural than the rest of the Empire. Harris, in his highly influential study *Ancient Literacy* (1989), reacted against what he perceived to be overly optimistic estimates of literacy levels in the Roman Empire by suggesting a maximum literacy level of anywhere between two to ten percent.[13] Harris based his minimalist approach on the fact that in every early-modern or modern country, majority literacy has only been achieved through an extensive network of state or religious schools. In Sicily in 1871, for example, illiteracy levels were male 79 percent and female 91 percent (Sardinia, male 81 percent and female 92 percent).[14] No comparative school network existed anywhere in the ancient world to what we now know, Harris argues, for the simple reason that there was no incentive on the part of the ancient elite to aim for mass literacy.

---

11. Hezser, *Jewish Literacy*, 69. Contrast this with Drazin, who argues that universal elementary education was a goal of Second Temple Judaism (*Jewish Education*, 15–23, 49–53, 64–66). Before the destruction of the temple, schools were apparently funded through fees. After the destruction, they were funded through the temple tax, widening access and raising already comparatively high literacy levels.

12. Hezser, *Jewish Literacy*, 39–40, 496. So too, Keith, *Jesus' Literacy*, 73–75.

13. Harris, *Ancient Literacy*, 22, cf. 233–48.

14. Harris, *Ancient Literacy*, 23.

Harris's estimation of such low literacy levels has been called into question by recent studies of graffiti, ostraca, letters, and other forms of what may be termed everyday writing. Graffiti, according to Kristina Milnor, is the public expression of private voices typically denied access to public means of expression controlled by those in authority.[15] It is the voice of the non-elite, the prostitute, and the laborer. Roger Bagnall's study of graffiti at Smyrna indicates that it was found throughout the ancient world, barring temples, and that it covered all topics, including sex, sport, transportation, *tabulae ansatae*, prayers for the restoration of poor eyesight, and lots and lots of names, often in coded form (isopsephisms).[16]

According to Milnor, what marks out graffiti from Pompeii from modern graffiti is that much of it shows familiarity with elite Roman authors such as Virgil, Ovid, Propertius, and Ennius.[17] We may scratch our heads and wonder what the equivalent would be today! This gives us insight as to how far canonical texts penetrated beyond the social groups of their elite authors. Some of it includes incorrect spelling, evidence not of poor literacy levels but rather of the widespread practice of phonetic spelling.[18] Pompeiian graffiti also includes independent compositions of poetry that demonstrate, according to Milnor, "a real awareness of both the formal and thematic traditions of canonical poetry, while at the same time preserving a strong sense of themselves as emerging from and contributing to a different discourse of written art."[19] The presumption of producers of all forms of graffiti is that they have access to a broad readership able to understand what they have written. Hezser discusses the various forms of graffiti found at Herodion, Masada, Nahal Michmas and Wadi Haggag but does not significantly engage with the possibility that they may indicate, as argued by Bagnall and Milnor, higher literacy rates in Judea than Harris permits.[20]

The minimalist approach to ancient literacy levels of Harris and Hezser is also challenged by Philo and Josephus, who both claim that most Jewish children were taught letters from an early age to facilitate comprehension of the Torah.[21] Josephus, for example, links the Sabbath with the

15. Milnor, *Graffiti*, 1–44.

16. Bagnall, *Everyday Writing*, 7–26.

17. Milnor, *Graffiti*, 5.

18. Bagnall, *Everyday Writing*, 26.

19. Milnor, *Graffiti*, 6.

20. Cf. Hezser, *Jewish Literacy*, 413–19.

21. Josephus, *Ag. Ap.* 1.60; 2.204; Philo, *Leg.* 16.115–16; 31.210. Carr, *Tablet of the*

study of texts, a weekly opportunity for the community to "hear," "learn," and "reflect" upon the Torah (*Ant.* 16.43; *Ag. Ap.* 2.175). Hezser believes that such sources project an ideal rather than reality.[22]

Other scholars are less skeptical toward such evidence. Alan Millard, for example, states that "the literacy situation in Jewish society differed from that in the Greco-Roman world in a notable way because there was a strong tradition of education in order that men, at least, should be prepared to read from the Scriptures in synagogue services. In theory, every Jewish male was expected to do so."[23] While we may not be able to determine exact literacy rates, Hezser's position may well significantly underestimate Jewish literacy rates, especially when we consider its bookish nature in contrast to paganism in which there was, according to Robert Parker, an absence of equivalent canonical texts.[24]

Why this discussion matters is that it shapes our perceptions of the role texts played in early Christian discipleship practices. Larry Hurtado has argued that the early Christian movement was bookish from the start, with New Testament texts enjoying a high status within their community from the off.[25] Literacy was presumed. It is at the heart of discipleship. To be a student of Jesus is to be a reader of texts. We will now consider the Gospel in light of the key educational motifs of memorization of word and imitation of deed.

Memorization

Memorization was at the heart of ancient education. To help appreciate its importance, I will outline Birger Gerhardsson's model of rabbinic tradition transmission, which, first published in 1961, has proved remarkably enduring.[26] Gerhardsson's description of how the Jewish oral law was transmitted is extremely useful in that it provides us with a possible template for how Jesus transmitted his teachings to his disciples. How this occurs is, of

---

Heart, 246–48.

22. Hezser, *Jewish Literacy*, 46–47. So too, Keith, *Jesus' Literacy*, 75–77.

23. Millard, *Reading and Writing*, 157.

24. Parker, *On Greek Religion*, 1–39.

25. Hurtado, *Destroyer of the Gods*, 105–41.

26. Gerhardsson, *Memory and Manuscript*, 93–170; Byrskog, *Jesus the Only Teacher*, 17–21, 155–75; Jaffee, *Torah in the Mouth*, vii.

course, not explicitly presented in the Gospel. Nonetheless, it is implied in the teaching process.

Memorization was an integral element of education at all levels and the burden of proof lies on those who reject the idea that Jesus would have intentionally used memorization techniques to transmit his teachings to his followers. Jesus was a teacher and teaching through memorization is what teachers did. Gerhardsson states: "[Jesus] had—as teachers have—disciples (*mathētai*), and these were able to learn—which in this milieu included memorizing. They received from Jesus—known as a man of sayings . . .—specific words, statements, sayings. And these logia and parables he inculcated into them. Otherwise, in my view, Jesus was not a teacher, nor were they disciples."[27] The most basic of pedagogical assumptions was that material had to be memorized. This may well help explain why Jesus's parables and aphoristic sayings are so similar across the synoptic gospels. The sayings of Jesus in Matthew are very close to those in Mark. In contrast, the Evangelists demonstrate far more latitude in how they retell Jesus's deeds and actions. This suggests that Jesus may have repeated his teachings to the disciples until they had them memorized.

Understanding Follows Memorization

Prior to attempting to interpret or explain a tradition, it was first committed to memory. In *b. Avod. Zar.* 19a, we find the injunction to first study the Torah (i.e., memorization) and then to meditate on it afterwards.[28] The difference between memorization and understanding is illustrated by the role of the *tanna* ("instructor"). The Tannaim were living books who memorized the oral Torah and who served in rabbinic colleges. They were on hand to recite the oral law when requested by a rabbi. The mechanical way in which they repeated traditions is illustrated in the proverb found in the Talmud: "A Magus mumbles on but does not understand what he is saying, and a professional memorizer of Tannaite sayings repeats his tradition, and he too does not know what he is saying" (*b. Soṭah* 22a).[29]

Interpretation was taught at the higher levels of education. In fact, we find warnings against sharing interpretation with children. R. Eliezer warns against introducing children to "excessive reflection" on the Torah. Instead,

27. Gerhardsson, "Secret," 9. So too, Jousse, *Memory*, 72–74.

28. Gerhardsson, *Memory and Manuscript*, 127.

29. Gerhardsson, *Memory and Manuscript*, 95.

they are to be placed among the disciples of sages (*b. Ber.* 28b). A late Saboraic commentary (sixth century CE) on a saying of R. Kahana contains the maxim that a man should first study and then undertake analytic enquiry into what he has learnt (*b. Shabb.* 63a). At the Talmud level of education, students were expected to know Scripture and the Mishnah by heart and to be able to participate in dialectical discussion on the meaning of the text. They were expected to contribute to the teaching by asking questions and sharing their own observations.

Throughout the Gospel, the disciples question Jesus and contribute with their own opinions, even if these fall short of his understanding (e.g., Matt 13:10).[30] After delivering seven parables to the crowds, Jesus asks the disciples in 13:51 whether they have understood "all this." These interactions suggest the equivalent of talmudic or rhetor level education, a move beyond memorization toward understanding.

Conserve the Authentic Wording

In Hellenistic education, it was common practice when presenting the words of others to summarize and put their thoughts into one's own words. In contrast, rabbinic practice was to convey the person's words verbatim.[31] The result was that traditions were often transmitted without understanding. When the first-century R. Joshua was asked about the meaning of the term *shelashit*, he confessed that "I have heard (as authoritative tradition) it plain (i.e., without explanation)" (*m. Parah* 1.1). The use of "I have heard" emphasizes that we are here dealing with oral tradition. The student was required to repeat his rabbi's words verbatim, and the rabbi was responsible for ensuring that the student had learned his teachings correctly.

In order to ensure that memorization occurred the rabbi was required to repeat his material. R. Eliezer ben Hyrkanos required the teacher to repeat a doctrinal passage four times for the pupil (*b. Erub.* 54b). The Rabbi who tirelessly repeated chapters for his students was the object of praise. R. Perida, held up as a worthy example, repeated a passage four hundred times for a slow pupil, and when the pupil still failed to memorize the passage, he repeated it another four hundred times (*b. Erub.* 54b). This is of course hyperbole, but the point is made. We may add to this Marcel Jousse's observation that within this system, "nothing is detached from

---

30. Matt 13:10, 36; 15:12, 15; 17:19; 19:10, 25.

31. Gerhardsson, *Memory and Manuscript*, 130–36.

concretely defined persons."[32] Traditions were usually linked to persons, providing social references that helped reinforce memorization. The Gospel similarly provides an abundance of social, temporal, and geographical settings to aid memorization.

The Rule of Brevity

The emphasis on transmitting verbatim the words of a rabbi resulted in a corresponding emphasis on brevity and conciseness.[33] It is expressed as a pedagogical rule in b. Pesah 3b: "A person should always repeat a statement to his disciple in economical language." The rule was itself given a name, "the shortest way" (*derek qesarah*). This resulted in the practice of concisely summarizing large bodies of teachings. A good example of this is Matthew's version of the Lord's Prayer, well suited, Jousse suggests, for rhythmo-melodic memorization.[34] Many more examples of concise statements could be listed, particularly from the Sermon on the Mount.

We may distinguish between three elements in a teacher's instruction: (1) the lecture itself, frequently a discussion on a passage which has been memorized by the student; (2) a condensed memory text (Mishnah) which summarizes the contents of the lecture; and (3) a heading or a catchword by which to remember the lecture topic. Using the catchword, the student was thereby able to recall the Mishnah, the condensed summary of the lecture.

In the Gospel, key words are used to associate different narratives together (e.g., "bread" in Matt 14:17, 19; 15:2, 26, 33, 34, 36; 16:5, 7, 8, 9, 10, 11). While aiding memorization, such words do not function as catchwords because they are not limited to any one narrative. There is also little evidence that catchwords were used in early Christian writings when referring to the Gospel. Nevertheless, the usefulness of this technique should not be discounted by today's readers of the Gospel in that modern Bible translations partly reflect this ancient practice when they include titles to different pericopes (e.g., NRSV, "Feeding the Five Thousand," "The Canaanite Woman's Faith," "Peter's Declaration about Jesus"). These are based on key themes, characters or settings derived from the narrative and reflect the common practice of referring to narratives by name (cf. Jesus's reference to "the thorn-bush" in Luke 20:37.).

---

32. Jousse, *Memory*, 26.

33. Gerhardsson, *Memory and Manuscript*, 137–48; Jousse, *Memory*, 50.

34. Jousse, *Memory*, 51.

The Principle of Association

Rabbinic material was typically structured according to a defining principle signaled at the beginning of a literary section. A very common method was to order material according to the order of a known biblical passage. Scripture becomes the principle of arrangement of oral teachings. This is how midrash was organized—it simply followed the order of the Torah.

The Evangelist employs a similar devise by ordering material according to the plot of Jesus's life. The missions to Galilee, Jerusalem, and the nations provide a narrative frame or principle of arrangement into which various episodes may be inserted and remembered more easily. The Evangelist employs journey narratives and significant time periods or sequences to associate material together. The events in chapters 5 to 9 occur over a two-day period (cf. Matt 8:16). Chapters 12 and 13 occur during a very busy Sabbath. Jesus anticipates and undertakes a journey to Jerusalem (cf. 16:21). The events leading up to and including the crucifixion are set over a memorable sequence of days associated with Passover and the Sabbath (Matt 21:18; 22:23; 26:17, 20; 27:1, 45, 57, 62; 28:1).

Another method was to associate together material topically for the simple reason that material of a similar nature is easier to remember when grouped together. This is the case, for example, in Isa 40–55, where material is grouped on a factual basis while at the same time being grouped according to catchwords. In the Talmud, material is grouped thematically into six tractates. Similarly in the Gospel, material is grouped into major discourses on a thematic basis.

Written Notes

As elsewhere in the ancient world, written notes were used as a mnemonic device.[35] In general, the rabbis resisted the written transmission of the oral Torah, possibly motivated by the use of writing in magical rituals. In *b. Git.* 60b, the writing down of the oral Torah is prohibited (cf. *b. Tem.* 14b). Not a single written copy of the Mishnah is referred to in the Talmud covering the Tannaitic and Amoraic periods. By keeping a text oral, it remained a secret text with restricted access. The oral Torah was Israel's precious secret.

---

35. Gerhardsson, *Memory and Manuscript*, 159–63; Gamble, *Books and Readers*, 26–27; Jousse, *Memory*, 57.

Nevertheless, there is extensive evidence that students used writing tablets and notebooks. Parallels may be drawn to Papias's account of the use of notes (*hypomnēma*) by those who heard Peter to record his words (*Pap.* 21.1). Rainer Riesner suggests that Jesus attracted individuals who were most probably literate such as Joanna, Joseph of Arimathea, and Zacchaeus, individuals who had the ability to and means of taking notes of his teachings.[36]

Reading Aloud

In the ancient world, material was always read aloud. This pertained regardless of whether material was read in public or in private. Words were meant to sound. To read something in a whisper was to indicate that you were transmitting secret doctrines, doctrines that needed to be kept away from an "immature human public."[37] As a result, material was written with an ear to how it would sound, as was the case with the King James Version of the Bible. In *b. Ber.* 13a, we find the striking principle in relation to the use of the Shema that "one should make his ears hear what his mouth says," and so say the Shema out loud.

There is good evidence that the Gospel was written with consideration to how it would sound. Bernard Brandon Scott and Margaret Dean have produced a sound map for the Sermon on the Mount, arguing that, at least in the Greek, the sermon was written with an ear to how it would sound.[38] They posit a highly literate Evangelist who deliberately imitated the conventions of orality.

In light of the widespread use of these various memorization techniques I have outlined we may assume that the first step in achieving the call of the Gospel Commission to "teach them to obey everything that I have commanded you" (Matt 28:20) is the memorization of Jesus's teachings. Such an emphasis requires a huge commitment of time and effort. Emphasizing memorization results in a reader who is less a critic and more a preserver of the text. It results in humility before the text. The text dominates the reader rather than the reader the text. There is less time for theoretical reflection.[39]

36. Riesner, *Jesus als Lehrer*, 491–98. So too, Millard, *Reading and Writing*, 225–29.

37. Gerhardsson, *Memory and Manuscript*, 166.

38. Scott and Dean, "Sound Map," 311–78.

39. I am indebted to my colleague, Oliver Glanz, for these observations.

In comparison, in most contemporary Christian communities there is limited emphasis on the memorization of Scripture. Any memorization tends to be far less systematic than that undertaken in elementary education in the ancient world and is often restricted to memory texts removed, sometimes violently, from their literary contexts. Adult converts are typically not subjected to this process and instead jump directly to understanding. More time is spent talking about the text than learning the text. For the ancients, this is putting the cart before the horse. Memorization precedes reflection.

Teaching through Word and Deed

Teachers in the ancient world taught through two media—words and deeds. The teacher presented his subject through the spoken or written word and the student's responsibility was to memorize and understand these words. Achieving understanding would usually occur through questions and answers. The teacher would also, especially at higher levels of education, attempt to model in deed the meaning of his words. The student would imitate these deeds.

	Teacher	Student
Words	speaks, reads repeats, explains	hears, reads memorizes, understands
Deeds	acts	observes, imitates

Good teachers sought to ensure that their deeds matched their words and served as an example worthy of imitation. If the teacher was not himself the object of imitation, the text-based words and deeds of others were used to secure the same outcomes. Numerous biographies were written to provide readers with *lives* worth imitating. This educational philosophy lies behind the Evangelist's presentation of Jesus as a teacher who taught through both word and deed.[40] As an educational philosophy, it stresses the transfer of both theoretical and experiential knowledge from the teacher to the student. Its goal, however, extends beyond the transfer of knowledge. Knowledge is to be applied by the student in different situations. Judicious

40. *OCD*, s.v. "*Imitatio*," 727–28. See also Byrskog, *Jesus the Only Teacher*, 261–75; Talbert, *Reading the Sermon*, 18–20; Pitts, "Origins of Greek Mimesis," 109–29.

judgments are to be made. This is what the ancients called wisdom, the subject of our next chapter.

The Evangelist alternates between of the words and deeds of Jesus.[41] As noted above, he presents five major discourses:

Major Discourses

Matt 5:1—7:29	The Sermon on the Mount
Matt 10:1—11:1	Discipleship discourse
Matt 13:1–53	Parables discourse
Matt 18:1—19:1	Community discourse
Matt 24:1—26:1	Prophecy discourse

Interspersed between these "word" sections are accounts of Jesus's "deeds of power" (Matt 11:20), additional explanations and warnings, and examples of those who understand or fail to understand his words and/or who imitate or reject his actions.

The Gospel is ideally suited to such a didactic setting and aligns the reader with the idealized student through two literary mechanisms. First, in response to the Evangelist's presentation of Jesus's words and deeds, the reader is invited to connect the two. When we read of Jesus's actions, we are invited to question which of his teachings they illustrate. When we read his teachings, we are expected to look elsewhere in the Gospel to see where they are put into practice. The result of such a reading strategy is a lifetime of memorization and meditation in which the reader is increasingly immersed in a rich network of connections between Jesus's words and deeds. In literary critical terms, this is an extended and ever deepening second-reading experience.[42] In this manner, the Evangelist hopes that we will conclude that, unlike the Pharisees whose deeds do not match their words (23:3), in Jesus we have a consistent teacher worthy of imitation, one who, in the words of Cleopas on the road to Emmaus, was truly "mighty in deed and word before God and all the people" (Luke 24:19).

Secondly, the Evangelist hopes that the reader will increasingly align his or her own words and deeds with those of Jesus. This is how discipleship

41. Many scholars have posited topical readings of Matthew focusing on his alternation between narrative and discourse. Cf. Lohr, "Oral Techniques," 427; Bauer, *Structure*, 26–45; Davies and Allison, *Matthew 1–7*, 59–61.

42. Iser, *Implied Reader*, 281–82. A first reading is, as implied, when the reader first reads the text.

is practically experienced by the reader. Motivation to engage in this process is provided through a range of characters who illustrate the blessings associated with implementing Jesus's words and the dangers of rejecting them. The wise reader is, in Jesus's words, one "who hears these words of mine and acts on them" (Matt 7:24; cf. Luke 6:47). Such a reader is like a wise man who built his house on the rock, the house possibly an allusion to the House of Israel and the rock to God as the "Rock of Israel" (2 Sam 23:3).[43] When the storms and floods attack, his house will not fall. In contrast, a foolish man is one who "hears these words of mine and does not act on them" (Matt 7:26; cf. Luke 6:49). He is like a man who built his house on sand. When the floods come and the wind blows, his house will fall, and "great was its fall" (Matt 7:27; cf. Luke 6:49). The idealized student not only hears the words of Jesus but acts on them. He aligns his deeds to Jesus's words. What this looks like in practice is illustrated in the deeds of Jesus provided as actions to imitate.[44]

Learning from the Negative Words and Deeds of Others

Throughout the Gospel, we encounter characters who serve as foils—negative examples illustrating the dangers of neglecting Jesus's teachings. Three examples serve to illustrate. First, Matthew's retrospect of Herod's beheading of John the Baptist (Matt 14:1–12) is a story packed with allusions to the Sermon on the Mount.[45] Herod illustrates the dangers of ignoring Jesus's teachings on adultery and lust in that he has committed adultery with his brother's wife and was "pleased," whatever this may imply, with his stepdaughter's birthday performance (14:3–4; cf. 5:27–28). Jesus taught his audience not to "swear by heaven, for it is his footstool, or by earth, for it is the city of the great King. And do not swear by your head, for you cannot make one hair white or black. Let your word be 'Yes, yes', or 'No, no', anything more than this comes from the evil one" (5:34–37). In contrast,

43. See *oikou Israēl* "House of Israel" in Matt 10:6 and 15:24. The use of *oikos* "house" in Matt 12:29, 44; 13:57 may also allude to Israel.

44. For parallels between the Sermon on the Mount and the rest of the Gospel, see Allison, *Sermon on the Mount*, 9–10.

45. In general, most commentators ignore or attach minimal significance to these allusions in preference for historical and redactional discussion. See Hill, *Matthew*, 242–45; Beare, *Matthew*, 322–25; Harrington, *Matthew*, 216–18; Davies and Allison, *Matthew 8–18*, 463–77; Yamasaki, *John the Baptist in Life and Death*, 129–32; Carter, *Matthew and the Margins*, 310; Schnackenberg, *Matthew*, 138–40; Nolland, *Matthew*, 578–85.

Herod promises an oath to grant the daughter of Herodias whatever she might ask (14:7). He is a parody of the one who is evil but knows how to give good gifts to his children (7:11). Finally, he ends up executing a prophet, reminding the reader of those Jesus earlier described as persecuting "the prophets who were before you" (5:11–12). The reader can safely conclude that Herod is not part of Israel's remnant! There is barely an incident in this story which is not anticipated in the Sermon on the Mount.

Jesus's encounter with the rich young man is another story illustrating the Sermon on the Mount.[46] The rich young man asks Jesus what he must do to have life of the new age (Matt 19:16). Jesus responds in part by emphasizing the need to keep the commandments. The young man questions which commandments (19:18). Jesus answers, "You shall not murder, You shall not commit adultery, You shall not steal, You shall not bear false witness, Honor your father and mother, also, You shall love your neighbor as yourself" (14:18–20). This reminds the reader of a number of the "antitheses" of 5:21–48 which focus on the need not just to keep the Decalogue in deed only, but to internalize respective attitudes ("You have heard that it was said to those of ancient times, 'You shall not murder': and 'Whoever murders shall be liable to judgment.' But I say to you, if you are angry with a brother you are liable for judgment . . . ," 5:21–22).[47]

The rich young man is told by Jesus that if he wants to be perfect (19:21; cf. "Be perfect, therefore, as your heavenly Father is perfect," 5:48), he must go, sell his possessions and give the money to the poor, and he will have treasure in heaven; then he is to come and follow him (19:21). This equates to Jesus's teachings in chapter 6 on the need to store up treasures in heaven rather than on earth and his warning not to worry about the practicalities of life, what you will eat, drink, or wear. Instead, the reader is encouraged to strive first for the kingdom of God and the Father's righteousness (6:19, 25–33). Again, a story in which there is hardly any element which can be read in isolation from the Sermon on the Mount.

Finally, the depiction in Matt 23 of the scribes and the Pharisees includes multiple allusions to the Sermon on the Mount:[48]

---

46. Olmstead, "Jesus," 51.

47. Nolland, *Matthew*, 790.

48. Marguerat, *Le Jugement*, 354; Harrington, *Matthew*, 326; Newport, *Sources*, 158–77; Kampen, *Matthew*, 162–69. For parallels specifically to Matt 6, Davies and Allison, *Matthew 19–28*, 266.

- They are unwilling to lift the burdens of others (Matt 23:4; cf. the need to carry someone else's burden the second mile in Matt 5:41)

- They practice piety before others to be seen by them (Matt 23:5; cf. the warning against practicing "your piety before others in order to be seen by them" in Matt 6:1)

- They swear by the sanctuary and altar (Matt 23:16–22; cf. the warning against making oaths in Matt 5:33–37)

- They keep every letter and stroke of the law but neglect its essence (Matt 23:23; cf. the essence of the Law and Prophets in Matt 7:12)

- They are guilty of poor judgment ("straining gnats and swallowing camels," Matt 23:24; cf. with those who seek the speck in their neighbor's eye while not noticing the log in their own, Matt 7:3)

- Jesus calls them "hypocrites"! (Matt 23:25, 27, 29; cf. "the hypocrites" and their behavior in Matt 6:2–18)

- On the outside they are like whitewashed tombs but on the inside, they are full of bones and all kinds of filth (Matt 23:25–27; cf. those whose exterior appearance differs from their inner state in Matt 7:15–19)

- They are the descendants of those who murdered the prophets (Matt 23:32; cf. the identification to those who revile the righteous as persecutors of the prophets in Matt 5:11–12)

What is particularly striking about these three passages is that their most prominent themes are all found in the Sermon on the Mount, and we have not even started considering possible links between these three passages and any of the Gospel's other discourses.

We may conclude that Matthew's intention in including these passages was not merely for information purposes. His willingness to go beyond what we find in Mark, as in the case of chapter 23, would indicate that he has intentionally included these passages as didactic devices whose primary purpose is to illustrate in negative terms the dangers of neglecting the words of Jesus. The idealized student is taught not just by observing the deeds of Jesus, but also through contrasting the words and deeds of other contrasting characters.

Multiplying Jesus's Words

Let us return to the idea of the idealized student as one who acts upon the words of Jesus. This concept is found in several instances in the Gospel in which multiplication occurs. In the parable of the sower, the seed produces an abundant harvest, "some a hundredfold, some sixty, some thirty" (Matt 13:8, cf. 13:3–9, 18–23). The multiplication motif may be interpreted in several ways. One option is that the seed represents the words of Jesus, and the multiplied seeds represent the interpretation of his words. The true disciple not only faithfully transmits the traditions of Jesus, he also faithfully interprets them. This suggestion is certainly in line with Gerhardsson's model of rabbinic education in which traditions were intentionally transmitted and interpreted. Evidence in favor of such an interpretation is found in Jesus's explanation of the seed which landed on the path as representing anyone who "hears the word of the kingdom and does not understand it" (13:19). In contrast, the good seed represents the "one who hears the word and understands (*synieis*) it" (13:23). Accepting this interpretation, we may draw a parallel to Matthew's own implementation of the process. Traditions are to be handed on faithfully just as Matthew has transmitted his sources. Matthew has done more, however, than simply replicate his Jesus-sources. He has incorporated his own understanding, interpreting them in a manner intended to bring glory to his master teacher.

The Evangelist intends this multiplication motif to be more, however, than just an allusion to his own scribal practices. A preferable approach is to recognize a third stage beyond transmission and interpretation.[49] This is alluded to in Matt 13:23 in that the one who hears the word (stage one) and understands it (stage two), also "bears fruit and yields, in one case a hundredfold, in another sixty, and in another thirty" (stage three). The use of the participles *akouōn* and *synieis*, "hears and understands," and the accompanying pair of indicative verbs, *karpophorei* and *poiei*, "bears fruit and produces," would suggest that the participles represent the conditions which permit the production of fruit. Bearing fruit occurs after understanding and interpretation has been achieved. For Ulrich Luz, here we have the fundamental text for Matthean hermeneutics in that "hearing,

---

49. Byrskog draws our attention to the fact that Jesus traditions are largely limited to the Gospels and that other New Testament authors did not feel at liberty to radically expand or adapt such traditions (*Jesus the Only Teacher*, 18).

understanding and doing go together for him, as they do for Judaism."[50] Doing follows hearing and understanding.

It is a little more difficult to identity the nature of multiplication in the parable of the talents in which the master entrusts, according to his servants' abilities, five talents to one servant, two talents to another, and one talent to a third (Matt 25:14-30).[51] Upon his return, the first and second servants present their doubled talents to their master, ten and four talents respectively. The third servant is castigated for not multiplying his talent, instead presenting his sole talent to his master. In the absence of an explicit explanation of the talents, early Church Fathers interpreted them as teachings from or about Jesus and the multiplication process as an allusion to the need to teach and preach them to others. Clement of Alexandria, for example, refers to them, quoting from 2 Tim 2:1-2, as "the things which you have heard of me [Jesus]."[52] Origen describes them as the "dispensation of the Word."[53] The implication of such interpretations is that they imply that different servants receive varying amounts of teachings from or about Jesus. Alternatively, the faithful servants may be understood with reference to the "faithful and wise servant" of Matt 24:45-47 who demonstrates his faithfulness through the good care of his fellow servants, in which case the additional talents may also be likened to deeds consistent with Jesus's teachings.[54]

Imitation

How does the Evangelist portray the process of imitation? Imitation was central to education in the ancient world. We find in the Pseudepigrapha the demand to imitate good men (T. Ash. 4:3) and the mercy of God (T. Benj. 4:1). Philo proposes Moses as the perfect king, lawgiver, high priest, and prophet, a perfect model and *typos* for "all those who were inclined to imitate him" (*Mos.* 1:158-59). Josephus portrays Moses as the perfect example

---

50. Luz, *Matthew 8-20*, 250.

51. In Song Rab. 7.14.1, a woman is entrusted with talents by her husband, who goes away. She multiplies the talents, representing the Torah. This would support a reading of Matthew's talents as referring to the teachings of Jesus.

52. Clement of Alexandria, *Strom.* 1.2.5.

53. Origen, *Comm. ser. Matt.* 2.14.12.

54. Luz, *Matthew 21-28*, 257. On the talents as representing special gifts, the Word of God, or the ability to make converts, see Davies and Allison, *Matthew 19-28*, 401-11.

of one who seeks to imitate the ways of God (*Ant.* 1:19). Numerous other Old Testament characters are presented as suitable examples to imitate.

In Greek education, children were taught the epics of Homer as a means of providing them with heroes they could imitate.[55] Pliny extols the virtues of a "living model" (*Ep.* 8.13) and Dio Chrysostom exhorts his readers to imitate, among others, clever artists (*4 Regn.* 83–95). In this context, the good teacher sought to embody his teachings or philosophy in his actions, thereby providing a living example for his students to imitate. The poor teacher was one who shared his teachings but failed to provide a *bios* "life" in harmony with his teachings. Jesus criticizes the scribes and Pharisees for such a failure when he tells the crowds and his disciples to do whatever the scribes and Pharisees "teach you and follow it but do not do as they do, for they do not practice what they teach" (Matt 23:3). It is a moot point as to which teachings of the scribes and Pharisees the disciples of Jesus should accept. Nevertheless, the scribes and Pharisees are imperfect exemplar figures who should, at best, be heard but not imitated.

The Evangelist encourages imitation through the explicit convergence between Jesus's own words and deeds and his stated expectations for his idealized followers. This is most clearly seen during the mission to the cities of Galilee in the missionary discourse of Matt 10 and during the mission to Jerusalem in Jesus's teachings on the cross and self-denial in Matt 16. I will highlight several parallels between Jesus's stated expectations for his idealized followers and his own words and deeds.

Imitation of Jesus's Ministry to Galilee (Matt 10:1–42)

Matthew 10 represents a transition in the nature of the disciples' experience. Dorothy Weaver notes that prior to chapter 10, the disciples were those who simply "followed" Jesus. Now they are "sent out" by Jesus to minister.[56] Their purpose is to imitate him, a theme made explicit in 10:24–25 in which he states that "a disciple is not above the teacher, nor a slave above the master; it is enough for the disciple to be like the teacher and the slave like the master." It is not necessary that we deal with the whole of the chapter to demonstrate that Jesus is in effect duplicating his own ministry in his disciples. Nevertheless, there are several very clear instances in this chapter

---

55. Joyal et al., *Education*, 132–33; Barrow, *Education*, 31–56.

56. Weaver, *Matthew's Missionary Discourse*, 82.

in which the experience of the idealized follower of Jesus reflects the words and deeds of Jesus.

First, in Matt 10:1, Jesus summons the Twelve and gives them authority over unclean spirits, "to cast them out, and to cure every disease and every sickness." This commission is expanded from 10:5 onward. These instructions to the disciples evoke Jesus's earlier deeds in chapters 8 and 9. This collection of deeds and its counterpart in the words of Jesus in chapters 5 to 7 are bracketed by two summary statements:

> Jesus went throughout Galilee, teaching in their synagogues and proclaiming the good news of the kingdom and curing every disease and every sickness among the people. So his fame spread throughout all Syria, and they brought to him all the sick, those who were afflicted with various diseases and pains, demoniacs, epileptics, and paralytics, and he cured them. And great crowds followed him from Galilee, the Decapolis, Jerusalem, Judea, and from beyond the Jordan. (Matt 4:23–25)

> Then Jesus went about all the cities and villages, teaching in their synagogues, and proclaiming the good news of the kingdom, and curing every disease and every sickness. (Matt 9:35; cf. 8:16–17)

It is these deeds of Jesus that the disciples are to imitate (10:8).[57] This imitation is, however, only partial. In comparison to Jesus who, in 4:23, teaches, preaches, and heals, the disciples are commissioned to heal and to preach (10:1, 7). They are not yet in a position to teach.[58] Nevertheless, they are to "cure the sick" as Jesus healed the centurion's servant (8:5–13), the paralytic (9:1–8), the woman with an issue of blood (9:20–22), and the two blind men (9:27–31). They are to "raise the dead" as Jesus raised the "sleeping" daughter of the leader of the synagogue (9:18–26). And they are to "cast out demons" as Jesus cast demons out of the Gadarene demoniacs (8:28–34) and the mute demoniac (9:32–34).

Secondly, Jesus commissions the disciples to proclaim the good news that the kingdom of heaven has come near (Matt 10:7). This proclamation evokes the earlier proclamation of Jesus: "Repent, for the kingdom of heaven has come near" (4:17; cf. 3:2). Their words are to match his words.

Thirdly, the disciples have freely received from Jesus and are to imitate him by freely giving to others. Jesus did not require payment from

---

57. Beare, *Matthew*, 242; Davies and Allison, *Matthew 1–7*, 150; and, *Matthew 8–18*, 62–63.

58. McKnight, "Extending Jesus," 18–19.

those he healed, neither are the disciples to take payment from those they help (10:9).

Fourthly, Jesus warns the disciples that when you face a hostile response, you are to "shake off the dust from your feet as you leave that house or town" (10:14). In contrast with the first three parallels I have highlighted, which all have their precedence in earlier words or deeds of Jesus, this warning anticipates the subsequent hostile reactions toward Jesus. In 12:9–14, Jesus heals a man with a withered hand on the Sabbath. The result is that the Pharisees depart and conspire against him, "how to destroy him." Jesus becomes aware of their intentions and likewise departs (12:15). He puts into practice his own instructions.

These examples illustrate the close link between the words and deeds of Jesus and that which he intends his followers to say and do. Other parallels may be identified. Luz, for example, states: "The disciples' behavior and fate correspond to the commands of the Sermon on the Mount. The disciples are defenseless (10:10, 16, cf. 5:38–42), poor (10:9–14, cf. 6:19–34), and persecuted (10:16–23, 38–39, cf. 5:10–12). They are under God's care (10:28–31, cf. 6:25, 31) and do not need to worry (10:19, cf. 6:25–34)."[59] Do the Twelve fulfill this commission? In short, no. This opens the possibility for readers to step into the shoes of the Twelve and adopt this idealized identity for themselves.

Imitation of Jesus's Ministry to Jerusalem (Matt 16:21–28)

The mission to Jerusalem may be deemed to start in Matt 16:21 when Jesus began to show his disciples "from that time on" that he must go to Jerusalem, where he would suffer great things at the hands of the elders, chief priests, and scribes, be killed and on the third day be raised. In contrast to the mission to the cities of Galilee, in which there is at least the possibility of a positive welcome (10:40–42), in this mission only rejection is anticipated, as indicated by the "clear chronological sequence" of predicted events.[60] Jesus subsequently informs his disciples that, "If any want to become my followers, let them deny themselves and take up their cross and follow me" (16:24; cf. the call to take up the cross in 10:38).

By framing his teaching in an open manner to those, whoever they are, who desire to follow him (16:24), Jesus is, in effect, speaking over the

59. Luz, *Matthew 8–20,* 59.
60. Davies and Allison, *Matthew 8–18,* 656.

heads of the Twelve and directly to the reader.[61] He has introduced the possibility that the Twelve may not, in fact, qualify according to this new definition of the ideal student. Idealized students are those willing to imitate Jesus to the extent that, just as he will lose his life in Jerusalem, they too will lose their lives. He motivates readers to imitate him in this manner by warning that those who try to save their life will in fact lose it and those who lose it "for my sake" will find it (16:25). He then invokes the image of the final judgment when the Son of Man will "repay everyone for what he has done" (*kata tēn praxin autou*, 16:27), the key issue being one's willingness to imitate Jesus's *praxis*, his journey to Jerusalem.

The idealized student cannot pick and choose between imitating Jesus in his mission to Galilee or in his mission to Jerusalem. In the Sermon on the Mount, set within the context of the mission to Galilee, the reader is warned in Matt 7:21–23 that it is not enough to prophesy like Jesus (cf. 10:19–20), to cast out demons like him (cf. 8:28–34; 9:32–34; 10:8), or to do many deeds of power ("cure the sick, raise the dead," 10:8; cf. "deeds of power" in 11:20, 21, 23; 13:54, 58).[62] It is not enough, in effect, to replicate the ministry of Jesus to the cities and villages of Galilee if you are not doing the will of his Father in heaven. This raises the question as to the nature of the will of his Father in heaven. We will return to this topic in chapter 5 in our consideration of binding and loosing and the interaction between heaven and earth. For the time being, it suffices it to say that Jesus affirms his obedience to his Father's will in the Garden of Gethsemane (26:39, 42), this being his willingness to see through the mission to Jerusalem. Thus, reading 7:21–23 in light of later plot-related developments in the Gospel, the reader is required to combine the discipleship ideals of the mission to Galilee with its emphasis on prophesy, casting out demons, and deeds of power (10:1, 8, 19–20), with that of the mission to Jerusalem with its focus on denial and the willingness to take up one's cross and follow Jesus (16:24). This warning indicates an awareness on the part of the Evangelist that certain readers may limit their imitation of Jesus to his more positive mission to Galilee.

---

61. In Mark 8:34, Jesus addresses his teachings on discipleship to the crowds.

62. Many scholars unnecessarily take Matt 7:21–23 as a description of the behavior of the false Christian prophets of 7:15. See Gundry, *Matthew*, 128; Davies and Allison, *Matthew 1–7*, 702–4; Luz, *Matthew 1–7*, 442–43. While applicable to later Christian contexts, the passage follows Jesus's warning in 5:17–20 against the perversion of the Law and the Prophets and should therefore be viewed as a continuation of this general polemic. So Nolland, *Matthew*, 335–37.

The Limitations of Imitation

The ancients were quite aware that learning through imitation was subject to certain pedagogical limitations. An early critique is provided by Philolaches, a character in a comedy by Plautus written toward the end of the third century BCE. Philolaches highlights one weakness of imitation which is that its effectiveness is often minimal and that it does not continue once the student has left the company of his teacher (Plautus, *Most.* 127–46). This criticism is somewhat negated through the Evangelist's choice of the *bios* genre which enables imitation via the text of the Gospel without necessitating the imminent physical presence of the teacher. Jesus is always accessible to the reader through the text. This assumes, of course, ready access to the text. Tacitus, prone to exaggeration, points out another problem. Imitation is only of value if the teacher has qualities worth imitating (*Dial.* 29). Each reader of the Gospel must decide whether this is in fact the case. These criticisms, while valid, should be set within a context of widespread support in the ancient world for imitation as a didactic technique (cf. Petronius, *Sat.* 57).

The Evangelist sets two further limitations on the reader's ability to imitate Jesus. First, an implicit limitation results from the tension between Jesus's emphasis on correcting your inner world and the fact that the reader is virtually never allowed into the inner world of Jesus's own thoughts. Jesus, for example, moves beyond a critique of the act of adultery to criticize the act of looking at a woman with lust, the equivalent of "committing adultery in the heart" (Matt 5:28). Intention is to be judged as deed, a position, suggest Davies and Allison, closer to the school of Shammai than the school of Hillel (cf. *b. Qidd.* 43a).[63] Jesus distinguishes between the exterior of false prophets who appear in sheep's clothing and their interior disposition as ravenous wolves (7:15). Similarly, he criticizes the scribes and Pharisees for being externally as clean cups while on the inside they are full of "greed and self-indulgence" (23:25). Outwardly they are like whitewashed tombs but inwardly they are "full of the bones of the dead and of all kinds of filth" (23:27). These critiques focus on the need to reform the inner world of your thoughts and intentions. Only once this is done will good fruit be produced ("only good trees can bear good fruit," 7:17).

This emphasis on the inner world of others is not matched by a corresponding presentation of Jesus's own inner world. Matthew, reflecting

---

63. Davies and Allison, *Matthew 1–7*, 523.

Jewish narrative storytelling techniques, characterizes Jesus by "showing" us his words and deeds. Mark's emphasis is similarly on "showing" rather than "telling."[64] Occasionally, however, Mark invites us into the inner world of Jesus. In contrast, Matthew consistently removes such references, closing what limited access to Jesus's inner world that Mark provides. Compare the following examples:

> *Moved with pity*, Jesus stretched out his hand and touched him. (Mark 1:41, italics supplied)

> He stretched out his hand and touched him, saying . . . (Matt 8:3)

> *He looked around at them with anger; he was grieved at their hardness of heart* and said to the man, "Stretch out your hand." He stretched it out, and his hand was restored. (Mark 3:5, italics supplied)

> Then he said to the man, "Stretch out your hand." He stretched it out, and it was restored, as sound as the other. (Matt 12:13)

> *Immediately aware that power had gone forth from him*, Jesus turned about in the crowd and said, "Who touched my clothes?" . . . But the woman, knowing what had happened to her, came in fear and trembling, fell down before him, and told him the whole truth. (Mark 5:30, 33, italics supplied)

> Jesus turned, and seeing her he said, "Take heart, daughter; your faith has made you well." And instantly the woman was made well. (Matt 9:22)

> Jesus, *looking at him, loved him* and said, "You lack one thing; go, sell what you own, and give the money to the poor, and you will have treasure in heaven; then come, follow me." (Mark 10:21, italics supplied)

> Jesus said to him, "If you wish to be perfect, go, sell your possessions, and give the money to the poor, and you will have treasure in heaven; then come, follow me." (Matt 19:21)

How is the reader to imitate the inner life of the Matthean Jesus when it is so inaccessible? Through the dictum that "you will know them by their fruit" (Matt 7:16; cf. 12:33).[65] Evidence for the health of the inner life is to

---

64. Marguerat and Bourquin, *How to Read Bible Stories*, 69–71.

65. This dictum was a commonplace. Davies and Allison cite Sir 27:6; Matt 12:33; Luke 6:43–45; and Jas 3:10–12 as examples where "fruit" is speech and people are judged

be found in its outward expression in word and deed. Jesus's inner world is not on trial. And yet the reader must still determine Jesus's motives to aid their imitation of him. Are his public deeds of power of chapters 8 and 9, for example, motivated by a desire to let his light shine before other so that they may give glory to his Father in heaven or by a desire to be seen by others (5:16; 6:1)? We are not told. Such gaps in the text serve the didactic function of delaying the reader's assessment of Jesus's motives, enticing the reader into the process of judging the motives of the central character of the Gospel. In so doing, the Jesus of the text is appropriated as the reader's own Jesus. The Evangelist supplies his words and deeds, the reader his motives. By supplying his motives, the reader implicitly decides whether or not to imitate Jesus.

A second limitation on the reader's ability to imitate Jesus relates to the restricted access to his words. Jesus obviously said more than is recorded in the Gospel. This limitation involves more, however, than the Evangelist's inability to include all of Jesus's words in the Gospel (cf. John 21:25). We find a tension in Jesus's teachings between his expectation that his disciples will transmit his words even when in difficult situations and his warning that sometimes there will be situations in which they should not worry about finding appropriate words of his to share. According to Matt 10:24–34, their duty as students is to share their teacher's words. In Matt 10:25, Jesus informs his followers that if he as head of the house has been called Beelzebul, they, as his students, should not expect to be treated any better. Nevertheless, what he says to them "in the dark," they are to tell "in the light," and what they hear whispered, they are to proclaim from the housetops (10:27). Even in difficult situations, they are to transmit the words of Jesus, without fear of those who can kill the body but who cannot kill the soul (10:28). Instead, they are to "fear him who can destroy both soul and body in Gehenna" (10:29).

Earlier, however, in Matt 10:16–20, Jesus warns the disciples that they will be handed over to councils and flogged in their synagogues. They will be dragged before governors and kings "as a testimony to them and the Gentiles" (10:18). When handed over, his followers are not to worry "how you are to speak or what you are to say; for what you are to say will be given to you at that time" for, in prophetic manner, it will not be them speaking but rather

---

by their words. In Matt 7:16–20; John 15; and Gal 5:19–23, fruit are general deeds (*Matthew 1–7*, 706).

"the Spirit of your Father speaking through you" (10:19–20; cf. Exod 4:12). There will be times when followers of Jesus must function as prophets.[66]

The reader must thus decide whether to choose the idealized identity of a student who faithfully transmits the words of Jesus or that of a momentarily inspired prophet transmitting the words of the Spirit. The "what" of imitation is dependent upon the reader's choice as to which discipleship role he or she chooses to adopt at any one point in time. These two limitations to imitation, one resulting from the characterization of Jesus and the other from the varied persona or roles offered the reader, indicate a degree of openness in the imitation process. This characteristic of Matthean imitation is further highlighted when we compare it with the Johannine discipleship ideal in which Jesus, sent into the world from above, only speaks the words he hears and does the works he sees his heavenly Father say and do.[67] He correspondingly expects his followers, having been reminded of his words and works by the Paraclete, to replicate his deeds (and words implied) before others.[68] In the Gospel of John, the reader is permitted far less discretion in the imitation process. He or she is called to replicate in total the words and deeds of Jesus. In contrast, the Gospel of Matthew requires the reader to continually assess the what, why, when, and how of imitation.

Implications

This chapter has demonstrated how a picture of the idealized student-teacher emerges from the text when it is analyzed in terms of prominent educational motifs within the ancient world. The educational emphasis on memorization is implied in the Evangelist's use of narrative techniques aimed at aiding the memorization process. The grouping of thematically similar material, the use of memorable time and place settings, and the alternation between word and deed, all facilitate memorization. Memorization is the basis for achieving understanding. While the thrust of the Gospel's plot is the impending judgments of Galilee and Jerusalem, the alternation between word and deed invites the reader to enter into his or her own judgment process, weighing the meaning of Jesus's own words embodied in his deeds. Achieving understanding involves readers judging their teacher: Do his words represent an attractive proposition upon which

---

66. Davies and Allison, *Matthew 8–18*, 185.

67. John 3:17, 34; 5:19. See Klink, "Light of the World," 87–88.

68. John 14:16; 16:13–15; 17:18.

to base your own life? Do his deeds match his words? If readers decide "no" to these questions, then their educational experience remains at the level of understanding. If they decide "yes," they are in a position to move to the next stage of their educational experience, putting them into practice in their own lives and sharing the words of Jesus with others.

In terms of imitation, the Evangelist presents an idealized student-teacher who is more than just a competent scholar who understands the text. Highly sympathetic readers who seek to embody his educational ideal will alternate between listening to the text and judging their own inner motivations and exterior words and deeds. They undertake two alignments: (1) their exterior words and deeds with those of Jesus; and (2) their interior motivations with their own reshaped exterior. In this circuitous manner, they align their inner worlds with that of Jesus. The result of this process is not just a good student-teacher trained to a high educational level. It is a transformed teacher who models for the community the words and deeds of Jesus.

The challenge that this picture of discipleship presents is that it requires far more interpersonal contact than industrial or postindustrial societies typically permit. Extended working hours, two-income households, multiple career changes, and nuclear families, all put pressure on interpersonal relationships and leave little time to invest in others. As a result, memorization is neglected and there are few opportunities for teachers to model in their own lives the words and deeds of Jesus for their students. Imitation is time-hungry and difficult to determine whether it has been pedagogically successful. It is easier to teach content and determine whether the student has gained understanding.

A focus on word over deed can result in followers of Jesus who know enough to commit to him but whose discipleship experience is highly cerebral and almost exclusively word focused. This leaves them vulnerable to other belief systems that offer more accessible deeds to imitate. It also produces followers of Jesus who lack the confidence to say with Paul, "Be imitators of me, as I am of Christ" (1 Cor 11:1).[69] This is, as far as I can see, one of the greatest challenges facing contemporary missiological practice. How do we create the time so that we can affirm with Paul that we have not just shared the word of the Lord, but we have provided our own students with a *life* to imitate? Paul's use of educational practices to disciple the Thessalonians is particularly striking: "So deeply do we care for you that we

---

69. On imitation, see 1 Cor 4:16; Eph 5:1; Phil 3:17; 1 Thess 1:6; 2:14; and 2 Thess 3:7, 9.

are determined to share with you not only the gospel of God but also our own selves because you have become very dear to us." (cf. 1 Thess 2:8). He shares both word and deed. Teachers must share their personal lives with their students, running the risk of rejection, not just of the contents of their teaching, but of their own lives as lives worthy of imitation.

5

The Wise Man

Leading the Nation on Behalf of Its King

Introduction

A NATION THAT ACCEPTS the sovereignty of Jesus requires spiritually discerning leaders. This chapter focuses on the wise man as national or community leader or, in the words of the Evangelist, the "faithful and wise servant, whom his master has put in charge of his household" (Matt 24:45). The motif of the wise man as a teachable leader is widespread in the Old Testament and Second Temple literature.[1] Joseph was promoted to high office by Pharaoh because of his wisdom (Gen 41:39–40). King Solomon was given a "wise and discerning mind" for the purpose of ruling his people (1 Kgs 3:12; cf. 2 Chr 1:11–12). Daniel was a wise man who evokes the ideal of Joseph (Dan 2:18, 21).[2] Both were in a foreign land against their will. Both served pagan kings who had problematic dreams. Both interpreted dreams. Both served as prime minister, in the case of Daniel, under a succession of pagan kings or regents: Nebuchadnezzar (Dan 2:46–49); Belshazzar (5:14); Darius (6:3); and Cyrus (10:1). This picture of the wise man as a high-status community leader is reinforced in later traditions such as Sir 38:24—39:11, *J.W.* 1.648 and 2.118.

In Matt 23:34, Jesus promises to send wise men to Israel (cf. the absence of wise men in Luke's equivalent in Luke 11:49). The expectation that the followers of Jesus will serve as community or national leaders may set

1. Wilkins, *Concept of Disciple*, 72–89.
2. Heaton, *School Tradition*, 118–20.

off alarm bells for some readers concerned at the prospect of a theocratic dictatorship. How can such a danger be avoided? What checks and balances can be placed on religiously motivated community leaders? How can wise men avoid becoming tyrants drunk on the power that results from their spiritual mandate? We will address these significant concerns by affirming the Evangelist's vision of the wise man as someone who avoids the twin dangers of tyranny on the one hand, a perceived danger in the West that has resulted in the depoliticization of large sections of government, and on the other hand, an absence of power that results in chaos. The ancients were well aware of the dangers of social breakdown, that a divided house would fall (cf. Matt 12:25).[3]

With these concerns in mind, we will focus on the wise man as a maker of morally significant decisions, as one who understands the future and who protects the nation from the most of serious of threats—demonic and idolatrous activity.

The Idealized Wise Man and the Making of Significant Decisions

A key requirement of those who lead the nation is the ability to make significant decisions. Such a skill is portrayed in Matt 16:19 in which Jesus informs Peter that "whatever you bind (*dēsēs*) on earth, will be bound (*estai dedemenon*) in heaven, and whatever you loose (*lysēs*) on earth will be loosed (*estai lelymenon*) in heaven."[4] The translation of Jesus's words is somewhat problematic in that it includes a future perfect periphrastic construction ("will be bound," "will be loosed"). A future periphrastic construction includes the future tense of the verb "to be" followed by a perfect participle. The difficulty we face in translation may be stated thus. Should we anticipate a future response on the part of heaven to what is bound on earth by giving priority to the future tense of *eimi* "to be" ("will be bound in heaven"), as in the ESV, KJV, NKJV, and NRSV? Or should we emphasize that earth is only affirming something that has already been

---

3. O'Donovan, *Desire of the Nations*, 94.

4. Peter's status as community leader is further confirmed in this passage through his receipt of divine revelation ("flesh and blood has not revealed to you, but my Father in heaven," Matt 16:17), his status as the foundation upon which Jesus will build his *ekklēsia* (16:18), and his receipt of the keys of the kingdom (16:19). Wilkins understands the phrase "in heaven" to be a Semitic circumlocution for describing the action of God (*Concept of Discipleship*, 197).

bound in heaven by stressing the perfect form of the participle, e.g., "binding" ("shall have been bound in heaven") as in the CSB and NASB? Which comes first, the decision on earth or a decision made in heaven? In the first instance, significant decisions are required of the decision maker. In the second instance, those on earth are merely confirming decisions already made in heaven. Translation is made all the more difficult by the fact that we only have two other future periphrastic constructions in the New Testament—Matt 18:18 and Heb 2:3.

The answer to this difficult exegetical dilemma may well be found in the LXX in which we find a good number of future periphrastic constructions which are most naturally translated with a future sense.[5] Assuming a similar usage in the Gospel, we may reaffirm a translation of Matt 16:19 and its equivalent in 18:18 in which the things Peter and the other disciples bind on earth are then bound in heaven. The same applies to the loosing process. Heaven will respond to decisions made on earth.

Further clarification is necessary. Origen emphasized the superiority of Peter over the other disciples on the basis that whatever he binds on earth, will be bound "in the heavens" (*en tois ouranois*, 16:19), whereas whatever the other disciples bind on earth, will only be bound "in the heaven" (*en ouranō*, 18:18).[6] Origen concluded on the basis of the difference between singular and plural heavens that Peter's superiority lies in his ability to affect not just one heaven, but them all. Origen is right to draw our attention to this difference. He may, however, have overstated the significance of the difference. Against his reading, we may appeal to Jonathan Pennington's detailed study of heaven and earth in Matthew in which he shows that, barring a number of ambiguous examples, the Evangelist normally employs *ouranos* "heaven" to refer to the visible heavens and *ouranoi* "heavens" to refer to heaven as the dwelling of God or to the divine realm. When, however, heaven is used in a heaven-earth pairing, it may refer either to the physical heaven or to the divine realm.[7] This would suggest that when Jesus uses the singular form in Matt 18:18, it may still refer to the divine realm as implied in 16:19. Thus we may infer that all followers of Jesus are expected to bind and loose in significant ways that affect the heavenly realm.

5. E.g., LXX 2 Sam 7:16; 2 Chr 7:15; Isa 10:20; 22:24; 32:3; 58:14; Jer 14:16; 43:30; 51:14; Ezek 44:2; 46:1.

6. Origen, *Comm. Matt* 13.31. Pennington includes as ambiguous uses, Matt 3:16–17; 14:19; and 16:1, and as possible anomalies, 16:19; 22:30; and 23:22 (*Heaven and Earth*, 143–49).

7. Pennington, *Heaven and Earth*, 142.

The Meaning of "Binding" and "Loosing"

What does it mean to "bind" (*deō*) and to "loose" (*lyō*)? Several suggestions have been proposed. Burnett Streeter interpreted binding and loosing in terms of Luke 11:52 ("Woe to you lawyers! For you have taken away the key of knowledge; you did not enter yourselves, and you hindered those who were entering").[8] In this reading, Peter is given true insight into righteousness and to bind and loose is to expound the moral law in a manner on earth that results in heaven abiding by the decision. For Streeter, Peter is the supreme rabbi or wise man of the kingdom. Nuancing this position, Günter Bornkamm argued that Matt 16:19 refers primarily to Peter's *teaching* authority, whereas 18:18 relates to the *disciplinary* authority of the congregation.[9]

A more focused definition is provided by Davies and Allison who suggest that to bind and loose is "to declare what is permitted (i.e., the rabbinic *šĕrê/šĕrā*) and what is not permitted (i.e., the rabbinic *'āsar/'ăsar*)."[10]

In the Mishnah, to bind, while predominantly used with reference to the act of restricting someone's physical freedom, may also denote the act of binding someone to a particular course of action ('*sr* in *m. Šeb.* 4:13; cf. *b. Moʿed Qat.* 16a). Mark Allan Powell appropriately observes that it refers to "the application of scriptural commandments for contemporary situations."[11] It involved the "discernment of the law's intent and of the sphere of its application."[12] According to Powell, Jesus binds and looses on several occasions. These include binding the law on murder to include anger and insults (5:21–23); the law on adultery as applying to lust, divorce, and remarriage (5:27–28, 31–32); the prohibition against false oaths as applying to *all* oaths (5:33–37; cf. Lev 19:12); the command to love your neighbor as applying to your enemies (5:43–48); and the command to honor your father and mother as including caring for your parents when they are in old age (15:3–9).[13] Examples of loosing include the loosing of the prohibition against working on the Sabbath to include plucking grain to satisfy your

---

8. Streeter, *Primitive Church*, 63, referenced in Davies and Allison, *Matthew 8–18*, 637.

9. Bornkamm, "Authority to 'Bind' and 'Loose,'" 85–97. Cf. Stendahl, *School of St. Matthew*, 28.

10. Davies and Allison, *Matthew 8–18*, 638.

11. Powell, "Binding and Loosing," 439.

12. Powell, "Binding and Loosing," 439.

13. Powell, "Binding and Loosing," 441–42.

hunger, the tradition against performing works of healing on the Sabbath (12:1–14), and the laws on ritual hand-washing (15:1–2, 10–20).

When we take into consideration other Second Temple sources, we find that binding and loosing applies to more than just law-related decisions. Binding and loosing are used throughout the LXX and the writings of Josephus in relation to the physical acts of binding and loosing by those in authority of those in subjugation. The Philistines, for example, seek to bind Sampson (LXX Judg 15:10).[14] To bind and loose is to exert authority and control over someone else. The terms are used in a figurative sense by Josephus to refer to the exercise of authority. A very significant example is found in *Jewish War* in which to bind and loose is equated with the administration of public affairs:

> Beside Alexandra, and growing as she grew, arose the Pharisees, a body of Jews with the reputation of excelling the rest of their nation in the observances of religion, and as exact exponents of the laws. To them, being herself intensely religious, she listened with too great deference; while they, gradually taking advantage of an ingenuous woman, became at length the real administrators of the state, at liberty to banish and to recall, to loose and to bind [*lyein te kai desmein*], whom they would. In short, the enjoyments of royal authority were theirs; its expenses and burthens fell to Alexandra. (*J.W.* 1.111 [Thackeray, LCL])

In some pseudepigraphal writings binding is also used to refer to exorcisms: "And Beliar shall be bound (*dethēsetai*) by him. And he shall grant to his children the authority to trample on wicked spirits." (*T. Levi.* 18:12; cf. *T. Sol.* 1:14). The position that binding and loosing frequently refers in pseudepigraphal literature to control over demons has been persuasively argued by Richard Hiers. He is correct, however, to sound a note of caution when it comes to determining the Evangelist's intentions with respect to binding and loosing. For Hiers, binding and loosing in the Gospel could refer to control over demons. More likely, however, considering the use of the indefinite *ho ean* in Matt 16:19 ("*whatever* you bind," "*whatever* you loose"), it may have a "broader, indeterminate application."[15] We may thus affirm with Hiers that binding and loosing, while including the making of legal

14. Cf. LXX 2 Sam 3:34; 2 Kgs 17:4; Josephus, *Ant.* 2.63, 78; 5:299; 18:236.

15. Hiers, "'Binding' and 'Loosing,'" 246. Wilkins unnecessarily limits binding and loosing to the authority "to declare that sins are either forgiven or retained" (*Concept of Discipleship*, 197).

rulings and/or the control of demons, refers more generally to the process of making unspecified but nevertheless morally significant decisions.

How the Evangelist Constructs a Wise Decision Maker

Reading any text requires the reader to make a constant flow of interpretative decisions.[16] In a more specific sense, however, the Gospel presents the reader with explicit decisions to make. The making of these decisions requires great wisdom and the need, in a very general sense, to bind and loose.

Dale Allison provides a very useful analysis of internal tensions in the teaching of the Matthean Jesus:[17] (1) On the one hand Jesus often refers to the gentiles in a disparaging manner (cf. Matt 5:47; 6:7, 32; and 18:17). In Matt 10:5-6, he tells his disciples to avoid going to the gentiles and instead to go only to the "lost sheep of the house of Israel" (cf. 15:24). On the other hand, this avoidance of gentiles is reversed at the end of the Gospel where Jesus instructs his disciples to "go . . . and make disciples of all nations" (28:19). This tension is heightened by references throughout the Gospel to gentiles (cf. the gentile Ruth in the genealogy, the gentile magi in ch. 2; the use of Isa 9:1-2 in Matt 4:14-16, and Isa 42:1-4 in Matt 12:17-21). (2) On the one hand, Jesus vigorously defends the law, right down to its jots and tittles (5:17-19). On the other hand, he forbids oaths in Matt 5:33-37, even though the Torah permits them. Some have understood Jesus's words against the principle of "an eye for an eye" as going against the Torah. (3) Jesus teaches in 5:43-48 that God loves the wicked and yet throughout the Gospel the wicked are consigned to Gehenna (13:42; 22:13; 24:51; etc.). (4) In 6:17-18, Jesus provides instructions as to how to fast. In 9:15, he denies that his followers can fast while the bridegroom is with them. (5) Jesus warns against following the teachings of the Pharisees and Sadducees ("leaven" in 16:6, 12). In 23:2-3, he states that because the scribes and Pharisees sit on Moses's seat, we should do whatever they teach, but not as they do, because they do not practice what they teach. Lastly, (6) if the Son of Man is Lord of the Sabbath who permits "certain contingencies to override the Sabbath (12:1-8, 9-14), then why should the disciples worry whether their eschatological flight might be on a Sabbath (24:20)?"[18]

---

16. Iser, *Implied Reader*, 118; Eco, *Role of the Reader*, 47-65.

17. Allison, *Studies in Matthew*, 239-40.

18. Allison, *Studies in Matthew*, 240.

Commentators have responded to such tensions by either exaggerating, denying, or explaining them away.[19] Allison himself suggests two possible explanations. Firstly, the tensions in the Gospel reflect tensions within the law. Allison argues that Matthew knew only too well that commandments can conflict with each other, and that "to break the Torah is not to abolish it."[20] Here the tension lies within the law itself and the various moral dilemmas it seeks to address. Secondly, the tensions in the Gospel reflect tensions within the character of God. God is a God who both loves and judges. Both elements are reflected in the Gospel. The tension between love and judgment goes back to Jesus himself and, concludes Allison, "beyond him to the Jewish theology in which he was raised."[21] These two explanations are valid and may be affirmed. In addition, we may link many of these tensions to the developing plot of the Gospel. The tension between Jesus and the leaders in Jerusalem rises as the plot progresses and this is reflected in changes in the tone of Jesus's language.

While not addressing the specific tensions Allison identifies, I would like to add that textual tensions or paradoxes are also integral to wisdom literature. Ben Witherington notes that the book of Proverbs includes several significant paradoxes:

> On the one hand, one learns in the prologue that the purpose of the book is that human beings may know wisdom and receive instruction in wise dealings. On the other hand wisdom, in the persona of Woman Wisdom, is said to be seeking humankind. On the one hand, wisdom seems to involve the investigation of natural and human phenomena and deducing practical lessons from them, but on the other hand, wisdom is something that God must reveal if anyone is to know it. Wisdom is on the one hand a challenge to the listener, and in other contexts the required response of that same listener.[22]

---

19. Traditional exegetes viewed it as their job to explain away the apparent tension between the mission to the gentiles in Matt 28:16–20 and Jesus's command not to go among the Samaritans or gentiles (10:5–6). Some scholars have emphasized such contradictions as evidence of different traditions embedded within the Gospel (e.g., Manson, *Only to the House of Israel?*, 1–4). Other commentators have emphasized consistency in the Gospel (e.g., Allison, *Studies in Matthew*, 245–47; Boxall, *Discovering Matthew*, 32).

20. Allison, *Studies in Matthew*, 247.

21. Allison, *Studies in Matthew*, 249.

22. Witherington, *Jesus the Sage*, 22.

Such paradoxes lie at the very heart of wisdom literature, reflected in the tendency of providing different explanations for the same phenomenon. For example, Proverbs explains poverty as resulting from ignoring instructions (Prov 13:18), injustice (13:23); laziness (12:27), wickedness (13:25), too much talk (14:23), a failure to sow (20:4), the love of sleep (20:13), and the use of excuses to justify inaction (23:13; 26:13). Proverbs provides qualified advice on the disciplining of children. At one extreme, the rod is justified (13:24). This is qualified elsewhere in that it should only be used when there is hope that it will have a positive effect and when it is not wielded in anger (19:18–19). Reproof and training lie at the other end of the discipline spectrum (22:6). A final example in which the reader must make sense of contrasting advice is found in Proverbs 26:

> Do not answer fools according to their folly, or you will be a fool yourself.
> Answer fools according to their folly, or they will be wise in their own eyes.
> (Prov 26:4–5)

Here the reader is given contrasting counsel. We should avoid answering fools and yet we should also answer fools. The difference lies in the motivation. Don't answer fools so that you don't engage in foolish talk and appear a fool yourself. Answer fools or else they will leave you convinced that they have outfoxed you and that they themselves are wise.

The role of the wise reader is not to blindly implement such proverbs. To try to do so may result in misapplication. Instead, Proverbs presents before the reader different options, associated motives, and possible outcomes, and then expects the reader to make a wise choice. The wise man thus makes decisions while listening to the broad array of Wisdom's counsels. Commenting on this feature of wisdom literature, James Kugel suggests that such literature deliberately provides riddles to ponder in that this is a more effective way of holding the student's attention to that of inculcating knowledge through repetition.[23]

Contrasting Counsel in the Gospel of Matthew

Recognition both of the important role of wisdom in the Gospel and Matthew's characterization of Jesus's followers as wise men would suggest the possibility that the Evangelist has incorporated contrasting advice within the Gospel in order that the reader be required to make decisions

23. Kugel, "Ancient Israelite Pedagogy," 20–21.

of comparable significance to those found in biblical wisdom literature.[24] Several such tensions in the Sermon on the Mount illustrate this point:

   a. *Whether to perform your acts of righteousness in public or private?*

      i. "In the same way, let your (pl.) light shine *before others*, so that they *may see* your good works and give glory to your Father in heaven" (Matt 5:16);

      ii. "Beware of practicing your righteousness *before others* in order to *be seen* by them; for then you have no reward from your Father in heaven" (6:1).

Wise readers must question whether the performance of their righteous acts in the public space is motivated by a desire for self-glorification or the glorification of God and choose accordingly whether to perform publicly such works.

   b. *Whether to judge or withhold judgment?*

      i. "Do not judge, so that you may not be judged. For with the judgment you make you will be judged, and the measure you give will be the measure you get. Why do you see the speck in your neighbor's eye, but do not notice the log in your own eye?" (7:1–2);

      ii. "Beware of false prophets, who come to you in sheep's clothing but inwardly are ravenous wolves. You will know them by their fruits. Are grapes gathered from thorns, or figs from thistles?" (7:15–16).

Wise men must decide whether judgment is required to safeguard the community or whether passing judgment may be, in certain circumstances, the ultimate act of hypocrisy.

   c. *Whether or not to give to others when requested?*

      i. "You have heard that it was said, 'An eye for an eye and a tooth for a tooth.' But I say to you, Do not resist an evildoer. But if anyone strikes you on the right cheek, turn the other also; and if

24. Jesus characterizes his works as those of wisdom in Matt 11:2, 19 and evokes prominent wisdom motifs in 11:25–30. Cf. Suggs, *Wisdom*; Mack, "Wisdom, Christology and Law"; Deutsch, *Lady Wisdom*; Gench, *Wisdom*. On different approaches to decision making (e.g., consequential, deontological, and perfectionist) and related readings of the Sermon on the Mount, see Talbert, *Reading the Sermon on the Mount*, 27–31.

anyone wants to sue you and take your coat, give your cloak as well; and if anyone forces you to go one mile, go also the second mile. Give to everyone who begs from you, and do not refuse anyone who wants to borrow from you" (5:38–42);

ii. "Do not give what is holy to dogs; and do not throw your pearls before swine, or they will trample them under foot and turn and maul you" (7:6).

Readers must decide whether to respond positively to requests for help or to remain wary. They are called to judge the motives of both the supplicant and themselves as givers.

d. *Whether to ask your Father in heaven for help in the mundane areas of life?*

i. "Therefore do not worry, saying, 'What will we eat?' or 'What will we drink?' or 'What will we wear?' For it is the Gentiles who strive for all these things; and indeed your heavenly Father knows that you need all these things. But strive first for the kingdom of God and his righteousness, and all these things will be given to you as well" (6:31–33);

ii. "Give us this day our daily bread" (6:11).

Wise readers are presented with the choice of simply trusting in the Lord to deal with their needs while they focus on kingdom priorities or, as in the Lord's Prayer, actively seeking divine intervention in routine and mundane matters.

Such decisions require the reader to determine his or her own motives and then to choose accordingly. Knowledge is thereby applied in complex and ambiguous situations resulting in the development of wisdom. The idealized wise man is to consider carefully the decisions he or she makes and the intentions that lie behind particular choices.

Heaven and Earth in Creative Tension

Reading Jesus's injunctions to bind and loose in isolation of their wider theological context will result in community leaders beholden to their own desires. As such, limitations are placed on their binding and loosing.

Checks and balances are placed on leadership. This becomes apparent when we consider the interaction between heaven and earth within the Gospel.

Pennington has drawn our attention to the extensive and nuanced interaction between heaven and earth in the Gospel. He highlights an ongoing tension between the two which, he intriguingly argues, will only be finally resolved at the eschaton (*palingenesia*, Matt 19:28).[25] Several examples highlight this tension. In the Lord's Prayer we are introduced to a binary opposition of heaven and earth: "Our Father in heaven, hallowed be your name. Your kingdom come. Your will be done, on earth as it is in heaven" (Matt 6:10). In this verse, the will of our Father in heaven has priority over earth. His will is to be done on earth as it is in heaven (cf. 7:21–23). Jesus reaffirms this position in 12:50–51 when he identifies his true family in these terms, "Here are my mother and my brothers! For whoever does the will of my Father in heaven is my brother and sister and mother." Again, heaven has priority over earth. The will of our Heavenly Father is to be manifested upon earth.

These examples point to the need not only to imitate Jesus, but also to imitate his Father in heaven. So far, so good. But as readers progress in their reading from chapter 12 into the central section of the Gospel with its focus on discipleship, they encounter an apparent tension. Instead of heaven influencing earth, they find the reverse, earth influencing heaven. As noted above, Jesus delegates in 16:19 the prerogative to bind and loose to Peter. In this case, earth influences heaven (cf. 18:18). Whatever is bound or loosed on earth will be bound or loosed in heaven.

The apparent contradiction is this. At some points in the Gospel, heaven has priority over earth (e.g., in the Lord's Prayer). At other points, earth takes the lead over heaven. Why is it important to recognize and affirm this tension? A failure to appreciate and respond to Matthew's tension in the relationship between heaven and earth will result either in weak leaders who abdicate their responsibility to make decisions on earth by repeatedly appealing to some projection of heaven's position or to overly domineering leaders who bind and loose on earth while paying little attention to the desires of heaven.[26] It is this last position, that of tyrannical leadership, that is identified in the Gospel as the most serious of these two dangers.

---

25. Pennington, *Heaven and Earth*, 7, 210.

26. This reading differs somewhat from Pennington who equates earth with earthly kingdoms (*Heaven and Earth*, 7).

For Matthew, domineering leadership develops when those in positions of spiritual authority bind and loose for their own ends. Their motives are self-serving. In Matt 20:17–19, Jesus warns the disciples that he will be subjected to abuse by tyrannical national leaders—the chief priests and scribes. The disciples, however, are themselves liable to becoming tyrants. In Matt 20:21, the mother of the sons of Zebedee requests of Jesus that her sons be given the top positions of authority in the kingdom of Jesus, to sit on his right and on his left. When the other ten disciples find out about the request, they strongly express their anger with the two brothers. Jesus intervenes and warns the disciples, "You know that the rulers of the Gentiles lord it over them, and their great ones are tyrants over them. It will not be so among you" (20:25). Instead, they are to serve.[27] Tyrannical leadership develops in the absence of heavenly oversight and in the presence of selfish motives. Jesus rejects a command-and-control exercise of authority.

I have characterized the two spheres of heaven and earth as being in apparent tension. When this tension is embodied in the decisions of the wise man, it provides a magnificent foundation upon which he can model a healthy combination of humility—listening to the will of his Father in heaven, and conviction—binding and loosing on earth. The wise man is encouraged to act with boldness but within a framework of accountability and reformed personal motives.

Teaching the Mysteries of the Kingdom

The idealized wise man does more than apply the teachings of Jesus in complex and ambiguous situations. He is also the object of special revelation concerning God's plans for the future. These plans relate less to the fortunes of individuals and more to the status of cities, nations, kingdoms, and empires. Seán Freyne and David Orton have both argued that the Matthean disciples are portrayed as *maśkîlîm* equivalent to those found in Daniel.[28] A little bit of background information is necessary at this point. In the book of Daniel, a cognate of the Hebrew verb *śkl* "to make or be wise" is applied to Daniel and his friends (*maśkîlîm*, "wise," Dan 1:4).[29] Daniel is the *maskil*

---

27. See also the motif of "the first" and "the last" in relation to leadership within the Jesus movement (Matt 19:30; 20:16, 26–28).

28. Freyne, "Disciples in Mark," 7–23; Orton, *Understanding Scribe*, 148–53.

29. *HALOT*, 3.1328.

"wise man" par excellence, a national leader who receives special wisdom concerning the future.

The wisdom with which Daniel and his friends are endowed in Dan 1:4 is explained in 2:20–22 as originating from God: "Blessed be the name of God from age to age, for wisdom and power are his. He changes times and seasons, deposes kings and sets up kings: he gives wisdom to the wise and knowledge to those who have understanding. He reveals deep and hidden things . . ." God is the revealer of mysteries (cf. 2.28, 29, 47), the one who has revealed to Nebuchadnezzar a specific mystery (MT: *rāz*; LXX: *mystērion*, 2.18, 19, 27, 28) that relates to "what will happen at the end of days" (2.28) and "what is to be" (2.29). The mystery reveals that following a series of kingdoms, "the God of heaven will set up a kingdom that shall never be destroyed, nor shall this kingdom be left to another people. It shall crush all these kingdoms and bring them to an end, and it shall stand forever" (2.44). In this context, Otto Piper suggests that the term "mystery" does not denote something incomprehensible but rather the secret purposes of God which he formerly kept to himself but has now revealed to men. God reveals to the wise his plans.[30]

Orton believes with good justification that the disciples are portrayed as *maśkîlîm* in Matthew 13.[31] Matthew 12 is a key turning point in the Gospel which occurs when the Jewish authorities commit the unpardonable sin of blaspheming the Holy Spirit.[32] At this point, the vocabulary associated with the kingdom of heaven changes. It is no longer "near" (4.23; 9.35). Instead, the vocabulary of nearness is transferred to the *parousia* (24–25; 26.29). After chapter 13, Jesus is no longer described as preaching. Instead, he teaches in parables. In Matt 13:10, the disciples do not question the meaning of the parable of the sower but rather ask why Jesus uses parables as a means of communication. The rabbis typically used parables to explain law.[33] Jesus informs them that the reason he speaks in parables to the crowds is because the crowds, unlike the disciples, have not received the mystery or secret (*mystērion*) of the kingdom of heaven (Matt 13:11).

George Ladd observes in relation to this revelation that the "mystery of the Kingdom is the coming of the Kingdom into history in advance of its

---

30. Piper, "Mystery," 187.

31. Orton, *Understanding Scribe*, 148–53.

32. Kingsbury, "Plot," 351–52.

33. For examples of rabbinic parables used to explain points of law, see McArthur and Johnston, *They Also Taught*, 17–91.

apocalyptic manifestation."[34] Daniel predicted that God's kingdom would be established. This was no secret. It was the great hope of all Second Temple Jews. The mystery revealed to the disciples is that the kingdom will enter gradually (cf. the parables of the sower, wheat and tares, mustard plant, and yeast), coexisting with earthly kingdoms, and will only be fully established on a final climactic day of judgment (cf. the parable of the net). The beneficiaries of this revelation, the disciples, have thus attained the same status as Daniel, as *maśkîlîm* in receipt of God's plans for the future.

The mystery includes an important nuancing of expectations in the parable of the sower. This parable evokes Old Testament prophecies that Yahweh would replant Israel: "The days are surely coming, says the LORD, when I will sow the house of Israel and the house of Judah with the seed of humans and the seed of animals" (Jer 31:27); ". . . and I will sow him for myself in the land. And I will have pity on Lo-ruhamah, and I will say to Lo-ammi, 'You are my people'; and he shall say, 'You are my God'" (Hos 2:23). The parable of the sower nuances such predictions in that it informs the reader that much of Israel will prove resistant to Yahweh's planting of seed (Matt 13:3–9, 18–23). We also learn that Israel will be subject to demonic activity in the form of the evil one who will snatch away the seed that lands on the path (13:19). The restoration process of Israel will only be marginally successful. Many in Israel, represented by the first three soil types, will in fact reject Yahweh's intervention.

Teaching the Mysteries of God to Others

The Danielic mysteries of God are not to be kept to yourself. The idealized wise man teaches others such mysteries, typically during periods of great suffering. Two key passages toward the end of the book of Daniel point toward this end:

> The wise among the people shall give understanding to many; for some days, however, they shall fall by sword and flame, and suffer captivity and plunder. (Dan 11:33)

> Those who are wise shall shine like the brightness of the sky, and those who lead many to righteousness, like the stars forever and ever. (Dan 12:3)

---

34. Ladd, *Presence of the Future*, 222. See also Davies and Allison, *Matthew 8–18*, 388–91; Luz, *Matthew 8–20*, 245.

These texts anticipate a time when a group of the wise will teach others.[35] Their teaching will be undertaken during a time when a "contemptible person" usurps the throne of the northern kingdom and sends his forces to occupy the temple, abolishing "the regular burnt offering" and setting up "the abomination that makes desolate" (cf. Dan 11:21, 31). During this period, the *maśkîlîm* will "give understanding to many" (11:33). A similar scenario is found in Daniel 12. During a "time of anguish, such as has never occurred since nations first came into existence," Michael the great prince will arise and save his people. These include the wise of 12:3, described as "those who lead many to righteousness," an allusion to their teaching activities. This time of anguish will occur "at that time" (*bā 'ēt*), a reference back to the events of chapter 11.

Many of these motifs are found in the Gospel; "the desolating sacrilege" (Matt 24:15), "those who understand" (24:15), and a "time of anguish" (24:21).[36] When quoting Daniel's description of the time of anguish (24:21), Jesus adds the words "until now" (*heōs tou nyn*), an indication that he understood the tragic events described Dan 12:1 as referring in some way to the horrific suffering that would soon come upon Judea.

There is a twist, however. When the abomination of desolation is set up in Daniel 11, the wise are to counteract those who would violate the covenant, giving understanding to "the many" (Dan 11:31–33). They are to remain among God's people and curb malign external influences. In Matthew, however, when the desolating sacrilege is set up in the holy place, the wise are not to remain in Judea, but rather, as the righteous Lot fled Sodom, they are to flee to the mountains (Matt 24:17). This is not, however, the end of their mission. Orton suggests that in the Gospel Commission the disciples are commissioned to continue in their role as *maśkîlîm* by teaching the nations the revelations they have received from their Maskil.[37]

35. Cf. the Maskil of Qumran whose role was to teach the saints, test their understanding, and keep his knowledge obscure from the unrighteous (Orton, *Understanding Scribe*, 148–49).

36. On the extensive influence of Daniel on Matthew, see Pennington, *Heaven and Earth*, 285–93.

37. Orton, *Understanding Scribe*, 150.

The Wise Virgins and the Limits of Knowledge

Being in receipt of the mysteries of the kingdom does not imply that the idealized wise man can predict the timing of revealed events. Wise leaders understand the limits of their knowledge. The parables of Matthew 13 and the eschatological teachings of chapter 24 do not set out a detailed timetable. They indicate sequence, not timing. When teaching the mysteries of the kingdom to his community, the wise man must also define the boundaries of his knowledge. He must prepare the community for uncertainty. This is clearly the case in the parable of the ten virgins (25:1–13), organized in a chiasm in which two foolish acts are contrasted:

Prologue (25:1–2)

 Five foolish virgins and five wise virgins contrasted (25:3–4)

  All ten virgins sleep (25:5)

   The midnight cry, "Here is the bridegroom" (25:6)

  All ten virgins trimmed their lamps (25:7)

 Five foolish virgins and five wise virgins contrasted (25:8–12)

Exhortation to "keep awake" (25:13)

The foolishness of the five foolish virgins involves holding the belief that one can tell the timing of the coming of the bridegroom. In Matt 25:3–4, the foolish virgins believe that the bridegroom is coming soon, and so do not plan for a possible late arrival. They do not bring extra oil in case of a delay.[38] In contrast, the wise take extra oil in case the bridegroom is delayed. In 25:8–12, the foolish make the opposite mistake. They believe that the bridegroom will be further delayed, that they have sufficient time to go to the dealers to purchase extra oil. In both instances, their mistake is to believe that they can tell the timing of the bridegroom's arrival. This interpretation is made explicit in the final appeal: "Keep awake therefore, for you know neither the day nor the hour" (25:13). The wise man must instruct the community concerning the bridegroom's right to control the timing of his arrival (cf. 24:48; 25:14, 19). As such, the wise man should prepare his community for both eventualities, an early and a late arrival of the bridegroom.[39] The idealized wise man's awareness of the provisional nature of

---

38. Davies and Allison, *Matthew 19–28*, 397–98. To take the oil as a reference to good works seems to over interpret its significance. Contrast Gundry, *Matthew*, 499.

39. Howell, *Matthew's Inclusive Story*, 109; Davies and Allison, *Matthew 19–28*, 392.

his understanding of the future serves as another powerful restraint on the development of tyrannical leadership.

There is no doubt that the *maśkîlîm* of Daniel achieve an understanding or grasp of the wisdom given to them. In contrast, the disciples, despite the revelations they receive, remain blind to their significance (e.g., Matt 14:26, 31; 15:16; 16:8–9, 22–23; 17:19–20).[40] The effect is to invite readers, who through reading or hearing the Gospel have also been privy to Jesus's revelation of the secrets of the kingdom of heaven, to adopt the status of *maśkîlîm* and to teach others what they have received.

Idolatry and the Control of Demons

Good leaders focus their attention on the most serious threats to their communities. In the Gospel, this is the threat of idolatry. Idolatry is caused by demonic activity and ultimately results in demonic control. Throughout the Gospel we find summary statements indicating that Jesus cast out demons and that he commanded his followers to do likewise (Matt 10:8; cf. 7:22; 8:16). The Evangelist focalizes these statements and commands in five exorcism narratives (8:23–34; 9:32–34; 12:22–32; 15:21–28; 17:14–21).

In the Old Testament, demons are typically understood to be false gods (cf. Deut 32:17). To worship idols is to worship false gods.[41] LXX Ps 95:5 states that "all the gods of the nations are demons." They are to be distinguished from the Lord who created the heavens. Those that entered the promised land are criticized in LXX Ps 105:37 for mingling with the nations, learning their ways, serving their idols and sacrificing "their daughters to demons." In LXX Isaiah 65:1–3, Yahweh condemns his rebellious people for "sacrificing in gardens and burning on bricks to demons, which do not exist" (v. 3).[42] The reference to demons is an addition to the Hebrew text made on the part of the LXX translators for whom idol worship equated to demon worship.

---

40. Freyne, "Disciples in Mark," 11.

41. The exception is when idols are made as depictions of Yahweh, as in the golden calf incident of Exod 32.

42. Cf. LXX Isa 13:21 and 34:14, in which, as a result of divine judgment, the nations are made desolate and become the abode of demons.

The Demonic Possession of Israel

The parallels we explored in chapter 2 between the preexilic generation and the generation of Jesus's day are further evident when it comes to the identity and role of demons. With overtones anticipating the Gospel's "faithless and perverse" and "evil and adulterous" generation (Matt 12:39; 16:4; 17:17), the Deuteronomist warns that Yahweh's jealousy will be provoked by a "perverse" and "faithless generation" who will offer sacrifices to demons, which the biblical author equates with strange gods and unknown deities (LXX Deut 32:16–21). Israel's punishment for such idolatry would be exile at the hands of a foreign nation (cf. 32:21ff.). Jesus affirms the Deuteronomist's picture when he casts Israel's situation in terms of possession by unclean and evil spirits:

> When the unclean spirit has gone out of a person, it wanders through waterless regions looking for a resting place, but it finds none. Then it says, "I will return to my house from which I came." When it comes, it finds it empty, swept, and put in order. Then it goes and brings along seven other spirits more evil than itself, and they enter and live there; and the last state of that person is worse than the first. So will it be also with this evil generation. (Matt 12:43–45)

There are three stages in this parable: first, the person is possessed of an unclean spirit; second, the spirit departs and wanders through a waterless region, during which period its "house" remains "empty, swept, and put in order"; and the third and final stage when the original unclean spirit recruits seven other evil spirits to enter and dwell within the person. At which stage is Jesus's immediate audience? The least strained way to approach this question is from the point of view of the final warning: "So will it be also with this evil generation" (12:45). The future tense *estai* "it will be" would indicate that the third stage represents a potential state Jesus's audience is in imminent danger of entering. If so, then they are either in stage one of the parable, in a state of possession, or in stage two, free of possession but nevertheless empty. It goes without saying that none of the three stages are to be desired. If stage three is somewhat in the future, then how might we apply stages one or two to Jesus's immediate audience?

One interpretation of the parable is to understand it as a retelling of the Babylonian exile in which Israel, personified as the dwelling place of Yahweh, was swept clean through captivity, but, due to a failure to put its house in order, is now in an empty state.[43] The weakness of such an interpretation is that it ignores the numerous references to Satan and demons throughout the opening chapters of the Gospel. If Jesus and his disciples had not intervened, many would have remained possessed. The first act of Jesus's ministry was to confront not the Romans but rather the one variously identified as the devil, the tempter, and the Satan (4:1–11). Israel is certainly not empty of demons prior to the start of Jesus's ministry.

A less strained interpretation of the parable, and one held by many scholars, is to link the emptying of the house of the unclean spirit with Jesus's ministry of exorcisms.[44] When Jesus arrives on the scene, Israel is infested by Satan and his filthy demons. This fits stage one. Jesus's ministry of confronting Satan and his demons results in stage two. His exorcisms empty the house. A failure to accept Jesus will, however, result in an empty house being repossessed by the original unclean spirit and seven additional evil spirits. It boggles the imagination to conceive of such a stage when you consider the dire state in which Jesus first encounters Israel. Who or what, we may ask, are these additional spirits?

Wise Men, the Son of David, and Exorcisms

How does the Evangelist link the idealized wise man with the exorcism of demons? We have already mentioned how binding and loosing were frequently related in pseudepigraphal writings to the control of demons. A second and stronger association, however, is the parallel identities of Jesus as "son of David" and Solomon as "son of David" (cf. 2 Chr 1:1; 13:6; 35:3; Prov 1:1; Eccl 1:1). Important for our discussion is the belief in Second Temple Judaism, based on interpretations of 1 Kgs 4:29–34, that Solomon was able to control demons.

In noncanonical sources, Solomon, the "son of David," was understood to have received the ability to control demons as part of his great wisdom. In the Wisdom of Solomon, dated to the second century BCE, he knows astronomy and, among many other things, "the powers of spirits" (Wis 7:20). In a recension of Ps 91 found at Qumran, Solomon's name is included just before the term "demons" in column one.[45] Such traditions continued into the first century CE. Josephus describes Solomon as receiving

---

43. For scholars holding this position, see Luz, *Matthew 8–20*, 221–22.

44. Davies and Allison, *Matthew 8–18*, 359–62; Wahlen, *Impurity*, 128–30.

45. Duling, "Testament of Solomon," 945.

wisdom greater than the wisest men of his day, the Egyptians (*Ant.* 8.49). This wisdom included the ability to compose books of odes, songs, parables, and similitudes, and to speak parables upon every sort of tree and living creature. In addition, God enabled him to learn how to expel demons. His manner of driving away demons is, notes Josephus, "of great force unto this day" (*Ant.* 8.49).[46] Josephus recounts his own eyewitness testimony in which Eleazar used Solomon's instructions to drive away a demon in the presence of Vespasian. Eleazar followed Solomon's advice and placed a certain root in a ring. He then, invoking Solomon's name and reciting Solomonic incantations, used the ring to draw the demon out through the demoniac's nostrils. This demonstrated the "skill and wisdom of Solomon," abilities given to him by God.

A related tradition, while Christian and postdating the Gospel, is found in the Testament of Solomon (cf. *T. Sol.* 11:6; 12:3; 15:10–11). In this work, dated to the first to third centuries CE, Solomon was disturbed because a young boy of whom he was extremely fond and who inspired the artisans building the temple was having his "soul" sucked out of him by a demon named Ornias (1:1–4).[47] In response to Solomon's prayer for help, the archangel Michael gave him a magic ring, reminiscent of Josephus's ring, with which he was able to call up demons, interrogate them, and learn their tricks (1:5–9). Solomon gave the ring to the boy who used it to bind the demon and bring him bound to Solomon (1:10–13). With the archangel Ouriel's help, Solomon sentenced the demon Ornias to cutting stones in the quarry for the temple (2:4–8). Solomon then gave the ring to Ornias and commanded him to bind and bring before him the prince of the demons, Beelzeboul (2:9). This he did, where upon Solomon praised God for placing in "subjection all the power of the demons" (3:5). In chapters 4 to 25, Solomon, served by Beelzeboul who called up and bound the demons on his behalf, interrogated and learnt the secrets of a host of different demons responsible for various natural disasters, sinful attitudes and acts. The demon Asmodeus, for example, confessed to being responsible for causing the wickedness of men to spread throughout the world, for hatching plots against newlyweds, and marring the beauty of virgins and causing their hearts to grow cold (5:7). The account closes in chapter 26 with Solomon falling in love with a beautiful Shummanite woman. To add

46. According to Eve, there are few stories of demons being cast out in pre-Christian Jewish literature (*Jewish Context*, 326–49).

47. On dating and provenance, see Duling, "Testament of Solomon," 943–44.

her to his harem, he, under duress, sacrifices five locusts to the foreign gods Raphan and Moloch and builds a temple for her idols. God responds by withdrawing his glory from him. Solomon concludes with this confession and admonition to his readers:

> As a result I, wretched man that I am, carried out her advice and the glory of God completely departed from me; my spirit was darkened and I became a laughingstock to the idols and demons. For this reason I have written out this, my testament, in order that those who hear might pray about, and pay attention to, the last things and not to the first things, in order that they might finally find grace forever. Amen. (*T. Sol.* 26:7–8 [Charlesworth])

It is highly likely that the tradition of Solomon using Beelzeboul, the ruler of the demons, to control the demons, predates rather than originates in the Gospels (e.g., Mark 3:22; Luke 11:15). When Jesus casts out a demon from a mute demoniac, the Pharisees claim that "by the ruler of the demons he casts out the demons" (Matt 9:34). Their reaction contrasts with that of the crowds, who were amazed at what Jesus has done.

A similar scenario is found in chapter 12. In Matt 12:22, Jesus cures a demoniac who was blind and mute.[48] The crowds again respond with amazement and ask, "Can this be the Son of David?" (12:23). In view of the traditions we have just highlighted, it is likely that they are, in effect, asking whether Jesus is a new Solomonic Son of David able to control demons. The Pharisees affirm but then weaponize this point of view when they claim that "it is only by Beelzebul, the ruler of the demons, that this fellow casts out the demons" (12:24). Even if Jesus is like Solomon, "Son of David," he is only able to cast out demons by cooperating with the dark forces of Beelzebul. Jesus rejects the Pharisees' position and instead claims to cast out demons by the Spirit of God (12:25–29). His source of power is antithetical to the powers of darkness.

We may add to this reading the observation that in the Old Testament, faithful kings of Israel led spiritual revivals by destroying the groves and high places associated with demonic activity. Extensive allusions to the pre-exilic state of Israel elsewhere in the Gospel suggest that the exorcism narratives should probably be read as the equivalent to the reforms of Joash, Hezekiah, and Josiah in which, from a position of leadership, they cleansed the temple of unclean things, killed the priests of Baal, and destroyed the

---

48. When we contrast Jesus's control over the demons with other exorcisms, we are impressed with how easy they are for Jesus (cf. Philostratus, *Vit. Apoll.* 4.20).

groves and high places at which idolatrous representations of demons were worshipped.[49] Jesus did not, of course, go around knocking down idols. Nevertheless, Greg Beale is correct in his observation that "there were forms of idolatry in the first century that did not involve bowing down to literal images."[50] Jesus as kingly leader of his community was, in true Solomonic fashion, cleansing Israel of the objects of its idolatrous practices, whether or not this involved the presence of physical idols. He started with Satan in the wilderness and continued with those possessed by demons. This was essential to enable a nation in a state of idolatry and distant from God, possessed by Satan and his minions, to return back to him.

Implications

The Evangelist believes that nations need leaders who accept and promote the sovereignty of Jesus. This raises the question as to how such leaders can avoid the serious danger of tyranny. The answer is to be found in his concept of the idealized wise man and the various checks and balances placed upon his exercise of power.

First, when making decisions (i.e., binding and loosing), wise men are called to operate under the constraint of the will of their Father in heaven, to bind and loose on earth mindful of heaven's agenda. A second constraint placed upon national leaders is that their vision for the future is not to be a vision of their own making but rather one divinely revealed to them—the mysteries of the kingdom of heaven (Matt 13:11). This revelation, while detailed and prescriptive, nevertheless incorporates a degree of contingency that requires them to plan both for an imminent and a delayed parousia. Certainty is combined with uncertainty, confidence with caution. Room is thereby created for the ongoing manifestation of divine sovereignty through their humble leadership of the community.

The third and final constraint I have identified is that wise men are to focus on protecting the community from the most significant of dangers, idolatry. This represents the main challenge to the sovereignty of Jesus over the nation and is manifested in the Gospel in the presence of demons, the defeat of whom can only be ensured through faith in God (17:19–20). Wise men are thus called to a task which they cannot achieve in their own

49. Cf. Joash (2 Kgs 11:18; 2 Chr 23:17); Hezekiah (2 Kgs 18:3–5; 2 Chr 29:16; 31:1); and Josiah (2 Kgs 23:4–20; 2 Chr 34:3–7).

50. Beale, *We Become*, 161.

strength, a further constraint on the development of tyrannical leadership. Are these various constraints fail-safe? No! Which is why the critical voices of the prophet and the other discipleship roles are always required.

6

The Scribe

Promoting the King's Laws throughout the Nation

Introduction

THE HEBREW TERM *sōpēr* is widely used in the Old Testament to denote a scribe or secretary (e.g., 2 Kgs 25:19; Neh 13:13; Jer 52:25), a state scribe (e.g., "the king's scribe," 2 Kgs 12:11; 2 Chr 24:11), or one conversant with the scriptures (e.g., 2 Chr 34:13; Ezra 7:6; Neh 8:1).[1] The equivalent term in the LXX is *grammateus*. The emphasis is on the scribe's ability to read, write, and interpret.

Defining what the Gospel writers meant when they referred to scribes is, however, particularly challenging because there was no normative understanding of what it meant to be a scribe. We may take a narrow definition and limit it to professional writers. The problem with this approach is that it fails to include many of the tasks undertaken by scribes. Scribes functioned as private, public, and royal secretaries, as legal experts, teachers in elementary education, instructors, and sources of interpretative authority.[2] The challenge we face is determining the extent of scribal activity, a task made all the more difficult, according to Martin Jaffee, by the widespread emphasis on anonymity in scribal literary culture.[3] Ancient scribes do not tell us much about how they operated. A broader definition would

1. *HALOT*, 2:767. Cf. Wilkins, *Concept of Disciple*, 61–72.

2. Westerholm, *Scribal Authority*, 27. The LXX identifies scribes as supervising the Hebrew slaves in Egypt (e.g., LXX Exod 5:6, 10) and later organizing the people of Israel (e.g., LXX Num 11:16).

3. Jaffee, *Torah in the Mouth*, 15–61.

be to identify the scribes under the loose heading of "'Torah scholars."[4] The problem with such a broad definition is that it obscures the fact that not everyone who was educated and literate was a scribe, and not every scribe was an expert in law.

The absence of a uniform first-century understanding of the role requires us to be somewhat cautious when determining the intentions of the Matthean Jesus when he describes those involved in his mission as scribes:

> And he said to them, "Therefore every scribe (*grammateus*) who has been trained for the kingdom of heaven is like the master of a household who brings out of his treasure what is new and what is old." (Matt 13:52)

> Therefore I send you prophets, sages, and scribes (*grammateis*) . . . (Matt 23:34)

In this chapter I will argue that the missional purpose of Matthew's idealized scribes is to promote the law of their king. My reasoning is this. The Evangelist presents Jesus as a king, a king who expresses his sovereignty over his kingdom, as with any king, by means of law. A kingdom without law is unthinkable in that it soon degenerates into a playground for bandits and robbers and results in the abuse of the weak by the strong. A king whose law does not run writ cannot claim to have a kingdom or to be a king.

In this context, Jesus-scribes are commissioned to promote and implement their king's law. In Matt 13:52, the "scribe discipled for the kingdom" is graphically described as "throwing out" things from his treasure store. John Nolland suggests that this is the imagery of disposal rather than display: "the treasure he has gained is a treasure he passes out to others."[5] In other words, this is a scribe who promotes and distributes that which he has received. Anders Runesson distinguishes between public institutions, represented by the chief priests, elders, and scribes, and voluntary associations, represented by the Sadducees, Pharisees, and the disciples of John the Baptist and Jesus. In commissioning scribes, Jesus was thus seeking to influence Israel's institutions.[6] He was spreading his kingdom into the organs of government.

In this chapter, we will start by addressing why the Matthean Jesus saw a need for kingdom scribes. Why are they necessary within his polity?

4. Teeter, "Scribes and Scribalism," 1202.
5. Nolland, *Matthew*, 571.
6. Runesson, *Divine Wrath*, 210–13.

What marks out his scribes from those already operating in Israel? We will then address the nature of the king's laws by first considering the ritual and moral purity code, and then the "weightier matters of the law," those key values required to ensure that a nation is founded on secure legal principles that reflect its king.

The Problem of Lawlessness

The Evangelist is not, as suggested by Gerhard Barth, combatting, on the one hand, antinomians, and on the other hand, scribal and Pharisaic legalists.[7] The problem is more complex than this. Those in Israel whose purpose is purportedly to promote the law are in fact themselves lawless.[8] Jesus describes the scribes and Pharisees as being full of "hypocrisy and lawlessness" (Matt 23:28). A similar situation is anticipated in the mission to the nations. Jesus predicts that the love of many will grow cold "because of the increase of lawlessness" (*anomia*, 24:12). Lawlessness, not legalism, is the problem facing both Israel and the nations. More worryingly, lawlessness is also a potential danger for the followers of Jesus. On judgment day, many will be rejected despite having prophesied, cast out demons, and performed many deeds of power in his name. Why? Because, as "workers of lawlessness," they have failed to do the will of their Father in heaven (7:21–23; cf. LXX Ps 6:9). They have failed to implement the legal expression of the Father's will.

What are we to understand by "lawlessness"? In the LXX, *anomia* is frequently contrasted with righteousness.[9] When contrasted in this manner, lawlessness denotes an active and wilful rebellion against God. The problem of lawlessness is especially serious when we consider that the very ones charged with the promotion of God's ways, the scribes of Israel, are themselves lawless, in a state of active rebellion. This is not so apparent when Jesus encounters individual scribes, who are portrayed mostly in positive terms, as followers on the edge of the Jesus movement (Matt 8:19; 22:35; cf. Mark 12:32). Jesus also recognizes the authority of their position.

---

7. Barth, "Matthew's Understanding," 63, 76.

8. Runesson, "Purity, Holiness," 151.

9. Cf. LXX Isa 5:7; 33:15; Ezek 18:20–21, 24, 27; 33:12–13, 18–19. Marguerat, *Le Jugement*, 351.

The scribes "sit on the seat of Moses" and rightly interpret Scripture in this capacity (Matt 23:1; cf. 2:3–6; 17:10).[10]

Nevertheless, conflict between the scribes and Jesus drives the plot of the Gospel. They consistently oppose him, accuse him of blasphemy (9:3), demand a validating sign (Matt 12:38), and respond with anger to his wonders (21:15). In terms of legal interpretation, their teachings lack authority and, according to Jesus, they break the commandments of God for the sake of their traditions (7:29; 15:1–3). They focus on the mechanics of tithing while neglecting the weightier matters of the law: justice, mercy, and faith (23:23–24). The problem is not that their tithing halakhah is wrong.[11] It is that they have neglected the most important elements of the law. Jesus accuses them, along with the Pharisees, of hypocrisy (23:13, 15, 23, 25, 27, 29). His general accusation is that they do not practice what they preach, placing legal burdens on others which they are unwilling to bear themselves (23:3–4). They focus on external appearance, seeking the approval and honor of men (23:5–7; cf. 6:1–18), while internally they are full of all kinds of filth, such as greed, self-indulgence, and, most seriously, lawlessness (23:25–28). Their disregard for the law extends to murdering those who seek to uphold the law—they shed the innocent blood of the righteous (23:33–35). Finally, they collude with the chief priests and elders to have the innocent Jesus executed (16:21; 20:18; cf. 26:57; 27:41).

In contrast, the Evangelist insists that the righteousness of those who accept the teachings of Jesus is to exceed that as defined or practiced by the scribes and Pharisees (Matt 6:20). We may assume, considering his pointed critique, that idealized scribes are to be guided in their inner life by law, are to encourage and support the righteous, and are to promote the weightier matters of the law without neglecting the lesser commands (6:22–23, 33; 23:23). This represents a scribal agenda that is both deeply personal and deeply political, aligning the values of the nation with those values that guide the idealized scribe's inner life.

---

10. Some scholars limit this affirmation to a reference to their reading of Torah. Cf. Runesson, *Divine Wrath*, 247–49.

11. Halakhah (from the Hb verb *halakh*, "to go") were Jewish oral laws and ordinances that supplemented scriptural law.

Jesus and the Purity Code

Israel is portrayed throughout the Gospel as operating within a large and well-developed legal body of purity codes. My goal in this section is quite limited. It is not to get involved in the various discussions concerning how the purity code was understood. Rather, I will try to determine how the Matthean Jesus related to this code. Did he support purity regulations? If so, which of them? Ritual purity regulations? Moral purity regulations? The answers to these questions will help shape the agenda of the idealized scribe as he or she combats the problem of lawlessness.

Jesus the Law Observant Jew

The days when the dominant paradigm in Gospel scholarship projected Jesus as a champion of grace battling trenchant Jewish legalism have thankfully receded.[12] Scholars such as Geza Vermes and E. P. Sanders have helped "restore" the Jewish identity of Jesus. For Vermes, Jesus represents figures in charismatic Judaism such as Honi and Hanina ben Dosa, a figure who showed "a complete lack of interest in legal and ritual affairs."[13] In contrast, Sanders posits a Jesus who was "a law-abiding Jew."[14] He states, "Nothing which Jesus said or did which bore on the law led his disciples after his death to disregard it."[15] In favor of this position, he appeals to legal debates in early Christianity as evidence that Jesus did not seek to overturn the law:

> If Jesus had declared all foods clean, why did Paul and Peter disagree
> over Jews eating with Gentiles (Gal 2.11–16)? Or, put in terms of
> Acts rather than Galatians, why did it take a thrice-repeated revela-
> tion to convince Peter (or, rather, to leave him puzzled and on the
> way to conviction) (Acts 10.9–17)? And if Jesus consciously trans-
> gressed the Sabbath, allowed his disciples to do so, and justified

12. Bultmann describes Jesus's message as "a great *protest against Jewish legalism*" (*Theology*, 11).

13. Vermes, *Jesus the Jew*, 77.

14. Sanders, *Jewish Law*, 125.

15. Sanders, *Jesus and Judaism*, 268. Keith dismisses this position by characterizing it thus: "Jesus cannot have spoken positively about the law because of the controversy in the early church. Jesus also cannot have spoken negatively of the law because of the controversy in the early church. Here we have a historical Jesus who was a thoroughly Jewish first-century teacher and yet said nothing inherently positive or negative about the law" (*Scribal Elite*, 145).

such action in public debate, how could Paul's Christian opponents
in Galatia urge that the Sabbath be kept (Gal 4:10)?[16]

This position has found more recent expression in Jonathan Klawans's important work on impurity and sin. Klawans writes: "I still find it highly
unlikely that Jesus rejected Jewish law in any truly radical way. The reason
is not because this was an impossible approach for a first-century Jew to
adopt. Rather, it is because Jewish ritual laws were highly debated in early
Christianity (e.g., Acts 15), suggesting that Jesus had not set out to clearly
abrogate such laws."[17] The rationale of this argument is that if Jesus had
adopted an explicit position against food laws or the Sabbath, this would
have been clearly understood by his early followers and there would thus
have been minimal debate on such matters.

These pro-law readings are strongly reflected in Matthean scholarship.
Gerhard Barth states that the Evangelist "holds fast to the lasting validity of
the law."[18] For Phillip Sigal, Jesus was a proto-rabbi, who "taught halakhah
along with his haggadic preaching."[19] Andrew Overman judges that "Jesus
and his disciples do not break the law. They break with the Pharisees over
interpretation of the law, but not with regard to its validity or importance."[20]
David Sim understands the Gospel as originating from a Christian Jewish
group that "both accepted without question the validity of the Torah and
attempted to observe it in its entirety."[21] Anthony Saldarini affirms that the
Matthean "Jesus and his disciples are always fully observant of the Jewish
law, as it is understood and interpreted by Matthew."[22] Anders Runesson has
argued that the Gospel "endorses a life as a follower of Jesus *within* Judaism, with strict law observance in specific Second Temple period format as
its main focus."[23] While Runesson does not necessarily advocate that mainstream Christianity adopt such a way of life, he calls for its recognition
as an integral element within earliest Christianity and the canon.[24] More
recently, John Kampen has described Jesus as the one "who now takes

---

16. Sanders, *Jesus and Judaism*, 250.

17. Klawans, *Impurity and Sin*, 145.

18. Barth, "Matthew's Understanding," 64.

19. Sigal, *Halakhah of Jesus*, 187.

20. Overman, *Matthew's Gospel*, 81.

21. Sim, *Christian Judaism*, 123.

22. Saldarini, *Matthew's Christian-Jewish Community*, 125.

23. Runesson, *Divine Wrath*, xxv.

24. Runesson, *Divine Wrath*, xxv–xxvi.

persons back to Sinai to hear the authoritative message God gave to Moses."[25] The fulfillment of the law can only be achieved, for Kampen, by following Jesus's teachings on the law. While there are dissenting opinions, the dominant position in Matthean scholarship is that Jesus kept the law and expected his followers to follow suit.[26]

In support of such a position, Runesson lists the following specific legal practices and commandments Jesus affirms in the Gospel:[27]

Almsgiving (Matt 6:3–4)

Individual prayer using a fixed format (Matt 6:5–13)

Fasting (Matt 6:16–18; cf. 9:14–15)

The Sabbath (Matt 12:1–14; 24:20)

Dietary laws (Matt 15:1–20)

Laws on purification of individuals healed from leprosy (Matt 8:4)

Wearing tzitzit and, most likely, tefillin (Matt 9:20; 14:36; 23:5)

Tithing (Matt 23:23)

Impurity related to food vessels and corpses (implied in Matt 23:25–26)

Festivals (Passover, Matt 26:2, 17–35)

Laws regulating or related to the sacrificial cult, including the temple tax
(Matt 5:23–24; 12:3–5; 17:24–27; 23:16–22)

In addition, Jesus discusses the legal issues of

Adultery (Matt 5:27–30)

Divorce (Matt 5:31–32; 19:3–9)

Bloodshed (Matt 5:21–22)

Retribution (Matt 5:38–42)

Honoring father and mother (Matt 15:4; 19:19)

Greed (Matt 19:21–24)

---

25. Kampen, *Matthew*, 90.

26. Cf. Foster, *Community*, 94–143; Deines, "Not the Law," 57.

27. Adapted from Runesson, "Purity, Holiness," 167–68. See also Runesson, *Divine Wrath*, 74–75.

The assumption among such scholars is that, at a minimum, Jesus kept the law. At dispute is whether Jesus advocated the ritual purity codes. Those convinced that he did, argue that the burden of proof is on those who believe that Jesus departed from the common practices of Judaism.[28] We should assume, according to their reasoning, that Jesus kept such laws unless told otherwise. We will shortly consider some of the arguments for this position. First, however, a few observations on the nature of the purity code and its presence in the Gospel.

The Purity Code

A key verse for understanding the Old Testament purity code is Lev 10:10 in which God commanded Aaron to "distinguish between the holy and the common, and between the unclean and the clean" (so Ezek 22:26; 44:23). These two distinctions, the holy and the common, and the clean and the unclean, determined Israel's purity codes. Each pair has a neutral term and a more marked term. The "common" (Heb. *ḥōl* ; Gk *bebēlos*) is the neutral term and refers to ordinary spaces or to those things in the world accessible to all human beings. The "holy" (Heb. *qōdeš*; Gk *hagios*) is the more marked term and refers to spaces, people, or things that have been set apart from the common as belong in some way to God. The "clean" (Heb. *ṭāhôr*; Gk *katharos*) is the neutral term and refers to a person or thing in its normal state. The "unclean" (Heb. *ṭāmēʾ*; Gk *akathartos*) is the more marked term and involves a thing that is no longer in a normal state, which has entered for some reason into a state of pollution.

Jacob Milgrom suggests in relation to Lev 10:10 that the state of a person, place, or time period could be described using a combination of one term from each pair; holy and common, clean and unclean.[29] According to Milgrom, four possible combinations were possible. First, the holy could combine with the clean. For example, the food for the priests was to be both holy and clean. Second, the common could combine with the clean. This was the normal state of most Israelites.

A third combination of common and unclean resulted from ritual or moral acts of defilement. Ritually defiling acts included the eating of

---

28. Haber, "*They Shall Purify Themselves,*" 202, 206; Runesson, "Purity, Holiness," 157.

29. Milgrom, *Leviticus 1–16*, 616. I have adapted Milgrom's terminology to reflect that of the NRSV. Milgrom uses "sacred" for "holy," "pure" for "clean," and "impure" for "unclean."

unclean meat (Lev 11:1–47), childbirth (Lev 12:1–8), leprosy (Lev 13:1—
14:57; Num 5:2), menstruation (Lev 15:19–30), male discharges (Lev 15:1–
18) and contact with corpses (Lev 22:4; Num 9:6–14; 19:11–14, 16–20).[30]
Such forms of impurity were not sin and resulted from natural physical
processes. They also did not distinguish between social class. The means of
restoring one's cleanliness in such instances was usually through washing,
and, depending upon the seriousness of the impurity, sacrifice. Differences
in purification requirements signal the seriousness of the pollution. In contrast to these natural physical impurities, Lev 18 and 19 provide a list of
defiling sins which lead to moral impurity. These include sexual sins (Lev
18:6–23), idolatry (19:4), theft and fraud (19:11, 13), profaning the name
of Yahweh (19:12), maltreatment of the deaf and the blind (19:14), partial
justice (19:15–16), hatred of one's kin or neighbor (19:17–18), witchcraft
(19:26, 31), prostitution (19:29), oppression of the alien (19:33–34), and
cheating with measurements (19:35–37).[31] The result of such impurity is
defilement of, and expulsion from, the land (18:24–30).

A fourth combination, holy and impure, was never to occur. If the holy
temple came into contact with impurity, it was to be purified as quickly as
possible to avoid the whole community being blighted. This is when ritual
impurity could lead to sin.[32]

Milgrom argues that it was the job of priests to distinguish between
these four combinations and to shift the balance in favor of the holy over
the common, and the clean over the unclean: "the goal is that the categories
of common and impure shall largely disappear, by their respective conversion into the sacred and pure."[33] Israel was to be turned into a holy nation
in which everyone adopted the highest possible standards, those of the
priests (cf. Exod 19:6).

A difficulty we face when interpreting Lev 10:10 relates to the fact that
the term "common" (ḥōl) appears nowhere else in Leviticus, nor, for that
matter, in the rest of the Pentateuch. This makes it very hard to judge how it
relates to the other three categories. A further difficulty is that in Leviticus

30. Cf. Klawans, *Impurity and Sin*, 22–26.

31. Cf. Klawans, *Impurity and Sin*, 26–31.

32. Cf. Klawans, *Impurity and Sin*, 25. Deliberate violations against the purity code
constituted an offense against God himself. As a result, God punished the offender
through instituting *kerath*, "a conditional divine curse of extinction" in which a person
was "cut off from the midst of his people" (e.g., Exod 31:14). It was sometimes but not
always associated with the death penalty. Repentance ensured acquittal.

33. Milgrom, *Leviticus 1–16*, 617.

the respective distinctions are not used in combination. We do not find, for example, persons described as holy *and* clean. Instead, persons, spaces, or times are simply described with one descriptor, i.e., holy, clean or unclean. The norm is to apply just one term.

What purpose did this system of codes serve? Milgrom argues that the Levitical purity code reflects a priestly desire to promote life by isolating those things related to death.[34] More recently, Klawans, building on the insights of Milgrom et al., has sought to revive the distinction between ritual impurity and sin (i.e., ceremonial and moral law).[35] For Klawans, ritual or cultic impurity occurs through natural and unavoidable processes and is cleansed through rites of purification. It is only dangerous when it defiles the holy. In contrast, moral/ethical impurity occurs through idolatry, murder, and sexual sin, and cannot be cleansed through purification but instead defiles the land. The Sabbath and the food laws of Lev 11 are difficult to categorise in this two-category scheme in that both include ritual and moral elements.[36] The Sabbath involves ritual to the extent that it requires the cessation of all work. It is moral in that it affirms and celebrates the identity of Yahweh as creator of the heavens and the earth and the one who delivers the oppressed from bondage (Exod 20:8–11; Deut 5:12–15). In the case of the food laws, unclean meat is strongly prohibited in a manner appropriate for moral prohibitions (Lev 11:1–23). The result, however, of touching unclean meat is that the one defiled remains unclean only until evening (11:24–28, 39–40).[37] Klawans further stresses the ability of moral impurity to defile the land physically, as against simply metaphorically, an assumption foundational to understanding judgment in the Gospel.

Hyam Maccoby suggests that most Jews adopted a more relaxed approach to ritual impurity than assumed by many Gospel scholars and only really sought ritual purity in preparation for participation in Jerusalem-based festivals. Most ritual impurities resulted from natural processes (childbirth, menstruation, death) and involved no sin and thus were of little everyday concern. The joyous act of sexual intercourse which renders a

---

34. Milgrom, *Leviticus 1–16*, 766–67.

35. For critique, see Finlan, *Sacrifice and Atonement*, 6–7. Sanders calls the distinction between ritual and moral aspects of the law, anachronistic (*Jesus and Judaism*, 249).

36. Klawans, *Impurity and Sin*, 5–12, 32–35.

37. Klawans acknowledges difficulties in applying his distinction to the dietary laws of Lev 11 and Deut 14 (*Impurity and Sin*, 31–32).

husband and wife ritually impure for one day is, after all, often undertaken in obedience to the biblical command to be fruitful and multiply![38]

The Purity Code as a Central Element of the Gospel

The purity code is embedded within the thought world of the Evangelist. This is most plainly demonstrated in his choice of terminology. We find, for example, references to "the Holy Spirit" (Matt 1:18, 20; 3:11; 12:32; 28:19); "the holy city" (4:5; 27:53); "holy things" (7:6); "the holy place" (24:15); "to make holy" (6:9; 23:17, 19); "the clean of heart" (5:8); "to make clean" (8:2–3; 10:8; 11:5; 23:25–26); "a clean linen cloth" (27:59); "unclean spirits" (10:1; 12:43); and "uncleanness" (23:27).

The purity code, whether ritual or moral, is so integral to the world of the Evangelist, that little to no explanation is provided for the uninitiated reader. Mark provides his readers with an explanatory gloss on ritual purity practices in Mark 7:3–4. Matthew provides no such gloss, most likely motivated by his conviction that his readership is already conversant in such matters (cf. Matt 15:1–20). His engagement with the purity code extends, however, well beyond his use of terminology.

First, the Evangelist assumes the code applies to space. Jerusalem is called the "holy city" (4:5; 27:53), the reason being that it is the "city of the great king" (5:35), the God of Israel. In the Old Testament, the closer one was to the presence of God in the temple, the more severe the purity restrictions and the more holy one had to be to gain access. This is reflected in the division of the temple into a series of courts; a Holy Place and a Most Holy Place. This gradation in holiness explains how the desolating sacrilege of Matt 24:15 could trigger the final destruction of Jerusalem in that it profanes the holy place of the temple.[39] In contrast to the holy temple, the synagogue was clean but non-holy space.[40] In 6:5–6, it is described in terms appropriate to public space, the equivalent of a street corner, and contrasted with the private space of one's inner room. Finally, the graveyard of 8:28 is unclean space. Graves could transmit impurity and so were whitewashed to ensure that they were not stepped upon inadvertently (cf. Num 19:16, 18). This lies behind Jesus's comparison of the scribes and Pharisees with whitewashed tombs in Matt 23:27.

38. Maccoby, *Ritual and Morality*, viii.

39. Cf. Theophilos, *Abomination of Desolation*, 11–21.

40. Runesson, "Purity, Holiness," 154–55.

Second, the purity code is integral to time settings within the Gospel. The Sabbath, the seventh day of the week, was set apart as holy and was not to be treated as common by undertaking activities associated with the six common days of the week (Gen 2:3; Exod 20:8–11; 35:2; Lev 23:3; Deut 5:12–15). It was to be treated as holy by Israel as a reminder that it was Yahweh who made Israel holy (Exod 31:12–17). We may note the following Sabbath-related points: (1) Jesus disputes the nature of true Sabbath keeping when his disciples pluck grain on the Sabbath and when he heals a man with a withered hand (Matt 12:1–14). These two accounts should not be read as a criticism of the Sabbath *per se*. Rather, as cogently argued by a growing body of scholars, such disputes fell well within the range of first-century debates on permitted Sabbath behavior.[41] (2) Righteous persons are to pray that their Sodom-evoking flight from defiled Jerusalem is not on a Sabbath (Matt 24:20), an indication that Jesus expected his followers to honor the sanctity of the Sabbath well beyond his own mission to Jerusalem. (3) The Evangelist ensures through numerous references that the reader is aware that Jesus died on the day of Preparation (i.e., Friday), rested in the grave on the Sabbath, and rose on the third day (16:21; 17:23; 20:19; 27:62, 64; 28:1). Holy Sabbath rest is respected.

Third, Second Temple Judaism was characterized by differing applications of the purity code. The Evangelist is quite aware of such developments as revealed in Jesus's polemic against the traditions of the elders (Matt 15:2–3, 6). Klawans offers an insightful analysis of how the purity codes were variously understood in Second Temple Judaism. We will briefly summarize his views as they help us understand what Jesus meant when he referred to the traditions of the elders. One approach to the purity codes is found in sectarian literature from Qumran. This approach melded ritual *and* moral impurity and required someone who was ritually impure to not only purify himself, but also to make atonement.[42] Ritual impurity was treated as sin. Conversely, those who sinned were counted as ritually impure. Thus, to avoid ritual impurity/sin, one must withdraw from the general populace if they are deemed to be ritually impure or sinners.

In contrast to the sectarian literature from Qumran, in Tannaitic rabbinic legal material, most likely the traditions of the elders referred to by

---

41. Sigal, *Halakhah of Jesus*, 145–86; Moo, "Mosaic Law," 7–9, 16; Saldarini, *Matthew's Christian-Jewish Community*, 126–34; Loader, *Jesus' Attitude*, 202–4, 246; Sim, *Christian Judaism*, 137; Kazen, *Jesus*, 55–60; Runesson, *Divine Wrath*, 70–74; Sanders, *Jewish Law*, 8–31.

42. Klawans, *Impurity and Sin*, 67–91.

Jesus, we find an approach more in line with the Old Testament, in that ritual impurity is separated from sin (i.e., moral impurity), and ritual purification is separated from atonement.[43] This approach is further characterized by an extensive expansion of the ritual purity codes. The half-a-dozen chapters in the Old Testament covering ritual purity (Lev 11–15, Num 19) were expanded into a large body of purity rulings found in an order of the Mishnah, an order of the Tosefta, plus large portions of Tannaitic midrashim and talmudic passages. Klawans highlights the growth of new sources of ritual defilement, such as idols and gentiles, and new modes of transferring ritual impurity, such as *maddaf*—the transference of ritual impurity from a person with a discharge or a woman during menstruation to objects physically *above* the person.[44] The purification of earthenware vessels takes up thirty chapters in the Mishnah tractate Kelim (cf. Lev 11:32–35; 15:4–6, 22; Num 19:15) and the spread of corpse impurity within a tent occupies eighteen chapters in the Mishnah tractate Ohalot (cf. Num 19:14–15).

In contrast to the massive development in ritual purity regulations in Tannaitic rabbinic material, there is little to no parallel development of moral impurity ideas, the reason being, suggests Klawans, that the concept of moral impurity was not *halakhic*, and thus had no impact on issues of civil justice, ritual purity, or one's personal status.[45] In only a few instances do we find the idea of moral defilement articulated. Moral defilement is not mentioned at all in the Mishnah and when it is mentioned in other Tannaitic sources, it is usually in the exegesis of scriptural passages such as Lev 18:24–30 and 20:1–3. In such sources, moral impurity is deemed to occur as a result of the sins of idolatry, incest, murder, judicial deceit, and blasphemy. It defiles the land and leads to the withdrawal of the Divine presence and ultimately to exile.[46]

We should not assume that the Evangelist reflects either of these approaches. Instead, he should be understood on his own terms. Like the rabbis, he rejected the idea that ritual impurity implied moral impurity or sin (Matt 15:10–20). Leprosy, for example, never implies sin.[47] It does not require repentance and confession. In stark contrast, however, he rejected

---

43. Klawans, *Impurity and Sin*, 92–117.

44. Klawans, *Impurity and Sin*, 94.

45. Klawans, *Impurity and Sin*, 131.

46. Klawans, *Impurity and Sin*, 118–35.

47. Contrast, Borg, *Meeting Jesus Again*, 49–58; Crossan, *Jesus*, 78–83.

their expansion of the ritual purity code and heavily stressed the importance of moral impurity.

Did Jesus Promote the Ritual Purity Code?

We now need to address the question of Jesus's attitude to the ritual purity code. Before I set out my own understanding, let us consider some important arguments of Runesson in favor of the continuing validity of the ritual purity code. He proposes that ritual and moral purity issues were "active categories" for the Evangelist (and Jesus) rather than "rejected matters of the past."[48] Runesson cites three examples in favor of his position.[49]

First, Runesson appeals to Matt 8:1–4, a story in which Jesus heals a leper and then, keeping to the legal command that those with leprosy should follow the priests' instructions on such matters, sends the leper to the temple with the direction that he "show [him]self to the priest, and offer the gift that Moses commanded, as a testimony to them" (8:4). Runesson takes this as evidence that the Evangelist understood that Jesus was concerned with ritual purity laws and not just the law in general.

While Runesson is right to draw our attention to this as an instance of Jesus's observance of the ritual purity laws, he underplays the ambiguity involved in Jesus's motive for sending the leper to the priests. Jesus sent him "as a testimony to them" (*eis martyrion autois*, 8:4). This can be taken a number of ways. Some, like Runesson, have taken the Evangelist's use of the phrase in a positive sense, as Jesus affirming that he keeps the ritual purity code or the law in general.[50] Others have read it as focusing on the actions of the leper; he is to testify either to his own changed state or to the cleansing action of Jesus.[51] Others have taken it as a condemning testimony, as a warning that if the priests continue in their unbelief, then they will incriminate themselves, a meaning likely implied in the use of "as a testimony to them" in 10:18 and 24:14.[52] There is no reason why we must choose a single motive to Jesus's command. Jesus can equally affirm his adherence of the ritual purity code while at the same time publicizing to the priests his healing deed of power (cf. 11:20, 23), a cleansing deed which served as

48. Runesson, "Purity, Holiness," 157.
49. Runesson, "Purity, Holiness," 158–61.
50. Allen, *Matthew*, 75.
51. Nolland, *Matthew*, 350–51.
52. Davies and Allison, *Matthew 8–18*, 16.

a prophetic challenge, a testimony and warning. These various plausible interpretations indicate that, in this instance, preserving the ritual purity code need not have been uppermost in Jesus's mind.

The second example Runesson offers is Jesus's command to the disciples in Matt 10:1 that they cast out unclean spirits (*pneumatōn akathartōn*), identified in 10:8 as demons. This he takes as further evidence that a central component in Jesus's initiation of the kingdom involved the removal of impurity. The disciples were to continue this process. Whether this was a central concern for the Evangelist is cast into doubt, however, by his consistent preference for *daimon* terminology over that of unclean spirits.[53] Matthew drops Mark's account of Jesus casting out an unclean spirit from a man in a synagogue in Capernaum (Mark 1:21–28). He drops from his summary of Jesus's ministry the note that "whenever the unclean spirits saw him, they fell down before him and shouted, 'You are the Son of God!'" (Mark 3:11; cf. "demoniacs" in Matt 4:24). He also drops the accusation of the Markan scribes that Jesus had an unclean spirit (Mark 3:30; cf. Matt 12:22–32). In Mark 5:1–13, Jesus casts out an unclean spirit (vv. 2, 8), whereas in Matthew it is demons that are cast out (Matt 8:28–34). The daughter of Mark's Syrophoenician woman has an unclean spirit (Mark 7:25; cf. "demon" in v. 30). The daughter of Matthew's Canaanite woman is tormented by a demon (Matt 15:22). Following the transfiguration, the Markan Jesus commands an unclean spirit to depart from a boy (Mark 9:25). In Matthew's equivalent account, he rebukes a demon (cf. Matt 17:18). Assuming Matthew drew on Mark as a source, the consistent change from Mark's "unclean spirits" to Matthew's "demons" would suggest that for Matthew, maintenance of ritual purity language was not a central concern.

Finally, in Matt 15:1–10, the Pharisees and scribes question Jesus as to why his disciples break the traditions of the elders by not washing their hands before they eat (cf. Mark 7:1–23). The issue here is one of touch defilement.[54] There is nothing in the Torah to indicate that impurity could be contracted in such a manner. Instead, the question of the scribes and Pharisees relates to later developments to the purity code—the traditions of the elders. In response, Jesus calls the scribes and Pharisees to obey the commandment of God over their traditions and rejects the idea that you can

---

53. Wahlen, *Impurity*, 118–20, 138. Cf. Kazen, *Jesus*, 310–13.

54. Loader, *Jesus' Attitude*, 214–17; Klawans, *Impurity and Sin*, 147. For Sanders there was extensive disagreement over handwashing, an unimportant matter for most Jews (*Jewish Law*, 55).

defile yourself by eating with unwashed hands (15:3, 20). It is not the failure of eating with unwashed hands that defiles, but rather that which comes out of the heart, moral impurities such as "evil intentions, murder, adultery, fornication, theft, false witness, slander" (15:18–20). Runesson concludes: "Matthew's Jesus states clearly here what is both implicit and explicit elsewhere, namely that ritual impurity is less important, or urgent, than moral impurity."[55] Runesson's position is that while Jesus was concerned for ritual purity, moral defilement was the more serious issue. While we may affirm Runesson's prioritization of moral defilement over ritual defilement, it is altogether more problematic to use this polemical passage to gauge Jesus's understanding of the ritual purity code.

Jesus's Attitude to the Ritual Purity Code

Given this discussion, I would argue that the Matthean Jesus did not proactively advocate the ritual purity code. We do not find him modeling through his actions the ritual purity code for his disciples. He models what to say when praying but not how to ritually wash before praying (Matt 6:5–15). When he does address ritual purity issues, it is usually when challenged by the scribes and Pharisees for his perceived transgression of their expansionist traditions (e.g., 15:1–2). However, neither does he explicitly reject the ritual purity code (cf. 5:17–18). Instead, he consistently prioritizes the moral purity code over the ritual purity code and dismisses the traditions of the elders (cf. 15:1–20).[56] In Matt 23:23, Jesus criticizes the scribes and Pharisees for neglecting the weightier matters of the law, issues of moral impurity such as a lack of justice, mercy, and faith, without neglecting "the others". By "the others" (*kakeina*), he was specifically referring to the tithing practices sanctioned in the Old Testament for crops (cf. Lev 27:30; Deut 14:22–23), taken by the Pharisees to include such herbs as mint, dill, and cummin.[57] Jesus's reasoning seems to have been, according to Donald Hagner: "If the Pharisees wish to tithe even the smallest herbs, well and good—let them, as long as they give attention at the same time to the most important items of the law, items that bear directly on the welfare of others around them."[58]

55. Runesson, "Purity, Holiness," 159.
56. Collins, "Matthew's ἐντολαί," 1334; Kazen, *Jesus*, 197–98, 343–44.
57. On Pharisaic tithing practices, see Westerholm, *Scribal Authority*, 54.
58. Hagner, *Matthew 14–28*, 670.

Jesus's objective was not to overturn adherence to the ritual purity code. His concerns were far more serious. His problem was with those who, in a state of lawlessness, wilfully transgressed the moral purity code and placed the traditions of the elders and "human precepts [taught] as doctrine" over the commandments of God (Matt 15:2, 6, 9). Such traditions included expansions to the ritual purity code, as in the case of defilement through the washing of hands (15:2), and, more seriously, rules designed to negate the moral purity code, as in the attempts of the scribes and Pharisees to minimize the obligation to honor your father and mother (15:4). He presumably would not have objected to someone faithfully fulfilling the ritual purity code as well as the moral purity code.

Anticipated Changes in the Implementation of the Purity Code

An additional factor we need to consider is that the Matthean Jesus anticipates dramatic changes in the way in which the purity code would be implemented. While Jesus acknowledges the practice of sacrifice (Matt 5:23–24; 9:13; 12:7; 23:18–20), he foresaw a time when the temple would be defiled (cf. 24:15; 27:5), the holy presence of God would depart (23:38; 27:51), and the temple be destroyed (24:2). This has important implications for how the purity code would function.

Firstly, in the face of the imminent destruction of the temple, there is little time or need to develop, in the words of Ben Meyer, a "massively detailed *halaka* to guide the conduct of life."[59] Secondly, the destruction of the temple removes the ability of those who are morally impure to achieve atonement for their sins. It also removes the risk of defiling holy space through ritual uncleanness, one of the main drivers for maintaining ritual purity in Judea. Thirdly, the Evangelist presents Jesus as offering his blood as the inaugurating blood of the covenant, a covenant which provides for "the forgiveness of sins" (26:28; cf. Jer 31:34b). Moral impurity is covered. In contrast, no consideration is given to the removal of ritual impurity, possibly an indication that the Evangelist did not believe it represented an important category for post-destruction followers of Jesus.

Finally, we may argue that the Evangelist wrote with an eye on the future mission to the gentiles and that this shaped his presentation of the law. Morna Hooker argues for a widespread awareness in the ancient world of the important rhetorical effects of the beginnings and endings of literary

59. Meyer, *Aims of Jesus*, 120.

works.[60] As such, we may assume that the Evangelist wrote the earlier chapters of the Gospel fully aware that he would conclude with the mission to the nations in Matt 28:18–20. A plausible implication of this assumption is that he intentionally wrote the preceding chapters in a manner that would aid rather than hinder those involved in the continuing mission to Jerusalem and the mission to the nations. Let us also assume that he wrote his Gospel aware of the complex problems involved in integrating gentiles into Jewish communities of Jesus followers (cf. Acts 11:1–18; 15:1–35; 21:17–26).

Combining these assumptions helps explain from a missional perspective his portrayal of Jesus as one who (1) prioritized the need for moral purity, (2) abided by but remained largely silent on the necessity for ritual purity, and (3) criticized expansions to the ritual purity code, the traditions of the elders.

Such a position enabled his Gospel to appeal to a wide range of early Jesus followers.[61] All are held accountable for moral purity. On those issues which do not fit neatly into either the ritual or moral purity categories, such as the Sabbath and food laws, the Evangelist errs on the side of their continued validity. The absence in the Gospel of a critique of the Old Testament ritual purity code worked well for those many Jewish Christians who were either members of the sect of the Pharisees or highly "zealous for the law" (Acts 15:5; 21:20). It permitted them to continue in their observance according to the dictates of their conscience. It also worked for gentile Christians in that it did not burden them with a large body of ritual purity laws (cf. 15:10).

At no point does the Evangelist address the issue of circumcision. Some scholars have argued that male gentiles who entered the community would have been circumcised.[62] Circumcision, they believe, was simply presumed by the Evangelist (so Matt 23:15). Others have argued that it is not mentioned because the issue had been dealt with at the Jerusalem conference prior to when the Evangelist wrote his Gospel. Their reasoning is that by the time the Gospel was written, baptism had replaced circumcision as the rite of entry for gentiles into the Matthean community (so Matt 28:19).[63] Both

---

60. Hooker, "Beginnings and Endings."

61. Konradt, *Israel*, 358.

62. Sim, *Christian Judaism*, 253–54; Slee, *Antioch*, 136–40; Runesson, *Divine Wrath*, 31–36.

63. Meier, *Law and History*, 30; Saldarini, *Matthew's Christian-Jewish Community*, 156–60.

explanations are founded on arguments from silence. I would argue that the Evangelist has written his Gospel mindful of both the continuing mission to Jerusalem (23:34–35) and the mission to the nations (28:18–20). As such, his silence on circumcision offers a *via media* in that it does not dissuade Jewish believers from circumcision, an accusation made against Paul in Acts 21:21, but nor does it explicitly require circumcision of gentiles. He does not require Jewish Christians to desist from keeping the ritual purity laws but neither does he require observance on the part of gentile followers. Missiological considerations seem to have shaped his position.

What Every Scribe Should Know

The Evangelist is a scribe *par excellence*—scribally literate, well-versed in the Old Testament, and an authoritative teacher of Jesus traditions. The Evangelist does not, however, expect all scribes involved in the missions of Jesus to reach his advanced level of scribal literacy. While we cannot rule out professionally trained scribes being involved in the early Jesus movement, the Evangelist being a case in point, Jesus addresses the Twelve in Matt 13:52, elsewhere in the New Testament described as "uneducated and ordinary men" (Acts 4:13), as "scribes" who have been "discipled" for the kingdom of heaven.[64] There is little in the Gospel to indicate that the goal of the Twelve's education with Jesus was to achieve scribal literacy, the ability to both read *and* write to a high standard. Nevertheless, he calls them scribes!

Instead, the emphasis we find in the Gospel is on Jesus developing the Twelve's understanding of his teachings and on them learning to interpret the Scriptures in a manner modelled by Jesus himself. A central part of this entails understanding the central ethos of the Law and the Prophets, synthesized in the command to love and the "weightier matters of the law."

The Love Command

The command to love, the first and greatest of the commandments, is found in Matt 22:34–40 in which a lawyer (*nomikos*), presumably in the hearing of the Twelve (cf. 23:1), tests Jesus by asking which is the greatest of the commandments in the law. The significance of this challenge is that Jesus is being asked to create a hierarchy among the commandments, a practice

---

64. Cf. Hilton, *Illiterate Apostles*, 35–57, 65.

reflected in rabbinic literature.[65] Jesus responds by fusing the *Shema* of Deut 6:5, a text recited morning and evening by pious Jews, with Lev 19:18:

> He said to him, "You shall love the Lord your God with all your heart, and with all your soul, and with all your mind." This is the greatest and first commandment. And a second is like it: "You shall love your neighbor as yourself." On these two command-ments hang all the law and the prophets. (Matt 22:37–40).

As in the other synoptic gospels, love is a virtue chiefly directed by human-ity toward God and to our fellow human beings. To love God is to love Jesus, whom his followers are to love more than their own fathers, mothers, sons or daughters (10:37). They are to relate to Jesus as they would relate to God.

We find no equivalent to John 3:16 in the Gospel of Matthew. God is not described as loving humanity. The closest we come to a statement affirming divine love for humanity is in Jesus's justification of his call to love your enemies rather than just your neighbor (Matt 5:43–44). This call is modelled, he explains, on his Father's treatment of the unrighteous, who, along with the righteous, enjoy the benefits of divinely sent sun and rain (5:45), the implication being that such acts are expressions of love bestowed upon the deserving and undeserving alike, regardless of whether it results in a change in their spiritual disposition.

A further surprise, considering Jesus's affirmation of the importance of love, is that nowhere in the Gospel are we told that Jesus loves others.[66] In fact, it seems as though the Evangelist has intentionally downplayed this theme, possibly a reflection of his wider tendency to downplay Jesus's emotions. In Mark 10:21, Jesus looks at the rich man who questioned him concerning eternal life and "loved" him. Matthew drops Jesus's look of love (cf. Matt 19:21). Nevertheless, he is portrayed as having compassion toward those in need such as the crowds (9:36), the sick (14:14), the hungry (15:32), and the blind (19:29–34). In Jesus, the more generalized divine love of God expressed through the sun and the rain takes the form of context-specific acts of compassion to those in trouble.

65. Barth, "Matthew's Understanding," 76–77.

66. Cf. references to Jesus's love in John 11:3, 5, 36; 13:1, 23, 34–35; 14:21; 15:9, 12–13; 19:26; 20:2; 21:7, 20.

The Weightier Matters of the Law

The idealized scribe is to ensure that core principles of the Torah are incorporated into national life. In Matt 23:23, Jesus criticizes the scribes and Pharisees for being hypocrites because they tithe mint, dill, and cumin, but neglect or abandon the weightier matters of the law; judgment-justice (*krisis*), mercy (*eleos*), and faith (*pistis*). By weightier matters, Jesus implies the more important rather than the more difficult, a distinction corresponding to the rabbinic distinction between heavy commandments and small commandments.[67] Jesus identifies these not just as important matters in general, but specifically as weightier matters "of the law."[68] As such, they are prominent motifs in the Torah. They also, however, in a more narrow sense, reflect the relational dynamics of the Mosaic covenant: (1) judgment would come upon Israel if it failed to keep the covenant (cf. Deut 12:29—13:5; 28:15-68);[69] (2) Yahweh promised to show his *ḥesed* "steadfast love," frequently translated as *eleos* "mercy" in the LXX, to those who love him and honor his covenant (cf. Deut 5:10; 7:9, 12); finally, (3) obedience or faithfulness to the covenant was an expression of Israel's trust and faith in Yahweh (cf. 9:23).

These weightier matters are not just weightier matters of the law but are, reflecting the Evangelist's positive attitude to the law, weightier matters of the Gospel. We may, in fact, go beyond this and assert that the Evangelist, while maintaining the need to keep the law, intentionally refocuses its weightier matters on Jesus, who repeatedly judges, responds to appeals for mercy, and is the object of the faith of others. By the time a first-time reader arrives at Matt 23:23, he or she is overwhelmingly aware that faithfulness to the weightier matters of the law cannot be achieved apart from the person and teachings of Jesus.

---

67. Klawans draws our attention to the rabbis' accusation against the generation before the destruction of Jerusalem that they paid too much attention to ritual impurity and too little to grave sins such as bloodshed (*Impurity and Sin*, 122).

68. Mercy and justice are prominent themes in Lev 17–21. Cf. Lev 16:2, 13–15; 19:15, 18, 34. See Snodgrass, "Matthew and the Law," 106. Matthew's weightier matters are formulated as a group of three, a practice particularly common in prophetic calls to faithfulness to the law (cf. LXX Hos 2:21–22). For the prophets, the law still holds and needs to be read and applied in a manner sensitive to its main themes, its weightier matters (cf. Isa 56:1; Jer 4:2; Mic 6:8; Zech 7:9).

69. Num 14:11; 32:8; Deut 1:32; 9:23.

The Weightier Matter of Justice

The term *krisis* typically corresponds in the LXX to the Hebrew *mišpāṭ* (e.g., Exod 15:25) and can refer to either divine judgment or justice. There is little benefit in distinguishing between these two concepts in that both are inextricably bound together in the Gospel; justice both demands judgment and flows from judgment (cf. *krisis* in LXX Isa 42:1–2//Matt 12:18, 20). Justice is decidedly a weightier matter for the Evangelist, as indicated by its pervasive presence throughout the Gospel (e.g., Matt 3:7–10; 11:20–24; 12:18–20; 36, 41–42).

JUSTICE AS EQUIVALENT REPAYMENT OF DEEDS

Matthean justice involves the equivalent repayment of your deeds, whether in the form of equivalent reward or equivalent retribution. In sum, how you treat others is how you will be treated by God.[70] These deeds consist of, according to Runesson, external deeds (e.g., "good fruit," Matt 3:10; 7:17–19; hospitality, 10:40–42), verbal deeds (e.g., insults, 5:22; blasphemy, 12:32; careless words, 12:36), and internal deeds (e.g., those things that happen in secret, 6:2–4, 16–18).[71] Internal deeds include, as in the law, your intensions.

Just as differences in intention are used in the law to distinguish between two similar external deeds (e.g., murder and manslaughter, Num 35:6–34; Deut 19:4–13), so too in the Gospel. A good example of similar external deeds distinguished according to internal intention is the difference between those in Matt 5:16, who let their light shine before others in order that they may see their good works and give glory to their Heavenly Father, and those in 6:1, who practice their righteousness before others in order to be seen by them. In such instances, the internal deed takes precedence over the external deed for the purposes of judgment.

The principle of equivalent repayment is grounded in the Torah, an important example being the killing of Egypt's firstborn in retribution for the mistreatment of Yahweh's first-born, Israel (Exod 4:22–23). It is expressed succinctly in the *lex talionis*, the law of equivalent retribution ("If any harm follows, then you shall give life for life, eye for eye, tooth for

---

70. In the Old Testament, judgment is frequently portrayed as a repayment of your ways or deeds (cf. 2 Chr 6:30; Job 21:19; Pss 18:20, 24; 28:4; 94:23; Isa 59:18; Jer 17:10; Ezek 7:4, 7–9; 18:20, 30; 24:14; 33:20; Hos 4:9; 12:2).

71. Runesson, *Divine Wrath*, 165–71.

tooth, hand for hand, foot for foot, burn for burn, wound for wound, stripe for stripe," Exod 21:23–24; cf. Lev 24:19–20; Deut 19:16–21).

Throughout the Gospel, we find numerous expressions of the equivalent repayment of our deeds (cf. Matt 5:38).[72] The measure you give, in context a reference to how you judge others, will be the measure you receive (7:2). The essence of the Law and the Prophets is deemed to be reciprocity, expressed in the golden rule that we are to do to others as we would have them do to us (7:12). When the Son of Man comes, he will repay everyone for what they have done (*praxis*, "the totality of one's deeds," 16:27), whether good or evil. Judgment is when you receive from God what you have done to others. At its most serious, if you shed innocent blood, your blood will be shed (21:41; 23:29–36). The parable of the vineyard is a case in point in which the wicked tenants, representing the chief priests, elders, and Pharisees (21:23, 45), murder the Son, an act of rebellion against his Father the owner of the vineyard, as a result of which they will experience justice by themselves being put to "a miserable death" (21:33–41). Retribution is proportional to their own murderous actions.

The principle of equivalent repayment is also applied to how readers respond to Jesus. If they acknowledge him before others, he will acknowledge them before his Father in heaven (10:32). If they deny him before others, he will deny them before his Father (10:33). If communities, whether Jewish or gentile, extend hospitality to his followers, they have therein extended hospitality to Jesus himself and will, as a result, enjoy a hospitable welcome from him on judgment day (10:12–13; 25:34–40). If they refuse hospitality to him or his followers, he will refuse hospitality to them (cf. 10:14–15; 25:41–46).

The principle of equivalent repayment is, however, to be restricted in the case of equivalent retribution involving the reader's treatment of others. When responding to others, followers of Jesus are to avoid repaying evil for evil.[73] They are to "rejoice and be glad" in situations of persecution for a great reward awaits them in heaven (5:11–12). Rather than requiring an eye for an eye and a tooth for a tooth, they are to avoid resisting evil doers and instead are to turn the cheek when struck, give up their cloaks when sued, and go the extra mile when forced (5:38–42). They are to love their enemies and pray for those that persecute them (5:44). This suspension of equivalent retribution reflects the fact that prior to the day of judgment, the Father

72. Cf. Exod 11:5; 12:12, 29; 13:2, 12–15; 22:29; 34:19–20.
73. Cf. Rom 12:17, 21; 1 Thess 5:15; 1 Pet 3:9.

has himself suspended the strict application of equivalence in his treatment of others. He makes the sun to rise on the evil and the good, and sends rain on the righteous and on the unrighteous (5:45). This willingness to imitate the Father in setting aside the law of equivalent repayment in your treatment of others opens up the possibility that on judgment day, the day when the principle cannot be set aside, he will reciprocate to the reader the mercy he or she has extended to others. Reciprocity is maintained, although now grounded on the reader's deeds of mercy toward others.

Living according to the principle of equivalent repayment requires readers to question how their deeds will determine the manner of their own judgment on judgment day, and on this basis, to make micro-judgments that shape their daily actions and treatment of others. It raises the terrifying possibility that they will be judged by a divine judge seeking the specks in their eyes if they have tried to remove the specks from the eyes of others while ignoring the logs within their own eyes (7:3–5). In the words of Isabella in William Shakespeare's *Measure for Measure*, "How would you be, if He, which is the top of judgment, should but judge you as you are? O, think on that, and mercy then will breathe within your lips, like man new-made."[74] They are to be willing to suspend equivalent retribution of others to ensure their own survival on the day of judgment.

JUSTICE AS MORE THAN EQUIVALENT REPAYMENT

While justice involves equivalent repayment, it cannot be reduced to equivalent repayment. At its most positive, the day of judgment is also a day of abundant reward. It is the time when those who have left houses, brothers, sisters, fathers, mothers, children or fields for the sake of Jesus's name, will receive a *hundredfold* in return (Matt 19:29). It is an opportunity for the expression of divine goodness, a reflection of the abundant blessings that flowed when Israel was judged to be faithful to the covenant (Deut 28:1).

This principle of generosity in judgment is expressed in the parable of the laborers in the vineyard, which focuses on the relationship between hiring (Matt 20:1–7) and payment (20:8–16). All workers, whenever hired, worked in the vineyard and received a reward, or, as in 16:27, repayment for their works (cf. 5:12; 6:1; 25:29).[75] At issue is the landowner's right to dispro-

---

74. Shakespeare, *Measure for Measure*, act 2, scene 2.

75. Cf. Eubank, "What Does Matthew Say?" On New Testament scholarship's unease with the concept of reward, see Bornkamm, *Der Lohngedanke*, 3–5.

portionately reward his workers on judgment day, to pay them more than their due. The first section of the parable is divided into four divisions that focus on the different times when the landowner went out to hire laborers:

1. Matt 20:1–2:   he went out (*exēlthen*) early in the morning

2. Matt 20:3–5a: going out (*exelthōn*) about the third hour

3. Matt 20:5b: going out (*exelthōn*) about the sixth and the ninth hour

4. Matt 20:6–7:   about the eleventh hour, going out (*exelthōn*)

The order of (1) movement ("he went out," "going out") and (2) time (i.e., the hour) established for the first three divisions is reversed in the fourth division in which the (2) timing ("the eleventh hour") precedes the (1) movement of the householder. This final division is meant to catch the reader's attention.

Crucial to our discussion is the basis upon which the laborers are hired. The Evangelist presents those hired early in the morning as agreeing with the landowner to work for the usual daily wage (*ek dēnariou tēn hēmeran*, 20:2). In contrast, the landowner agrees to pay the group hired at the third hour "whatever is right" (*ho ean ē dikaion*, 20:4). This ambiguity invites readers to supply their own definition of what is meant by right payment, most likely the expectation of proportional reward, that those hired at the third hour will be paid one denarius less three-twelfths.[76] The same basis of employment is implied for those hired at the sixth and ninth hours. Finally, those engaged at the eleventh hour are simply sent out into the vineyard with no indication of how their pay will be determined (20:7).

This progression from clear contractual agreement (i.e., equivalent repayment), to promise of right payment, to complete ambiguity, prompts the reader to question on what basis rewards will be given. In the second half of the parable this question is addressed (20:8–16). The laborers are paid in the reverse order in which they were hired, a literary device that allows the first group hired to witness the payment of the last group hired. Those hired last are paid one denarius, a full day's wage for one hour's work (20:9). When the first group hired receive the same payment, they complain that the landowner has made those who only worked for one hour "equal" (*isos*) to those who had borne "the burden of the day and the scorching heat" (20:11–12). This "equal" treatment is to their detriment.

---

76. Marguerat, *Le Jugement*, 452; Carter and Heil, *Matthew's Parables*, 140; Luz, *Matthew 8–20*, 525.

Normal expectations are that "as one works, so one is paid."[77] For them, this equal treatment is in fact unequal treatment, the same payment for twelve hours of work as for one hour of work.

The landowner's response is twofold. First, he has not wronged them nor treated them with injustice in that he has remained faithful to his agreement, one denarius for a day's work (i.e., equivalent repayment), and second, he asks whether he has the right to do as he wishes with what belongs to him, to act out of his goodness (*hoti egō agathos eimi*, 20:15). The question as to whether the landowner can act with such goodness is left open for the reader to answer in that none of the laborers respond to the landowner's question. In essence, readers are invited to determine the nature of their own judgment. They may choose to define "right payment" purely in terms of payment proportional to their own work, as in the case of those first hired. The danger of such an approach is that it can result in envy of other laborers and resentment toward a landowner who has bestowed disproportionate goodness upon those who have achieved less (cf. "evil eye" in 20:15). If such resentment toward what may seem a very arbitrary employer is not plucked out, condemnation will result (cf. 5:29; 18:9).[78] Alternatively, they can rejoice in the landowner's goodness toward others and thereby open up the possibility, though not fulfilled in the parable, of a generous reward for themselves regardless of their own length of service.

In essence, this parable supports a *quid pro quo* theology of justice in which the manner of reward the reader permits the landowner to extend to others, whether it be strictly according to equivalent repayment or a reward in which the landowner is permitted the right to express his goodness, will be the way he or she is rewarded.[79]

JUDGMENT OF BOTH THE INDIVIDUAL AND THE COMMUNITY

Matthean justice applies to both the individual and the community. This reflects the Torah. Examples of judgment of individuals include Cain (Gen 4:8–16), Lot's wife (19:26), Pharaoh (cf. Exod 11:1), Nadab and Abihu (Lev

---

77. See Marguerat, *Le Jugement*, 457.

78. On the arbitrary nature of the agent of action in this parable, see Zehetbauer, "Befristete Barmherzigkeit," 235–37.

79. Bornkamm rejects the idea that the denarius paid to those hired last represented a combination of reward and gift. Instead, for him it is purely a gracious gift. Bornkamm, *Der Lohngedanke*, 17–26.

10:1–2), and Korah, Dathan, and Abiram (Num 16:23–34). Collective judgment is given against the generation of the flood (Gen 6:5–7), Sodom and Gomorrah (19:24–25), Egypt (cf. Exod 11:1), and the exodus generation (Num 14:22–30; Deut 1:34–35). Sometimes judgment of the individual aligns with judgment of the community, as is the case with Pharaoh and Egypt. Both were deemed worthy of punishment. Other times the individual compares favorably with his or her community and is saved while the community is destroyed (e.g., Lot and Sodom).

In the Gospel, cities and nations are singled out for judgment, whether it be Sodom and Gomorrah (10:15; 11:23–24), Tyre and Sidon (11:21–22), Chorazin (11:21), Capernaum (11:23), Nineveh (12:41), Jerusalem (23:37–39) or the nations (25:31–32). On the day of judgment, it will be more tolerable for Sodom and Gomorrah, and Tyre and Sidon, than for the cities of Galilee (10:15; 11:22, 24). Individuals are also clearly subject to judgment, as illustrated by the many judgment-related statements directed to a nonspecific audience (e.g., Matt 7:1–5, 24–27). The assumption is present, however, that the individual can survive judgment independent of the fate of their city. Nevertheless, these two levels of judgment enable multiple comparisons of different responses to God's mission to be undertaken: individual versus individual, community versus community, and individual versus community. Context is thereby taken into account.

Present and Future Justice

When Israel was deemed faithful to the covenant, blessings flowed (cf. Deut 28:1–14). Unfaithfulness, however, would result in mild and ongoing punishment through the withdrawal of covenantal blessings. Higher degrees of unfaithfulness would result in severe punishments such as pestilence, defeat by enemies, hunger, nakedness, and the dreaded "diseases of Egypt" (cf. 28:15–68). If this failed to effect change, punishment would climax in the loss of the land through exile. The severity of punishment thus varied at any one point in time depending upon Israel's level of commitment to Yahweh and his covenant. The Evangelist works within this basic framework, distinguishing between rewards and punishments in the here and now, and those dispensed on a future day of judgment (cf. Matt 10:15; 11:22).[80]

The distinction between present and future judgment is expressed in Jesus's ruling on the prohibition to murder ("Whoever murders shall be

---

80. Trilling, *Das wahre Israel*, 84–87; Runesson, *Divine Wrath*, 49–52.

liable to judgment," 5:21): "But I say to you that if you are angry with a brother, you will be liable to judgment; and if you say to a brother, 'Raka', you will be liable to the council; and if you say, 'You fool', you will be liable to the Gehenna of fire" (own translation, 5:22). This verse, one of the most disputed in the Gospel, indicates different forms judgment may take:

Offense	Punishment
Angry with a brother	Liable to judgment
Insult a brother (*rhaka*)	Liable to the council
Call them a fool (*mōre*)	Liable to the Gehenna of fire

Traditional readings affirm an increasing intensity of punishment that correspond to an increasing seriousness of offense. To be angry is taken as indicating an inward wrath, and the two words of abuse (*rhaka*, "empty head"; *mōre*, "crazy") point to an increasing degree of insult.[81] More recently, this reading has been rejected by those who argue that there is no progression in the severity of the offense (and for some interpreters no intensification of punishment).[82] Instead, Jesus is deemed to be using hyperbole to emphasize the serious nature of anger, a cause of murder, threatening an appearance before the Sanhedrin and even Gehenna for those who even use deprecatory expressions against their brother. In essence, he is warning that those who harbour anger will be treated as though they have murdered. Intentions count. For our purposes, it is sufficient to note that Jesus assumes present and future elements of judgment, whether it be an appearance before the Sanhedrin or the future horrors of Gehenna.

In some cases, future punishment may be avoided by undertaking self-imposed punishment in the present, as indicated in Jesus's hyperbolic image of self-mutilation: "If your right eye causes you to sin, tear it out and throw it away; it is better to lose one of your members than for your whole body to be thrown into Gehenna" (Matt 5:29; cf. v. 30). Other examples reinforce this distinction between present and future judgment. An example of a mild future judgment is the fate of those who break and teach others to break the "least of these commandments" (5:19). They will be called the "least in the kingdom of heaven." More severe punishments are the future destruction of Jerusalem and the Son of Man's judgment of the nations (23:33—24:2, 15–21; 24:29–31; cf. 25:31–46).

81. Augustine, *Serm. Dom.* 1.9.24. Cf. Gundry, *Matthew*, 84–85; Davies, *Setting*, 238.

82. Davies and Allison, *Matthew 1–7*, 515.

The general rule governing rewards is that faithfulness results in a willingness to forgo being rewarded in the present and to defer reward to the *palingenesia*, the "renewal of all things" (19:28–29; cf. 6:4, 6, 18). In contrast, the hypocrites, motivated by a desire for self-aggrandizement, receive their transient rewards in the present (6:2, 5, 16). The effect of these various examples is to present a network of punishment-reward relationships that distinguish between the present and the future, thereby enabling the reader to respond in the present in a manner that will prove advantageous in the future.

The Weightier Matter of Mercy

The second weightier matter of the law, *eleos*, usually translated, "mercy," is predominantly used in the LXX to translate *ḥesed* (e.g., Exod 34:7) and denotes the kindness, whether in attitude or in action, conferred by one party to another, usually, but not always, in a mutual relationship. In the Gospel, it is required to avoid punishment resulting from the divine application of the law of equivalent retribution. Justice and mercy have been portrayed throughout the history of biblical interpretation as uneasy bedfellows, with some interpreters prioritizing justice over mercy, and others prioritizing mercy over justice.[83] Still others have viewed them as operating as equal partners or in different spheres. The issue at stake is whether justice can be maintained without sacrificing mercy, or mercy extended without sacrificing justice. Such concerns are partly mitigated when we take into account the Evangelist's emphasis on faith.

Requesting Mercy in the Context of Divine Retribution

In the Torah, mercy enables you to survive judgment. Lot, for instance, thanks the angels who have come to deliver him from the destruction of Sodom for the mercy they have shown him (MT: *ḥēn*; LXX: *eleos*, Gen 19:19). When Yahweh threatens to strike unfaithful Israel with pestilence and to disinherit them, Moses appeals for mercy (Num 14:12, 19), a central attribute of the divine name (MT: *ḥesed*; LXX: *eleos*, Exod 34:7; cf. 20:6; Deut 5:10; 7:9). These two examples are significant in that they maintain a clear distinction between judgment and mercy. Mercy removes judgment's threat of punishment. Several scholars have blurred this distinction with

---

83. Hill, *Matthew*, 146; Levine, "Mercy/Justice Dichotomy."

respect to *eleos* in Matt 23:23. Pierre Bonnard, for example, reads *krisis* as "justice," a justice achieved through mercy. In such a reading, the connotations of judgment and punishment associated with *krisis* are unnecessarily minimized.[84] Alternatively, others have sought to distinguish between *krisis* "justice" as a standard of the law and mercy as something in tension with the law, something necessary to save us from the law.[85] Such approaches fail to give mercy its due place as a distinct weightier matter *of the law*.

Divine judgment is a present reality for many characters in the Gospel. The presence of the weak and sick in Israel is not just an unfortunate happenstance but rather, from a biblical theology perspective, a symptom of Israel's dire spiritual condition. In the Gospel, many inhabitants of Israel suffer from the "diseases of Egypt" (cf. Matt 4:23–25; 9:35; 10:1), an indication within a covenantal framework that Israel as a nation is viewed by the Evangelist as being in a state of apostasy and subject to severe divine displeasure.

In this reading, the cries for mercy directed to Jesus are the equivalent of appeals in the Old Testament to the God of Israel to turn away his wrath, to desist from administering punishment, his covenantal curses. Such cries evoke the psalmist's cry for mercy when subject to divine wrath (cf. *eleēson me, kyrie* in LXX Ps 6:3).[86] An appeal for mercy and the removal of divine retribution is found in the parable of the unforgiving servant (Matt 18:23–25), in which, as a result of his appeal, the servant, a stock image for God's people, receives mercy manifested in the removal of his great debt and punishment (Matt 18:26, 33). The principle of equivalent repayment is set aside.

In chapter 9, two blind men follow Jesus crying out, "Have mercy (*eleēson*) on us, Son of David!" (Matt 9:27). Jesus heals them after he has elicited a confession of faith in him (9:28). In chapter 15, a Canaanite woman cried out to Jesus, "Have mercy (*eleēson*) on me, Lord, Son of David; my daughter is tormented by a demon" (15:22). Jesus responds to her cry and heals her daughter after affirming her "great faith" (*megalē sou hē pistis*, 15:28). In chapter 17, the father of an epileptic boy kneels before Jesus after the disciples had failed to help him due to their lack of faith and requests, "Lord, have mercy (*eleēson*) on my son" (17:15). Jesus heals him. Finally, in chapter 20, two blind men sitting by the roadside shout out as Jesus passes by, "Lord, have mercy (*eleēson*) on us, Son of David!" (20:30). They repeat

84. Bonnard, *Matthieu*, 340.
85. Wengst, "Recht und Gerechtigkeit."
86. E.g., LXX Pss 9:14; 24:16; 25:11.

their appeal in response to the protestations of the crowds (20:31). Jesus, motivated by compassion, heals them and they follow him (20:34). These appeals for mercy are directed to Jesus in the same manner that characters in the Old Testament appealed to Yahweh for mercy.

Mercy Is Conditional

The dispensing of divine mercy is, counterintuitively, conditional. It is dependent upon us showing mercy to others. This dynamic introduces into the reader's practice of justice a "moment of self-criticism."[87] In the parable of the unforgiving servant, the servant was deluded in believing that he could repay his debt ("Have patience with me and I will pay you everything," Matt 18:26).[88] Great indebtedness is typically the norm. The king knew this and, instead of extending the time permitted to repay, cancelled the servant's debt out of compassion (18:27). The servant's failure, however, to extend mercy to his fellow servant, resulted in him becoming subject once again to the king's anger (18:34). The servant is under obligation to imitate his king by extending mercy to others, without which forgiveness of his own debts will be withdrawn (18:34–35; cf. 6:14–15). He is to treat others as he has been treated by the king.

If mercy removes divine wrath, forgiveness addresses the underlying cause of God's wrath—sin and debt. Provision for the cancellation of "debt" is alluded to in Matt 6:12, 14–15 ("Forgive us our debts . . . your heavenly Father will also forgive you"). This divine forgiveness of "debts" (*ta opheilēmata*, "obligations in a moral sense," 6:12) and "trespasses" (6:14, 15) is, like mercy, contingent on the debtor forgiving others. If you forgive others, "your heavenly Father will also forgive you" (6:14). But if you do not forgive others, "neither will your Father forgive your trespasses" (6:15). Forgiveness of sins is thus dependent upon two factors, divine compassion and the reader's willingness to treat others as he or she would want to be treated by God. The reciprocal nature of divine mercy ensures that it is still infused with justice. God treats us as we treat others.

87. O'Donovan, *Ways of Judgment*, 97.

88. Contrast with Eubank (*Wages*, 56–58), who believes that the debt could have been repaid.

The Weightier Matter of Faith

The noun *pistis* refers to "trusting" and "having confidence" in someone or something. Its cognate verb *pisteuō* means "to trust," "to rely on" somebody or something (e.g., Matt 8:13). Its passive form refers to being "worthy of trust" or "reliable," although this voice is not present in the Gospel.[89] Its adjective *pistos* means 'trustworthy' (cf. the "faithful and wise slave," 24:45; the "good and trustworthy slave," 25:21, 23).

In the Torah, faith in Yahweh is the marker of true Israel (cf. Gen 15:6). Elsewhere in the Old Testament, faith is treated in a similar vein. The righteous live by their faith and it is this virtue that enables Israel to survive the crisis of divine judgment.[90] It is a precondition for those who would cry out for mercy when subject to divine wrath. You do not, after all, appeal for mercy from someone you do not trust. Likewise, in the Gospel, faith and faithfulness mark out those who are true Israel. Most surprisingly from a traditional Jewish perspective, faith in God is now focalized on the person of Jesus. Matthew supplements a number of times Mark's use of "to believe" with "in me" or "in him" to reinforce the need for faith *in* Jesus (cf. Mark 9:42/Matt 18:6; Mark 15:32/Matt 27:42).[91]

THREE LEVELS OF FAITH

There are in the Gospel three levels of faith. The lowest level of faith is not just the absence of faith but rather the presence of an active and hostile unbelief. This is the case in Nazareth, where the unbelief (*apistia*) of the inhabitants of the town limits Jesus's ability to perform many deeds of power (Matt 13:58). It is not just Jesus who is affected by such unbelief. At the transfiguration, while Jesus was appearing in his glory at the top of a mountain in the presence of Moses and Elijah (17:1–8), this "faithless and perverse generation" (*genea apistos kai diestrammenē*, 17:17) inhibited at the bottom of the mountain the disciples' ability to heal an epileptic boy, a clear parallel to the faithless generation of the exodus who made and worshiped

---

89. According to Barth, the *pistis* concept denotes "trust in the fatherly kindness of God who cares for his creatures" ("Matthew's Understanding," 112). Barth unnecessarily excludes understanding from faith.

90. MT Hab 2:4; see "by Yahweh's faith" in LXX Hab 2:4.

91. Klein, "Das Glaubensverständnis," 30–33.

a golden calf at the bottom of the mountain while Yahweh, at the top of the mountain, was revealing the law to Moses (Exod 24:15–18; 32:1–6).[92]

The next level of faith includes those who have "little faith" (*oligopistoi*). In a general sense, this includes all those who fail to trust the Father to provide for their daily needs, whether it be for food, drink, or clothing (cf. *oligopistoi* in Matt 6:30). More specifically, however, a minimal faith in the Father is manifested in a failure to trust in Jesus. The disciples are described as "little faithers" due to their failure to trust in him when in two storms (8:26; 14:31). They also fail to trust in him to provide their daily bread (16:5, 8), the supply of which is taken elsewhere in the Gospel as a sign of the Father's care (6:11, 25–34). When surrounded by those without faith, they themselves have little faith as evidenced in their failure to help the epileptic boy because of the faithless crowds (cf. 17:20). Those of little faith are not subjected to immediate judgment, as is the case for those with hostile unbelief. Instead, they are provided evidence to strengthen their faith in the Father and in Jesus.[93]

Those in the Gospel with maximum faith are transparent exemplar figures, individuals who appear once in the narrative and then disappear and who model for the reader a positive character trait to imitate.[94] They are those who place their trust in Jesus and who, as a result, receive salvation from divine wrath (cf. "Your faith has saved you" in Matt 9:22).[95] These include:

The centurion in Capernaum (Matt 8:5–13; "faith" in 8:10, 13)

The paralyzed man (Matt 9:2–8; the "faith" of those who carry him in 8:2)

The woman suffering from hemorrhages (Matt 9:20–22; "faith" in 9:28, 29)

Two blind men (Matt 9:27–31; "mercy" in 9:27; "faith" in 9:28, 29)

The Canaanite woman (Matt 15:21–29; "mercy" in 15:22; "great faith" in 15:28)

---

92. Carter, *Matthew and the Margins*, 354.

93. Cf. Matt 6:30, 33; 8:26; 14:31–32; 16:8–10; 17:18–20.

94. Luz, *Disciples*, 126–27.

95. Heinz, "Matthew as Interpreter," 179. Luz provides a highly individualistic definition of Matthean faith as "the human attitude corresponding to the divine Power of salvation, whereas understanding is the presupposition for loyalty to the earthly Jesus, that is for Christian ethics" (*Disciples*, 124).

Strong faith is the basis upon which appeals for mercy are made, as in the cases of the two blind men and the Canaanite woman. The faith of the gentile centurion is contrasted with a lack of faith in Israel, a warning sign that gentiles will be accepted into the kingdom on account of their faith and that those parts of Israel that manifest a lack of faith will be rejected (8:5–13).[96] Faith functions as a community boundary marker. Recognition of gentile faith is further provided when the Canaanite woman is singled out for her faith. In contrast to Mark, in which no mention is made of her faith, Matthew explicitly links the healing of her daughter with her great faith ("Woman! Great is your faith!," Matt 15:28; cf. Mark 7:29). Janice Capel Anderson notes that as we progress through the Gospel, such marginal characters respond, "more and more positively to Jesus."[97] In contrast, the leaders become more hostile.

These examples clearly signal to the reader that as a weightier matter of the law, faith is to be directed to Jesus and is expected of both Jews and gentiles.[98] This has the important missiological implication that faith in the divine is to be practically manifested through faith in Jesus, regardless of your ethnic status.

MERCY AND COVENANTAL FAITHFULNESS

Faithfulness is also a necessary condition to receive mercy. Mercy on its own can be presumed upon, taken advantage of, by those who would appeal to their merciful treatment of others as the basis on which their cherished sins should be forgiven. They can cultivate sin but then claim forgiveness because they forgive others. Augustine counteracted just such a position when he argued against those who live a dissolute and iniquitous life, but claim that, due to their charitable works toward others, they should be forgiven. He characterizes them as appealing to Matthew's Lord's Prayer, claiming that because they have forgiven their debtors, their own debts should be forgiven, irrespective of the fact that they indulge their own sins (*Civ.* 21.27; Matt 6:12). A commitment to faithfulness counteracts such presumption.

In the Torah, the criterion for judging Israel is its faithfulness to God's will expressed through exclusive devotion to him and a willingness to obey

96. Barth, "Matthew's Understanding," 112.

97. Anderson, *Matthew's Narrative Web*, 183.

98. Runesson, *Divine Wrath*, 393, 401–7.

the various stipulations of his covenant (e.g., Exod 19:5; Lev 26:3–13; Deut 11:26–28; 13:4). Faith and obedience go hand in hand.[99] These stipulations are summarized in the Decalogue, which, in the Gospel, is refocused on Jesus. The first two commandments affirm exclusive covenant loyalty to the God of the exodus (Exod 20:1–6; Deut 5:6–10). In the Gospel, loyalty to Yahweh is similarly manifested in the believer's willingness to serve God alone (Matt 5:24). Now, however, such loyalty also includes a willingness to follow Jesus, itself an exodus allusion to those led by Yahweh out of Egypt (cf. "follow me" in Matt 4:19; 8:22; 9:9).[100] Torah faithfulness to Yahweh is thus reframed as faithfulness to the Father's Son. The third commandment's call to fealty to the name of Yahweh (Exod 20:7) is now expressed both in the desire that the name of our Father in heaven be hallowed (Matt 6:9; cf. 21:9; 23:39) and in loyalty to the name of Jesus (e.g., 10:22; 18:20). Both names are to be honored. In the epilogue of the Gospel, the reader is made aware that the Father and Son share the same name, a name which they also share with the Holy Spirit (28:19).[101] To honor the name of Yahweh is now to honor the name of Jesus.

In a similar vein, the keeping of the fourth commandment can no longer be undertaken purely based on Torah regulations. Now the Son of Man's lordship of the Sabbath must be considered (12:8). How you treat your neighbor, summarized in the second half of the Decalogue, is another criterion for judgment reframed around the person of Jesus. The observer of these commands must now take into account his numerous rulings on such matters as murder, anger, adultery, lust, and divorce (cf. 5:21–32; 19:1–12). These laws are, after all, the laws of the king.

JESUS THE DISCRETIONARY JUDGE

The effect of this reorienting of the weightier matters of the law around the person of Jesus is to expose readers to their future judge and the legal basis upon which they will be judged. The Matthean Jesus considers, as in

---

99. Bultmann and Weiser, "πιστεύω, πίστις, πιστός . . . ," *TDNT*, 6:197; Marguerat, *Le Jugement*, 138–39.

100. Exod 13:17–18, 21; 15:13; Judg 6:8; Jer 2:6; Ezek 20:10; Amos 2:10; 2 Esd. 3:17; 14:4; 15:10. See Kingsbury, "The Verb *Akolouthein*," 56–73; Wright, *Victory*, 647.

101. Davies and Allison, *Matthew 19–28*, 685–86. Against this reading Nolland (*Matthew*, 1268–69) argues that Matthew's language should be read as "in the name of the Father and the name of the Son and the name of the Holy Spirit."

the Torah, circumstantial factors when judging, whether it be your intention, your attitude toward him—primarily expressed in terms of faith, your treatment of others—whether you extend mercy and generosity to fellow servants, the response of your city, and the nature of the divine appeal. Jesus is a discretionary judge who, by nuancing judgment and tying it so closely to mercy and faith, invites readers to take the necessary steps to determine the nature and tone of the judgment to which they will be subjected on the Last Day.

Implications

The purpose of the idealized Jesus-scribe is to combat the problem of national lawlessness. This we defined as an active hostility on the part of those in authority toward divine sovereignty. The Evangelist's response to this problem is to appeal to the reader to adopt the identity of his idealized scribe. In Matt 23:34, Jesus informs the scribes and Pharisees that he would send them scribes as part of his final appeal to Jerusalem. We cannot rule out the possibility that this would have been interpreted by some of the Gospel's original audience as referring to scribally-literate followers of Jesus who were experts in Torah. Nonetheless, the solution to the problem of lawlessness is not more scribally-literate scribes or the production of a new body of detailed legal rulings (cf. 13:52). Instead, the Evangelist shapes the reader into an idealized scribe through his presentation of story after story focusing on the weightier matters of the law; justice, mercy, and faith. It is through establishing among the general population an awareness of, and a commitment to, these weightier matters, that lawlessness-as-rebellion is to be combatted at both the individual and national levels. A self-regulating populace results in national transformation.

The Gospel's emphasis on the weightier matters of the law has important implications for political theology. Biblical law may coexist with other judicial systems when it is defined in terms of weightier matters. An important precedent for overlapping legal jurisdictions is Ezra the scribe who was responsible for implementing both the laws of the king of Persia and the laws of his God. Idealized scribes involved in the mission to the nations are not required to seek the abolishment of national legal systems. Neither are they expected to promote their own detailed legal rulings, their own "traditions of the elders." Instead, they are to promote the weightier matters of the law, as oriented toward Jesus, in a manner that will result in the transformation rather than the replacement of national legal systems.

Oliver O'Donovan warns that when a political theology is based upon a single principle, there is a risk that, however good that principle may be (e.g., liberty, justice), it becomes a domineering and oppressive ideology.[102] The weightier matters of the law avoid this danger in that they are themselves in tension, each keeping the others in check. The weightier matter of justice requires the nation to incorporate into its legal and political culture the principles of personal accountability and punishment proportional to the crime. Situational factors must be considered when sentencing. It requires that the nation's leaders rule in the shadow of their own judgment, in the knowledge that one day they will be judged on the same basis they have judged others. Mercy requires that the principles of redemption and restoration be embedded within political culture and legal practices. Justice is to be tempered with mercy. Faith requires the nation to seek divine guidance and intervention and cede to God the right to determine the values that shape society. When a nation accepts these weightier matters, it is, in effect, entering a covenant relationship with God. It is no longer lawless.

102. O'Donovan, *Desire of the Nations*, 250.

7

Concluding Thoughts

The Gospel Commission and the
Establishment of Divine Sovereignty

IT IS WORTH US considering the central themes of the Gospel Commission before we identify the main implications of this study:

> And Jesus came and said to them, "All authority [*exousia*] in heaven and on earth has been given [*edothē*) to me. Go therefore and make disciples[1] of all nations [*panta ta ethnē*], baptizing them in the name of the Father and of the Son and of the Holy Spirit, and teaching them to obey everything that I have commanded you. And remember, I am with you always, to the end of the age." (Matt 28:18–20)

The Gospel Commission fuses allusions to two important Old Testament passages. First, Matt 28:18–20 includes clear intertextual allusions to LXX Dan 7 in which, as in the Gospel, one like a son of man "was given authority" (*edothē autō exousia*) over "all the peoples of the earth" (*panta ta ethnē tēs gēs*), so that they might serve him (LXX Dan 7:14, cf. vv. 26–27).[2] The Danielic Son of Man will liberate "the holy ones of the Most High" and share dominion with them over the beast-like nations (7:18; cf. v. 27).

---

1. In regular Greek usage, *mathēteuō* meant intransitively "to be" or "to become" a pupil. In the New Testament, it often takes on a transitive sense, "to make disciples." For discussion, see Wilkins, *Concept of Discipleship*, 160–62.

2. Gnilka, *Das Matthäusevangelium*, 507–8; Davies and Allison, *Matthew 19–28*, 682–83.

In the Gospel, Israel, rather than being liberated by the Son of Man from the nations, adopts beast-like characteristics and, in collusion with the fourth beast of Dan 7, betrays and kills the one sent to liberate it. Israel rejects the authority of the Son of Man.[3] Despite this rejection, the resurrected Jesus is given "all authority (*pasa exousia*) in heaven and on earth," an imperial authority which is to be established through the process of making disciples of "all nations" (*panta ta ethnē*, 28:18–19).[4] The goal of the Gospel Commission is to establish the sovereignty of Jesus as Son of Man over *all* the nations. It is to fulfill the hopes of Daniel despite the change in circumstances of Israel. It is deeply nation-focused in nature.

A second cluster of allusions turns the Moses-Joshua conquest-of-Canaan narrative on its head. Scholars have long noted parallels between the commissioning of the eleven disciples in the Gospel Commission and the commissioning of Joshua in the Old Testament. Davies and Allison highlight the parallels in these terms:

> Readers are to exercise their scripturally informed imaginations and set the end of Jesus beside the end of Moses. Just as Moses, at the close of his life, commissioned Joshua both to go into the land peopled by foreign nations and to observe all the commandments in the law, and then further promised his successor God's abiding presence, so similarly Jesus: at the end of his earthly ministry he told his disciples to go into all the world and to teach the observance of all the commandments of the new Moses, and then further promised his assisting presence[5]

These intertextual allusions are most clearly seen when we consider Josh 1:1–9.[6] Yahweh commands Joshua to "rise up and cross the Jordan" and to "observe and act as my servant Moses commanded you" (Josh 1:2, 7). Jesus commands his disciples to "go" and to teach the nations "to obey everything that I have commanded you" (Matt 28:19–20). Yahweh promises Joshua that "I will also be with you, and I will not forsake you or overlook

---

3. Matt 7:29; 9:6, 8; 21:23–24, 27.

4. Scholars question whether "all the nations" includes Israel. For Israel's inclusion, see Gnilka, *Das Matthäusevangelium*, 508; Stanton, *New People*, 158; France, *Gospel of Matthew*, 1114–15. For Israel's exclusion, Hare and Harrington, "Make Disciples," 361–63. Meier believes that while "all the nations" excludes rejected Israel, it includes individual Jews ("Nations or Gentiles," 101–2).

5. Davies and Allison, *Matthew 19–28*, 680.

6. Cf. Deut 31:23. On the relationship between Josh 1:5 and Matt 28:20, see Trilling, *Das wahre Israel*, 40.

you" (Josh 1:5). Jesus promises the eleven disciples that "I will be with you always, to the end of the age (Matt 28:20).

More speculatively, Jesus's command to baptize the nations into the name (*eis to onoma*) of the Father, Son, and Holy Spirit may well be understood within this context as a further conquest allusion, the equivalent of Joshua crossing over the Jordan.[7] Support for such a reading is found in 1 Cor 10:2 in which Paul, possibly drawing on earlier Christian traditions, allegorizes Israel's crossing of the Red Sea as a baptism "into Moses" (*eis ton Mōusēn*).[8] Jesus may well be suggesting a similar association, relating baptism into the name of the Father, Son, and Holy Spirit with the crossing of the Red Sea and the subsequent crossing of the Jordan. If this is the case, then the allusions in the Gospel Commission to the conquest of Canaan may be summarized thus:

Conquest of Canaan	Conquest of the Nations
Command to cross over the Jordan	"baptizing them in the name of the Father and of the Son and of the Holy Spirit"
The need to act in accordance with the law when they enter Canaan	"teaching them to obey everything that I have commanded you"
Yahweh's promise to always be with Joshua as he enters Canaan	"And remember, I am with you always, to the end of the age"

Those that entered the land of Canaan, excluding Joshua and Caleb, were a new generation that succeeded the evil generation of the exodus (Deut 1:35). In the Gospel, Israel is characterized as an evil and adulterous generation (e.g., Matt 12:39, 45; 16:4). It is only those who become like children, part of a new generation (18:3), who are to represent Jesus to the nations. This new and faithful generation are not to attempt a reconquest of Israel. Instead, they are to depart from the defiled land of Israel and are to enter the territories of the nations, which now function as the geographical equivalent of Joshua's land of Canaan.

We may conclude, based upon these extensive parallels, that the Gospel Commission anticipates a mission to the nations that extends the imagery of Israel's original conquest of Canaan. The crucial difference is, however, that instead of a law-abiding faithful generation driving out

---

7. Waetjen (*Matthew's Theology*, 293–94) unnecessarily rejects the Trinitarian formula as original.

8. Conzelmann, *1 Corinthians*, 165–66.

before them the wicked inhabitants from the land of Canaan, Jesus desires that a faithful remnant of Israel encourage the nations to accept him as sovereign and to become law-observant members of his kingdom, all the while retaining tenure of their own land.

I have chartered in previous chapters a process whereby several idealized roles combine to transform the nation and prepare it for the kingship of Jesus. The prophet invites a distant nation into a closer relationship with God and warns of the consequences of a failure to accept the invitation. The righteous person focalizes the nation's response. The extension of hospitality to righteous persons by the nation results in a deferral of judgment. In contrast, the shedding of the innocent blood of the righteous hastens judgment. The student-teacher draws the nation into a closer relationship with Jesus through an intensely personal process of internalization of word and imitation of deed. Education guards against nominalism. Wise men function as leaders of the nation, guided by the "mysteries of the kingdom of heaven" and protecting it from the most serious of threats, idolatry. Law-observant scribes ensure that the most important values of the covenant guide how the nation operates. Through these means, God's kingdom is established.

Space considerations mean that this reconstruction has necessarily underplayed the considerable first-century overlap in responsibilities and characteristics that existed between these different roles. For example, both wise men and righteous persons, as well as teachers, were known for teaching. The Evangelist himself describes the prophets, wise men, and scribes of Matt 23:34–35 as all being righteous. This qualification does not, however, invalidate the basic process set out.

The Status of Israel and the Identity of the *Ecclēsia*

The scenario I have painted raises questions as to the continuing status of Israel and the identity of the *ecclēsia*. First, a word on the status of Israel. Replacement or supersessionist theories developed by Christian writers such as Barnabas and Justin Martyr in the second century CE propose that Israel as a nation has been rejected in favor of the gentiles. The gentile church has replaced Israel as God's people. Most contemporary Matthean scholars have, in some way or other, reacted against such theories. The most convincing alternative to supersessionist theories is the proposal that while Israel as a nation has not been rejected, its leadership has been judged and replaced by the followers of Jesus.[9] There is a shift in the leadership of Israel from one group of Jews to another group of Jews.[10] In this reading, the Jerusalem-based shepherds of Israel are to be distinguished from the Jewish crowds, many of whom respond positively to Jesus and his disciples. They are part of a faithful remnant of Israel who accept the authority of the Son of Man.[11]

Support for this position is found in the parable of the wicked tenants (Matt 21:33–46).[12] The vineyard, a metaphor for Israel (cf. Ps 80:8–17; Isa 5:1–4), remains the property of the landowner even though he decides to replace the tenants due to their appalling treatment of his servants and his Son (Matt 21:1–46). The Evangelist concludes the parable with the observation that the chief priests and the Pharisees realized that the parable was about them (21:45; cf. "elders of the people" in 21:23). They are the object of the landowner's judgment. While the tenants are to be replaced, the vineyard nevertheless remains the property of the landowner. He does not sell it, nor does he purchase an alternative plot. The problem is not, as observed by Matthias Konradt, that "the vineyard produces bad grapes but rather that the tenants do not deliver the fruit."[13] The prophetic certainty of the impending judgment of Israel's leaders conveyed in the parable is later tempered in 23:34–35 with the slimmest of hopes that they may yet respond to one final appeal delivered by those prophets, wise men, and scribes sent by the resurrected Jesus. The possibility is at least implied that Israel's leadership may yet heed Jesus's warning and refrain from persecuting those he will send them. Nevertheless, the Evangelist expects that the leaders will act according to type and fill up the measure of their ancestors (23:32).

The parable of the wicked tenants raises the question as to whom the tenancy of the vineyard will be given? The text states that it will be given to another *ethnē* (Matt 21:43). But who is this *ethnē*?[14] The parable implies that

9. Saldarini, *Matthew's Christian-Jewish Community*, 200–201; Konradt, *Israel*, 1–15, 236; Runesson, *Divine Wrath*, 207–325. Cf. For alternative positions, see Hooker, *Son of Man*, 44; Levine, *Social and Ethnic Dimensions*, 168–69.

10. This reflects Kampen's view of the Jesus movement as being *within* sectarian Judaism (*Matthew*, 193, 199–202).

11. Some scholars suggest a shift from Israel as an ethnic entity to a religious entity defined by its beliefs. Meyer, *Aims of Jesus*, 221–23; Sim, "Attitudes to Gentiles."

12. I am in broad agreement with Konradt, *Israel*, 172–93.

13. Konradt, *Israel*, 176.

14. Much discussion has focused on the difference between *ethnē* and *laos*. Here I purposefully avoid this discussion and instead appeal to the narrative of the Gospel to determine the identity of the "people" envisaged by Jesus.

it will be those that "respect" (*entrepō*) the son of the landowner (21:37). Elsewhere in the Gospel, these are the Twelve who receive authority from Jesus and who are given the keys of the kingdom and the right to bind and loose (10:1; 16:19; 18:18). From God's perspective, they are the new leaders of Israel, an Israel whose circumstances have dramatically changed.[15] The disciples are now able, by faith, to command that "this mountain," an allusion to the temple and its authorities, "be lifted up and thrown into the sea" (21:21). Their mission does not depend upon the temple. Neither does it depend upon the fortunes of Jerusalem. They are to be willing to flee from the holy city rather than defend it when attacked (24:16). The Gospel presents a decoupling of faithful Israel from Jerusalem and the temple.

While the Evangelist affirms in Matt 23:34–35 an ongoing mission to that part of Israel that rejects the sovereignty of its king, and this includes both hostile sheep and shepherds, faithful Israel is now a movement on the move, spreading out among the nations. The land of Judea is defiled and so the righteous need to flee. But in fleeing from the land, faithful Israel, represented by the disciples and the crowds that followed Jesus out of the cities, becomes the means by which the nations may be saved. This is not the end of Israel, but rather the fulfillment of its commission, that through it, the nations will either be blessed or cursed (cf. Gen 12:3).

In this context, we should not interpret Gospel references to the *ekklēsia* as denoting a gentile Christian church separate from Israel (Matt 16:18; 18:15, 17, 21).[16] Rather, the *ekklēsia* represents that part of Israel that accepts the sovereignty of Jesus, paralleled in the Old Testament by the *ekklēsia* of Israel that accepted the sovereignty of Yahweh rather than that of other gods. While such an *ekklēsia* does not require adherence to the traditions of the elders, it is a deeply prophetic Sabbath-keeping and law-observant body. It honors righteousness. It is faithful Israel called to exert, in conjunction with the Son of Man, dominion over the nations.

In contrast, the fate of unfaithful Israel is to become subject to the dominion of those powers with whom it colluded to kill the Son of Man. These very same powers will attack Jerusalem and desolate the temple (24:15). As in the Old Testament, God will use the nations after which Israel lusted as tools of divine judgment. Its adulterous lovers will turn upon it, and, in the stark imagery of Ezekiel, strip it naked, stone it, and cut it into pieces with

---

15. Konradt, *Israel*, 191.

16. In certain instances the term *ekklēsia* was used to refer to Jewish synagogues. Runesson, *Divine Wrath*, 11.

their swords (cf. Ezek 16:35–43). The Evangelist does not address the long-term post-judgment status of that part of Israel that might continue to resist the sovereignty of its king. This is less likely an oversight and more likely a ploy on his part to leave the status of this part of Israel ambiguous to allow for a future change of heart.

The Mission to the Nations

We have intimations throughout the Gospel of the nature of the mission to the nations.[17] The missions to Galilee and to Jerusalem involved a multi-pronged attempt aimed at bringing an evil and adulterous generation to repentance. In both missions, we are presented with an idealized description of followers of Jesus. In Matt 10:41–42, it includes prophets, righteous persons, and student-teachers. In 23:34, it includes prophets, wise men, and scribes. These missions failed, however, to bring Israel to repentance.

Contrasting this failure of the mission to Galilee with the positive response of gentiles, we are told that the cities of Tyre, Sidon (11:21–22), and Sodom (11:23–24), would have repented in response to such a climatic appeal.[18] Nineveh, the embodiment of moral evil and cruelty in the Old Testament, is lauded for responding to the appeal of a prophet—and an unwilling prophet at that (12:41). The queen of the South is praised for responding to Solomon's wisdom (12:42).[19] These positive examples of gentiles who respond to restricted missional initiatives are further reinforced during the mission to Galilee through representative foreigners responding positively to the ministry of Jesus. Jesus commends a centurion in Capernaum for demonstrating a degree of faith unfounded elsewhere in Israel (8:5–13).[20] A Canaanite woman from the district of Tyre and Sidon demands mercy from Jesus despite never having heard him preach or seen him act (15:21–28).[21]

In contrast, representatives of the nations are portrayed less favorably during the mission to Jerusalem.[22] Jesus implicates them in his impend-

17. Meier, *Law and History*, 28.

18. Tyre was known in the Hebrew Scriptures, like Sidon, for its wealth and hubris and, paradoxically, like Jerusalem, as a God-fearing city. Guillaume, "Dislocating Jerusalem's Memory," 257–66.

19. Lövestam, *Jesus*, 26–37.

20. Wilson, *Healing*, 51–64.

21. Levine, *Social and Ethnic Dimensions*, 131–64; Duling, *Marginal Scribe*, 40–41.

22. General statements about the gentiles tend to be negative (e.g., Matt 5:7; 6:7, 32;

ing death when he predicts that the Jerusalem authorities will "hand him over to the gentiles (*tois ethnesin*) to be mocked and flogged and crucified" (20:19). The disciples will likewise be put to death and "hated by all nations" (*hypo pantōn tōn ethnōn*, 24:9). Many false prophets will arise and there will be an increase in lawlessness (24:11–12). Nevertheless, the followers of Jesus are to proclaim the gospel of the kingdom throughout the world as a testimony to all the nations, even though it will result in persecution (24:9, 14). Evidence is provided to the reader of the veracity of these dark predictions when Pilate, despite his protestations of innocence, participates in the shedding of innocent blood (27:19, 24–26). Nevertheless, the centurion and those with him charged with keeping watch over the crucified Jesus, see the earthquake and "what took place," and in terror confess Jesus to be God's Son (27:54).

This mixed characterization of the gentiles indicates that the nations have not yet achieved the perilous state of Galilee and Jerusalem. They are in a state of flux. They have not yet achieved the status of an "evil and adulterous generation" and may well yet respond to prophetic appeals to repent, the presence of righteous persons and teachers within the nation, and the leadership of wise men and scribes.

Motivating Readers for Mission

The Evangelist has written his Gospel in such a way as to encourage his readers to participate in mission. First, mission involves multiple discipleship roles. The educator is affirmed as being of equal importance to the prophet. The presence of the righteous person complements that of the scribe and the wise man. If the reader does not readily identify with any of these roles, a composite identity may be constructed drawing on a selection of disciple-related motifs within the Gospel. The history of interpretation testifies to the popularity of this approach. In distinguishing between various discipleship roles, the Evangelist has relieved the reader of the burden of fulfilling all the tasks involved in the mission to the nations. Responsibility for the mission does not rest on any one pair of shoulders. It is a communal venture.

Secondly, the Gospel presents a broad range of missional scenarios. It models mission to the village, town, city, and nation. It models mission to different levels of society, to the sheep and to the shepherds. It models

18:17; 20:25). Sim goes too far, however, in suggesting that this reveals an anti-gentile attitude (*Apocalyptic Eschatology*, 198–209).

entering a community, remaining there when accepted, and withdrawing when rejected. It models different psychological stances toward the community, whether it be the more distant and critical mindset of the prophet, to the more intimate mindset of the educator and the protective mindset of the wise man. It models mission undertaken by the literate and the illiterate, the educated and the uneducated. It models mission independent of monetary resources. In presenting such a diverse range of missional scenarios, the Evangelist reduces the ability of the reader to claim that the Gospel does not address his or her situation in some way.

Thirdly, the Evangelist assigns great theological significance to the various reactions of the nations to this mission. On the positive side, I have argued that the Evangelist holds out the possibility that the judgment of the nations may be deferred through a process of national transformation. Prophets diagnose the problem and warn the nation of the consequences of rejecting divine sovereignty. Righteous persons function as the salt of the earth. Their presence matters. When the nation extends hospitality to them, the nation itself is counted as righteous and preserved from judgment. When the nation ignores the needs of the righteous, future judgment will be more severe. Persecution of the righteous results in a hastening of judgment. Teachers guard against nominal allegiance by inviting the wider population into an intensive and intimate process of imitation. Wise men guide the nation, aware of their sovereign's plans for the future. Finally, scribes ensure that the public and legal culture of the nation is grounded upon a covenant relationship with their king as expressed in the weightier matters of justice, mercy, and faith. They seek to integrate divine legal principles within existing legal systems and among the general populace. Acceptance of this initiative leads to national transformation as the sovereignty of King Jesus is established over the nation.

This transformation process reflects the Old Testament in which Yahweh sent prophets and other representatives to Israel in order to bring the nation back to himself. When Israel responded positively, judgment was deferred. Similarly, when the nations accept the sovereignty of King Jesus, there is a deferral of judgment, a delay of the *parousia*.

This vision of national transformation extends beyond a narrow preoccupation with the salvation of individuals and instead provides us with a rich picture of what a restored nation might look like. It is a vision in which individuals are saved *within* rather than *from* their national contexts. It involves the whole of the nation accepting the sovereignty of Jesus and challenges those political theologies which focus on withdrawal from society or the separation of church and state. Such political theologies leave large parts of the nation outside the sovereignty of King Jesus. The Evangelist's vision is for the whole of the nation to accept divine sovereignty and this is reflected in the broad range of discipleship roles and missional scenarios he presents. Both home and palace, village and council, are to be encouraged to accept the sovereignty of their king.

This positive and optimistic portrayal of the nations' future is counterbalanced by a more sombre message. The nations are in a state of idolatrous lawlessness and are already under divine judgment. The Gospel warns that they are highly likely to respond to the disciples in the same way as the leaders of Israel responded to Jesus. They will reject their appeals to repent and instead will persecute them and shed their innocent blood. God will not, however, allow this to go unpunished. Justice will be restored when the Son of Man treats the nations in the same way they have treated his envoys. Those who have extended mercy to his followers will receive mercy. Those who rejected them will be rejected.

The factor that precipitates the *parousia*, if we take Jesus's mission to Jerusalem as the template for the mission to the nations, is the shedding of innocent blood. Over the generations, this blood pollutes the land to the extent that it becomes uninhabitable. Innocent blood cries out for justice. Only judgment can restore the land to an inhabitable state. We may infer from the multifaceted mission of Jesus to Israel that prior to the final judgment, God will send a host of different envoys reflecting the discipleship roles we have discussed, a climax of revelation, a testimony to the nations, a loud cry, in an attempt to turn a generation that reflects the generation of the flood away from their lawless ways. God responds to the cry of innocent blood with his own loud cry to the nations, a final and desperate appeal for them to change. When this initiative is rejected and more blood is shed, judgment becomes the only means by which divine sovereignty may be established.

The Evangelist does not anticipate a distant time in the future when Jesus will call his followers to participate in this mission. Instead, the call is always in the present, made any time someone reads his Gospel and feels the conviction that they should participate in this mission. In this sense, there is always the possibility that a community of readers will read the Gospel and together feel convicted to embody all the discipleship roles I have described. When a community responds in this manner, they become a climax of revelation, a condemning testimony, a threat to those among the nations who would resist the sovereignty of King Jesus. Those who resist will likely respond with hostility. This hostility precipitates judgment.

In this sense, hastening the *parousia* requires two conditions, a community of followers who share the vision of the Evangelist, and nations which respond with ultimate cruelty and violence. When these two conditions align, God is justified in judging the nations. When only the first condition is fulfilled, the final judgment will be more severe, but nevertheless may not be precipitated. This theology enables the followers of Jesus to contribute to the timing of the *parousia* but not to control it. They too must accept the sovereignty of the one who ultimately decides when it will occur. They too must respect the will of their Father in heaven.

Bibliography

Allen, Willoughby C. *A Critical and Exegetical Commentary on the Gospel according to Matthew*. 3rd ed. Edinburgh: T. & T. Clark, 1912.

Allison, Dale C. *The New Moses: A Matthean Typology*. Minneapolis: Fortress, 1993.

———. *The Sermon on the Mount: Inspiring the Moral Imagination*. New York: Crossroad, 1999.

———. *Studies in Matthew: Interpretation Past and Present*. Grand Rapids: Baker Academic, 2005.

———. "Was There a 'Lukan Community'?" *IBS* 10 (1988) 62–70.

Anderson, Janice Capel. *Matthew's Narrative Web: Over, and Over, and Over Again*. JSNTSup 91. Sheffield, UK: JSOT Press, 1994.

Bagnall, Roger S. *Everyday Writing in the Graeco-Roman East*. Berkley: University of California Press, 2011.

Barrow, Robin. *Greek and Roman Education*. London: Bristol Classics, 1996.

Barth, Gerhard. "Matthew's Understanding of the Law." In *Tradition and Interpretation in Matthew*, edited by Günther Bornkamm et al., 58–164. London: SCM, 1982.

Barton, Stephen C. "Can We Identify the Gospel Audiences?" In *The Gospels for All Christians: Rethinking the Gospel Audiences*, edited by Richard Bauckham, 173–94. Edinburgh: T. & T. Clark, 1998.

Bauckham, Richard. "For Whom Were Gospels Written?" In *The Gospels for All Christians: Rethinking the Gospel Audiences*, edited by Richard Bauckham, 9–48. Edinburgh: T. & T. Clark, 1998.

Bauer, David R. *The Structure of Matthew's Gospel*. Sheffield, UK: Sheffield Academic, 1988.

Beale, Gregory K. "Isaiah 6:9–13: A Retributive Taunt against Idolatry." *VT* 41 (1991) 257–78.

———. *We Become What We Worship: A Biblical Theology of Idolatry*. Downers Grove: IVP Academic, 2008.

Beare, Francis Wright. *The Gospel according to Matthew: A Commentary*. Oxford: Blackwell, 1981.

Behm, Johannes, and Ernst Würthwein. "Μετανοέω." In *TDNT* 4:975–1009.

Bibliography

Blank, Sheldon H. "The Death of Zechariah in Rabbinic Literature." *Hebrew Union College Annual* 12–13 (1937) 327–46.

Bonnard, Pierre. *L' Évangile Selon Saint Matthieu.* Neuchatel, Switzerland: Delachaux & Niestlé, 1963.

Borg, Marcus J. *Meeting Jesus Again for the First Time: The Historical Jesus & the Heart of Contemporary Faith.* New York: HarperCollins, 1994.

Bornkamm, Günther. "The Authority to 'Bind' and 'Loose' in the Church in Matthew's Gospel." In *The Interpretation of Matthew,* edited by Graham N. Stanton, 85–97. Philadelphia: Fortress, 1983.

———. *Der Lohngedanke im Neuen Testament.* Göttingen: Vandenhoeck & Ruprecht, 1961.

Boxall, Ian. *Discovering Matthew: Content, Interpretation, Reception.* Grand Rapids: Eerdmans, 2015.

Bultmann, Rudolf. *The Theology of the New Testament.* Vol. 1. London: SCM, 1952.

Bultmann, Rudolf, and Artur Weiser. "Πιστεύω, πίστις, πιστός [. . .]." In *TDNT* 6:174–229.

Burnett, Fred W. *The Testament of Jesus-Sophia: A Redactional-Critical Study of the Eschatological Discourse in Matthew.* Washington, DC: University Press of America, 1981.

Burridge, Richard A. *What Are the Gospels? A Comparison with Graeco-Roman Biography.* 2nd ed. Grand Rapids: Eerdmans, 2004.

Byrskog, Samuel. *Jesus the Only Teacher: Didactic Authority and Transmission in Ancient Israel, Ancient Judaism, and the Matthean Community.* Coniectanea Biblica New Testament 24. Stockholm: Almqvist & Wiksell, 1994.

Cargal, Timothy B. "'His Blood Be upon Us and upon Our Children': A Matthean Double Entendre?" *NTS* 37 (1991) 101–12.

Carr, David M. *Writing on the Tablet of the Heart: Origins of Scripture and Literature.* Oxford: Oxford University Press, 2005.

Carter, Warren. "Evoking Isaiah: Matthean Soteriology and an Intertextual Reading of Isaiah 7–9 and Matthew 1:23 and 4:15–16." *JBL* 119 (2000) 503–20.

———. *Matthew and the Margins: A Sociopolitical and Religious Reading.* Maryknoll: Orbis, 2000.

Carter, Warren, and John P. Heil. *Matthew's Parables: Audience-Oriented Perspectives.* CBQMS 30. Washington, DC: Catholic Biblical Association of America, 1998.

Charette, Blaine. *The Theme of Recompense in Matthew's Gospel.* JSNTSup 79. Sheffield, UK: JSOT, 1992.

Collins, R. F. "Matthew's ἐντολαί: Towards an Understanding of the Commandments in the First Gospel." In *The Four Gospels 1992: Festschrift Frans Neirynck,* edited by F. Van Segbroeck et al., 1325–48. Leuven: Leuven University Press, 1992.

Conzelmann, Hans. *1 Corinthians: A Commentary on the First Epistle to the Corinthians.* Hermeneia 67. Philadelphia: Fortress, 1975.

Cope, O. Lamar. *Matthew: A Scribe Trained for the Kingdom of Heaven.* Washington, DC: Catholic Biblical Association of America, 1976.

Cousland, J. R. C. "The Feeding of the Four Thousand Gentiles in Matthew? Matthew 15:29–39 as a Test Case." *NovT* 41 (1999) 1–23.

Crossan, John Dominic. *Jesus: A Revolutionary Biography.* New York: HarperCollins, 1994.

Davies, William D. *The Setting of the Sermon on the Mount.* Brown Judaic Studies 186. Atlanta: Scholars, 1989.

Davies, William D., and Dale C. Allison. *A Critical and Exegetical Commentary on the Gospel according to Saint Matthew: Commentary Matthew 1–7*. Edinburgh: T. & T. Clark, 1988.

———. *A Critical and Exegetical Commentary on the Gospel according to Saint Matthew: Commentary on Matthew 8–18*. Edinburgh: T. & T. Clark, 1991.

———. *A Critical and Exegetical Commentary on the Gospel according to Saint Matthew: Commentary on Matthew 19–28*. Edinburgh: T. & T. Clark, 1997.

Deines, Roland. "Not the Law but the Messiah: Law and Righteousness in the Gospel of Matthew—an Ongoing Debate." In *Built upon the Rock*, edited by Daniel M. Gurtner and John Nolland, 53–84. Grand Rapids: Eerdmans, 2008.

Deutsch, Celia. *Hidden Wisdom and the Easy Yolk: Wisdom, Torah and Discipleship in Matthew 11:25–30*. JSNTSup 18. Sheffield, UK: JSOT Press, 1987.

———. *Lady Wisdom, Jesus, and the Sages: Metaphor and Social Context in Matthew's Gospel*. Valley Forge, PA: Trinity Press International, 1996.

Downs, David J. *Alms: Charity, Reward, and Atonement in Early Christianity*. Waco, TX: Baylor University Press, 2016.

Drazin, Nathan. *History Of Jewish Education from 515 BCE to 220 CE (During the Periods of the Second Commonwealth and the Tannaim)*. Baltimore: Johns Hopkins University Press, 1940.

Duling, Dennis C. *A Marginal Scribe: Studies in the Gospel of Matthew in a Social-Scientific Perspective*. Eugene, OR: Cascade, 2012.

———. "Matthew as Marginal Scribe in an Advanced Agrarian Society." *Hervormde Teologiese Studies* 58 (2002) 520–75.

———. "Testament of Solomon." In *The Old Testament Pseudepigrapha: Apocalyptic Literature and Testaments*, edited by James H. Charlesworth, 935–59. New York: Doubleday, 1983.

Eco, Umberto. *The Role of the Reader: Explorations in the Semiotics of Texts*. Bloomington: Indiana University Press, 1979.

Edwards, Richard A. *Matthew's Narrative Portrait of Disciples: How the Text-Connoted Reader Is Informed*. Harrisburg, PA: Trinity Press International, 1997.

Elliott, Mark Adam. *The Survivors of Israel: A Reconsideration of the Theology of Pre-Christian Judaism*. Grand Rapids: Eerdmans, 2000.

Eubank, Nathan Paul. *Wages of Cross-Bearing and Debt of Sin: The Economy of Heaven in Matthew's Gospel*. BZNW 196. Berlin: de Gruyter, 2013.

———. "What Does Matthew Say about Divine Recompense? On the Misuse of the Parable of the Workers in the Vineyard (20.1–16)." *JSNT* 35 (2013) 242–62.

Evans, Craig A. "Jesus and the Continuing Exile of Israel." In *Jesus and the Restoration of Israel: A Critical Assessment of N. T. Wright's Jesus and the Victory of God*, edited by Carey C. Newman, 77–100. Waco, TX: Baylor University Press, 2018.

Eve, Eric. *The Jewish Context of Jesus' Miracles*. JSNTSup 231. Sheffield, UK: Sheffield Academic, 2002.

Finlan, Stephen. *Sacrifice and Atonement: Psychological Motives and Biblical Patterns*. Minneapolis: Fortress, 2016.

Foley, John M. *Immanent Art: From Structure to Meaning in Traditional Oral Epic*. Bloomington: Indiana University Press, 1991.

Foster, Paul. *Community, Law and Mission in Matthew's Gospel*. WUNT 2/177. Tübingen: Mohr Siebeck, 2004.

France, R. T. *The Gospel of Matthew*. NICNT. Grand Rapids: Eerdmans, 2007.

Bibliography

Freyne, Sean. "The Disciples in Mark and the Maskilim in Daniel." *JSNT* 16 (1983) 7–23.

Gallagher, Sarita D. "Blessing on the Move: The Outpouring of God's Blessing through the Migrant Abraham." *Mission Studies* 30 (2013) 147–61.

Gamble, Harry Y. *Books and Readers in the Early Church: A History of Early Christian Texts*. New Haven: Yale University Press, 1995.

Garrison, Roman. *Redemptive Almsgiving in Early Christianity*. JSNTSup 77. Sheffield, UK: JSOT Press, 1993.

Gärtner, Judith. "'Keep Justice!' (Isaiah 56:1): Thoughts regarding the Concept and Redaction History of a Universal Understanding of Ṣedaqa." In *Ṣedaqa and Torah in Postexilic Discourse*, edited by Susanne Gillmayr-Bucher and Maria Häusl, 86–99. London: Bloomsbury T. & T. Clark, 2017.

Gench, Frances Taylor. *Wisdom in the Christology of Matthew*. Lanham, MD: University Press of America, 1997.

Gerhardsson, Birger. *Memory and Manuscript: Oral Tradition and Written Transmission in Rabbinic Judaism and Early Christianity; with, Tradition and Transmission in Early Christianity*. Grand Rapids: Eerdmans, 1998.

———. *The Mighty Acts of Jesus according to Matthew*. Eugene, OR: Wipf & Stock, 2016.

———. "The Secret of the Transmission of the Unwritten Jesus Tradition." *NTS* 51 (2005) 1–18.

Gnilka, Joachim. *Das Matthäusevangelium*. Vol. 1. Freiburg: Herder, 1986.

———. *Das Matthäusevangelium*. Vol. 2. Freiburg: Herder, 1988.

Goodman, Martin. *Mission and Conversion: Proselytizing in the Religious History of the Roman Empire*. Oxford: Clarendon, 1994.

Goulder, Michael D. *Midrash and Lection in Matthew*. Eugene, OR: Wipf & Stock, 2004.

Gray, Sherman W. *The Least of My Brothers: Matthew 25:31–46; A History of Interpretation*. SBL Dissertation Series 114. Atlanta: Scholars, 1989.

Grundmann, Walter. "Δύναμαι/δύναμις." In *TDNT* 2:284–317.

Guillaume, Philippe. "Dislocating Jerusalem's Memory with Tyre." In *Memory and the City in Ancient Israel*, edited by Diana V. Edelman and Ehud Ben Zvi, 257–66. Winona Lake, IN: Eisenbrauns, 2014.

Gundry, Robert H. *Matthew: A Commentary on His Literary and Theological Art*. Grand Rapids: Eerdmans, 1982.

Haber, Susan. *"They Shall Purify Themselves": Essays on Purity in Early Judaism*. Early Judaism and Its Literature 24. Atlanta: SBL, 2008.

Hagner, Donald A. *Matthew 14–28*. WBC 33B. Dallas: Word, 1995.

Hamilton, Catherine Sider. "Blood and Secrets: The Re-telling of Genesis 1–6 in *1 Enoch* 6–11 and Its Echoes in Susanna and the Gospel of Matthew." In *"What Does the Scripture Say?": Studies in the Function of Scripture in Early Judaism and Christianity; The Synoptic Gospels*, edited by Craig A. Evans and H. Daniel Zacharias, 90–141. LNTS 469. London: Bloomsbury T. & T. Clark, 2013.

———. *The Death of Jesus in Matthew: Innocent Blood and the End of Exile*. SNTSMS 167. Cambridge: Cambridge University Press, 2017.

———. "'His Blood Be upon Us': Innocent Blood and the Death of Jesus in Matthew." *CBQ* 70 (2008) 82–100.

Hannan, Margaret Ann. *The Nature and Demands of the Sovereign Rule of God in the Gospel of Matthew*. LNTS 308. London: T. & T. Clark, 2006.

Hare, Douglas R. A., and Daniel J. Harrington. "Make Disciples of All the Gentiles (Mt 28:19)." *CBQ* 37 (1975) 359–69.

Harrington, Daniel J. *The Gospel of Matthew*. Collegeville, PA: Liturgical, 1991.

Harris, William V. *Ancient Literacy*. Cambridge: Harvard University Press, 1989.

Hauge, Matthew Ryan. "Fabulous Parables: The Storytelling Tradition in the Synoptic Gospels." In *Ancient Education in Early Christianity*, edited by Matthew Ryan Hauge and Andrew W. Pitts, 89–106. LNTS 533. London: Bloomsbury T. & T. Clark, 2017.

Hays, Richard B. *Echoes of Scripture in the Gospels*. Waco, TX: Baylor University Press, 2016.

———. *Echoes of Scripture in the Letters of Paul*. New Haven: Yale University Press, 1989.

Heaton, Eric William. *The School Tradition of the Old Testament: The Bampton Lectures for 1994*. Oxford: Oxford University Press, 1994.

Heil, John Paul. "The Blood of Jesus in Matthew: A Narrative-Critical Perspective." *Perspectives in Religious Studies* 18 (1991) 117–24.

———. *The Death and Resurrection of Jesus: A Narrative-Critical Reading of Matthew 26–28*. Minneapolis: Fortress, 1991.

———. "The Double Meaning of the Narrative of Universal Judgment in Matthew 25.31–46." *JSNT* 20 (1998) 3–14.

Heinz, Joachim Held. "Matthew as Interpreter of the Miracle Stories." In *Tradition and Interpretation in Matthew*, edited by G. Bornkamm et al., 165–299. London: SCM, 1982.

Herzer, Jens. "The Riddle of the Holy Ones in Matthew 27:51b–53: A New Proposal for a *Crux Interpretum*." In *"What Does the Scripture Say?": Studies in the Function of Scripture in Early Judaism and Christianity: The Synoptic Gospels*, edited by Craig A. Evans and H. Daniel Zacharias, 142–57. London: Bloomsbury T. & T. Clark, 2013.

Hezser, Catherine. *Jewish Literacy in Roman Palestine*. Tübingen: Mohr Siebeck, 2001.

———. "The Torah versus Homer: Jewish and Greco-Roman Education in Late Roman Palestine." In *Ancient Education and Early Christianity*, edited by Matthew Ryan Hauge and Andrew W. Pitts, 5–24. LNTS 533. London: Bloomsbury T. & T. Clark, 2016.

Hiers, Richard H. "'Binding' and 'Loosing': The Matthean Authorizations." *JBL* 104 (1985) 233–50.

Hill, David. *The Gospel of Matthew*. NCB. London: Oliphants, 1972.

Hilton, Allen R. *Illiterate Apostles: Uneducated Early Christians and the Literates Who Loved Them*. LNTS 5431. London: T. & T. Clark, 2018.

Holmberg, Bengt. *Sociology and the New Testament: An Appraisal*. Minneapolis: Fortress, 1990.

Hooker, Morna D. "Beginnings and Endings." In *The Written Gospel*, edited by Markus N. A. Bockmuehl and Donald A. Hagner, 184–202. Cambridge: Cambridge University Press, 2005.

———. *The Son of Man in Mark: A Study of the Background of the Term "Son of Man" and Its Use in St Mark's Gospel*. London: SPCK, 1967.

Howell, David B. *Matthew's Inclusive Story: A Study in the Narrative Rhetoric of the First Gospel*. JSNTSup 42. Sheffield, UK: Sheffield Academic, 1990.

Hurtado, Larry W. *Destroyer of the Gods: Early Christian Distinctiveness in the Roman World*. Waco, TX: Baylor University Press, 2016.

Iser, Wolfgang. *The Implied Reader: Patterns of Communication in Prose Fiction from Bunyan to Beckett*. Baltimore: Johns Hopkins University Press, 1974.

Jaffee, Martin S. *Torah in the Mouth: Writing and Oral Tradition in Palestinian Judaism 200 BCE–400 CE*. Oxford: Oxford University Press, 2001.

Bibliography

Jeremias, Joachim. *Jesus' Promise to the Nations.* Philadelphia: Fortress, 1982.

Jousse, Marcel. *Memory, Memorization, and Memorizers: The Galilean Oral-Style Tradition and Its Traditionists.* Eugene, OR: Cascade, 2018.

Joyal, Mark, et al. *Greek and Roman Education: A Sourcebook.* New York: Routledge, 2009.

Kampen, John. *Matthew within Sectarian Judaism.* AYBRL. New Haven: Yale University Press, 2019.

Kazen, Thomas. *Jesus and Purity Halakhah: Was Jesus Indifferent to Impurity?* Winona Lake, IN: Eisenbrauns, 2010.

Keener, Craig S. *The Gospel of Matthew: A Socio-Rhetorical Commentary.* Grand Rapids: Eerdmans, 2009.

Keith, Chris. *Jesus Against the Scribal Elite: The Origins of the Conflict.* Grand Rapids: Baker Academic, 2014.

———. *Jesus' Literacy: Scribal Culture and the Teacher from Galilee.* LNTS 413. London: T. & T. Clark, 2011.

———. *The Pericope Adulterae, the Gospel of John, and the Literacy of Jesus.* Leiden: Brill, 2009.

Kingsbury, Jack Dean. "The Plot of Matthew's Story." *Int* 46 (1992) 347–56.

———. "The Verb *Akolouthein* ('To Follow') as an Index of Matthew's View of His Community." *JBL* 97 (1978) 56–73.

Kinney, Robert K. *Hellenistic Dimensions of the Gospel of Matthew: Background and Rhetoric.* WUNT 2/414. Tübingen: Mohr Siebeck, 2016.

Kirwan, Michael. *Political Theology: An Introduction.* Minneapolis: Fortress, 2009.

Klawans, Jonathan. "Idolatry, Incest, and Impurity: Moral Defilement in Ancient Judaism." *Journal for the Study of Judaism in the Persian, Hellenistic and Roman Period* 29 (1998) 391–415.

———. *Impurity and Sin in Ancient Judaism.* Oxford: Oxford University Press, 2000.

———. *Purity, Sacrifice, and the Temple: Symbolism and Supersessionism in the Study of Ancient Judaism.* Oxford: Oxford University Press, 2006.

Klein, Hans. "Das Glaubensverständnis im Matthäusenvangelium." In *Glaube im Neuen Testament: Studien zu Ehren von Hermann Binder anlässlich seines 70 Geburtstags,* edited by Ferdinand Hahn et al., 29–42. Neukirchen-Vluyn: Neukirchener Verlag, 1982.

Klink, Edward W. "Light of the World: Cosmology and the Johannine Literature." In *Cosmology and New Testament Theology,* edited by Jonathan T. Pennington and Sean M. McDonough, 74–89. London: T. & T. Clark, 2008.

Knowles, Michael P. *Jeremiah in Matthew's Gospel: The Rejected-Prophet Motif in Matthean Redaction.* JSNTSup 68. Sheffield, UK: JSOT Press, 1993.

Konradt, Matthias. *Israel, Church, and the Gentiles in the Gospel of Matthew.* Waco, TX: Baylor University Press, 2014.

Kugel, James. "Ancient Israelite Pedagogy and Its Survival in Second Temple Interpretations of Scripture." In *Pedagogy in Ancient Judaism and Early Christianity,* edited by Karina Martin Hogan et al., 15–58. Early Judaism and Its Literature 41. Atlanta: SBL, 2017.

Ladd, George Eldon. *The Presence of the Future; The Eschatology of Biblical Realism.* Grand Rapids: Eerdmans, 1974.

Leim, Joshua E. *Matthew's Theological Grammar: The Father and the Son.* WUNT 2/402. Tübingen: Mohr Siebeck, 2015.

Levine, Amy-Jill. *The Social and Ethnic Dimensions of Matthean Salvation History: Go Nowhere among the Gentiles (Matt 10:5b).* Lewiston, NY: Mellon, 1988.

Levine, Samuel Jay. "Looking beyond the Mercy/Justice Dichotomy: Reflections on the Complementary Roles of Mercy and Justice in Jewish Law and Tradition." *Journal of Catholic Legal Studies* 45 (2006) 455–71.

Loader, William R. G. *Jesus' Attitude to the Law: A Study of the Gospels.* WUNT 2/97. Tübingen: Mohr Siebeck, 1997.

Lohr, C. H. "Oral Techniques in the Gospel of Matthew." *CBQ* 23 (1961) 403–35.

Lövestam, Evald. *Jesus and "This Generation": A New Testament Study.* Coniectanea Biblica New Testament Series 25. Stockholm: Almqvist & Wiksell, 1995.

Luz, Ulrich. "The Disciples in the Gospel according to Matthew." In *The Interpretation of Matthew,* edited by Graham Stanton, 98–128. London/Philadelphia: SPCK/Fortress, 1983. Reprinted in *Studies in Matthew* by Ulrich Luz, 115–42. Grand Rapids: Eerdmans, 2005.

———. "Discipleship: A Matthean Manifesto for a Dynamic Ecclesiology." In *Studies in Matthew,* 143–64. Grand Rapids: Eerdmans, 2005.

———. *Matthew 1–7: A Commentary.* Hermeneia 61A. Minneapolis: Augsburg, 1989.

———. *Matthew 8–20: A Commentary.* Hermeneia 61B. Minneapolis: Fortress, 2001.

———. *Matthew 21–28: A Commentary.* Hermeneia 61C. Minneapolis: Fortress, 2005.

Maccoby, Hyam. *Ritual and Morality: The Ritual Purity System and Its Place in Judaism.* Cambridge: Cambridge University Press, 1999.

Mack, Burton L. "Wisdom, Christology and Law in Matthew's Gospel." *JBL* 90 (1971) 353–55.

Malherbe, Abraham J. *Moral Exhortation; A Greco-Roman Sourcebook.* Philadelphia: Westminster, 1986.

Marcus, Joel. *The Way of the Lord: Christological Exegesis of the Old Testament in the Gospel of Mark.* Louisville: Westminster John Knox, 1992.

Marguerat, Daniel, and Yvan Bourquin. *How to Read Bible Stories: An Introduction to Narrative Criticism.* London: SCM, 1999.

Marguerat, Daniel. *Le Jugement dans l'évangile de Matthieu.* Le Monde de la Bible 6. Geneva: Labor et Fides, 1981.

Mason, Steve. "Pollution and Purification in Josephus's *Judean War.*" In *Purity, Holiness, and Identity in Judaism and Christianity: Essays in Memory of Susan Haber,* edited by Carl S. Ehrlich et al., 181–207. WUNT 305. Tübingen: Mohr Siebeck, 2013.

McArthur, Harvey K., and Robert M. Johnston. *They Also Taught in Parables: Rabbinic Parables for the First Centuries of the Christian Era.* Eugene, OR: Wipf & Stock, 2014.

McKnight, Scot. "Extending Jesus." In *Devotions on the Greek New Testament: 52 Reflections to Inspire and Instruct,* edited by J. Scot Duvall and Verlyn D. Verbrugge, 18–19. Grand Rapids: Zondervan, 2012.

Meier, John P. *Law and History in Matthew's Gospel: A Redactional Study of Mt. 5:17–48.* Rome: Biblical Institute, 1976.

———. "Nations or Gentiles in Matthew 28:19." *CBQ* 39 (1977) 94–102.

Metz, Johannes Baptist. *Theology of the World.* New York: Herder and Herder, 1969.

Meyer, Ben F. *The Aims of Jesus.* London: SCM, 1979.

Milgrom, Jacob. *Leviticus 1–16.* WBC 3. New York: Doubleday, 1991.

Millard, Allan. *Reading and Writing in the Time of Jesus.* Sheffield, UK: Sheffield Academic, 2000.

Milnor, Kristina. *Graffiti and the Literary Landscape in Roman Pompeii.* Oxford: Oxford University Press, 2014.

Mitchell, Margaret M. "New Testament Envoys in the Context of Greco-Roman Diplomatic and Epistolary Conventions: The Example of Timothy and Titus." *JBL* 111 (1992) 641–62.

Moltmann, Jürgen. "Covenant or Leviathan? Political Theology for Modern Times." *Scottish Journal of Theology* 47 (1994) 19–41.

Moo, Douglas J. "Jesus and the Authority of the Mosaic Law." *JSNT* 20 (1984) 3–49.

Newport, Kenneth G. C. *The Sources and Sitz im Leben of Matthew 23*. JSNTSup 117. Sheffield, UK: Sheffield Academic, 1995.

Nolland, John. *The Gospel of Matthew: A Commentary on the Greek Text*. Grand Rapids: Eerdmans, 2005.

O'Donovan, Oliver. *The Desire of the Nations: Rediscovering the Roots of Political Theology*. Cambridge: Cambridge University Press, 1996.

———. *The Ways of Judgment: The Bampton Lectures*. Grand Rapids: Eerdmans, 2005.

Olmstead, Wesley G. "Jesus, the Eschatological Perfection of Torah, and the *Imitatio Dei* in Matthew." In *Torah Ethics and Early Christian Identity*, edited by Susan J. Wendel and David M. Miller, 43–58. Grand Rapids: Eerdmans, 2016.

Orton, David E. *The Understanding Scribe: Matthew and the Apocalyptic Ideal*. Sheffield, UK: Sheffield Academic, 1989.

Overman, J. Andrew. *Matthew's Gospel and Formative Judaism: A Study of the Social World of the Matthean Community*. Minneapolis: Fortress, 1990.

Parker, Robert. *On Greek Religion*. Ithaca, NY: Cornell University Press, 2011.

Pennington, Jonathan T. *Heaven and Earth in the Gospel of Matthew*. Leiden: Brill, 2007.

Piotrowski, Nicholas G. *Matthew's New David at the End of Exile: A Social-Rhetorical Study of Scriptural Quotations*. NovTSup 170. Leiden: Brill, 2016.

Piper, Otto A. "The Mystery of the Kingdom of God: Critical Scholarship and Christian Doctrine." *Interpretation* 1 (1947) 183–200.

Pitts, Andrew W. "The Origins of Greek Mimesis and the Gospel of Mark: Genre as a Potential Constraint in Assessing Markan Imitation." In *Ancient Education in Early Christianity*, edited by Matthew Ryan Hauge and Andrew W. Pitts, 107–36. LNTS 533. London: Bloomsbury T. & T. Clark, 2016.

Powell, Mark Allan. "Binding and Loosing: A Paradigm for Ethical Discernment from the Gospel of Matthew." *Currents in Theology and Mission* 30 (2003) 438–45.

Przybylski, Benno. *Righteousness in Matthew and His World of Thought*. SNTSMS 41. Cambridge: Cambridge University Press, 2004.

Reinhartz, Adele. *Cast Out of the Covenant: Jews and Anti-Judaism in the Gospel of John*. Lanham, MD: Lexington/Fortress, 2018.

Riesner, Rainer. *Jesus als Lehrer: Eine Untersuchung zum Ursprung der Evangelien-Überlieferung*. WUNT 2/7. Tübingen: Mohr (Paul Siebeck), 1981.

Rosner, Brian S. "The Concept of Idolatry." *Themelios* 24 (1999) 17–29.

———. *Greed as Idolatry: The Origin and Meaning of a Pauline Metaphor*. Grand Rapids: Eerdmans, 2007.

Rowland, Christopher. "Scripture." In *The Cambridge Companion to Christian Political Theology*, edited by Craig Hovey and Elizabeth Phillips, 157–75. Cambridge: Cambridge University Press, 2015.

Runesson, Anders. *Divine Wrath and Salvation in Matthew: The Narrative World of the First Gospel*. Minneapolis: Fortress, 2016.

———. *The Origins of the Synagogue: A Socio-Historical Study*. Coniectanea Biblica New Testament Series 37. Stockholm: Almqvist & Wiksell, 2001.

———. "Purity, Holiness, and the Kingdom of Heaven in Matthew's Narrative World." In *Purity, Holiness and Identity in Judaism and Christianity: Essays in Memory of Susan Haber*, edited by Carl S. Ehrlich et al., 144–80. WUNT 305. Tübingen: Mohr Siebeck, 2013.

Ryan, Jordan J. *The Role of the Synagogue in the Aims of Jesus*. Minneapolis: Fortress, 2017.

Saldarini, Anthony J. *Matthew's Christian-Jewish Community*. Chicago: University of Chicago Press, 1994.

Sandelin, Karl-Gustav. "The Jesus-Tradition and Idolatry." *NTS* 42 (1996) 412–20.

Sanders, E. P. *Jesus and Judaism*. Philadelphia: Fortress, 1985.

———. *Jewish Law from Jesus to the Mishnah: Five Studies*. Minneapolis: Fortress, 2016.

Scheck, Thomas P. *St. Jerome's Commentaries on Galatians, Titus, and Philemon*. Notre Dame, IN: University of Notre Dame Press, 2010.

Schnackenburg, Rudolf. *The Gospel of Matthew*. Grand Rapids: Eerdmans, 2002.

Scott, Bernard Brandon, and Margaret E. Dean. "A Sound Map of the Sermon on the Mount." In *Treasures New and Old*, edited by David R. Bauer and Mark Allan Powell, 311–78. Atlanta: Scholars, 1996.

Scott, James M., ed. *Exile: A Conversation with N. T. Wright*. Downers Grove: IVP Academic, 2017.

Sigal, Phillip. *The Halakhah of Jesus of Nazareth according to the Gospel of Matthew*. Atlanta: SBL, 2007.

Sim, David C. *Apocalyptic Eschatology in the Gospel of Matthew*. Cambridge: Cambridge University Press, 1996.

———. "Gentiles, God-Fearers and Proselytes." In *Attitudes to Gentiles in Ancient Judaism and Early Christianity*, edited by David C. Sim and James S. McLaren, 9–27. LNTS 499. London: Bloomsbury T. & T. Clark, 2013.

———. *The Gospel of Matthew and Christian Judaism: The History and Social Setting of the Matthean Community*. Edinburgh: T. & T. Clark, 1998.

Slee, Michelle. *The Church in Antioch in the First Century CE: Communion and Conflict*. JSNTSup 244. London: T. & T. Clark, 2003.

Snodgrass, Klyne. "Matthew and the Law." In *Treasures New and Old: Contributions to Matthean Studies*, edited by David R. Bauer and Mark Allan Powell, 99–127. Atlanta: Scholars, 1996.

Stanley, Christopher D. *Arguing with Scripture: The Rhetoric of Quotations in the Letters of Paul*. London: T. & T. Clark, 2004.

Stanton, Graham N. *A Gospel for a New People: Studies in Matthew*. Louisville: WJKP, 1992.

———. "Revisiting Matthew's Communities." In *SBL 1994 Seminar Papers*, edited by E. H. Lovering, 9–23. Atlanta: Scholars, 1994.

Stendahl, Krister. *The School of St. Matthew and Its Use of the Old Testament*. 2nd ed. Ramsey, NJ: Sigler, 1991.

Strecker, Georg. *Der Weg der Gerechtigkeit: Untersuchung zur Theologie des Matthäus*. FRLANT 82. Göttingen: Vandenhoeck & Ruprecht, 1962.

Streeter, Burnett H. *The Primitive Church, Studied with Special Reference to the Origins of the Christian Ministry*. New York: Macmillan, 1929.

Suggs, M. Jack. *Wisdom, Christology, and Law in Matthew's Gospel*. Cambridge: Harvard University Press, 1970.

Talbert, Charles H. *Reading the Sermon on the Mount: Character Formation and Decision Making in Matthew 5–7*. Columbia: University of South Carolina Press, 2004.

Teeter, D. Andrew. "Scribes and Scribalism." In *EDEJ*, 1201–4.

Theophilos, Michael P. *The Abomination of Desolation in Matthew 24:15*. LNTS 437. London: Bloomsbury T. & T. Clark, 2012.

Trilling, Wolfgang. *Das wahre Israel: Studien zur Theologie des Matthäus-Evangeliums*. 3rd ed. SANT 10. Munich: Kösel, 1964.

Turner, David L. *Israel's Last Prophet: Jesus and the Jewish Leaders in Matthew 23*. Minneapolis: Fortress, 2015.

Ulmer, Rivka, and Moshe Ulmer. *Righteous Giving to the Poor: Tzedakah ("Charity") in Classical Rabbinic Judaism, Including a Brief Introduction to Rabbinic Literature*. Piscataway, NJ: Gorgias, 2014.

Urbach, Ephraim E. *The Sages: Their Concepts and Beliefs*. Cambridge: Harvard University Press, 1987.

Vermes, Geza. *Jesus the Jew: A Historian's Reading of the Gospels*. London: Collins, 1973.

Vine, Cedric E. W. *The Audience of Matthew: An Appraisal of the Local Audience Thesis*. LNTS 496. London: Bloomsbury T. & T. Clark, 2014.

———. "Repatriating the Canaanite Woman in the Gospel of Matthew." *AUSS* 58 (2020) 7–32.

Waetjen, Herman C. *Matthew's Theology of Fulfillment, Its Universality and Its Ethnicity: God's New Israel as the Pioneer of God's New Humanity*. London: Bloomsbury T. & T. Clark, 2017.

Wahlen, Clinton L. *Jesus and the Impurity of Spirits in the Synoptic Gospels*. WUNT 2/185. Tübingen: Mohr Siebeck, 2004.

Watts, Rikki E. *Isaiah's New Exodus in Mark*. Grand Rapids: Baker Academic, 2000.

Weaver, Dorothy J. *Matthew's Missionary Discourse: A Literary Critical Analysis*. JSNTSup 38. Sheffield, UK: JSOT Press, 1990.

Wengst, Klaus. "Recht und Gerechtigkeit—Gericht und Erbarmen: Beobachtungen im Matthäusevangelium." *Theologische Quartalschrift* 195 (2015) 119–34.

Westerholm, Stephen. *Jesus and Scribal Authority*. Lund: CWR Gleerup Forlag, 1978.

Westermann, Claus. *Basic Forms of Prophetic Speech*. Louisville: WJKP, 1991.

Wilkins, Michael J. *The Concept of Disciple in Matthew's Gospel As Reflected in the Use of the Term Μαθητής*. NovTSup 59. Leiden: Brill, 1988.

Wilson, Walter T. *Healing in the Gospel of Matthew: Reflections on Method and Ministry*. Minneapolis: Fortress, 2014.

Witherington, Ben. *Jesus the Sage: The Pilgrimage of Wisdom*. Minneapolis: Fortress, 1994.

Wright, N. T. *Jesus and the Victory of God*. London: SPCK, 1996.

———. *The New Testament and the People of God*. London: SPCK, 1992.

Yamasaki, Gary. *John the Baptist in Life and Death: Audience-Oriented Criticism of Matthew's Narrative*. JSNTSup 167. Sheffield, UK: Sheffield Academic, 1998.

Yoder, John Howard. *The Priestly Kingdom: Social Ethics as Gospel*. Notre Dame, IN: University of Notre Dame Press, 1984.

Zehetbauer, Markus. "Befristete Barmherzigkeit: Die scheinbar willkürliche Ungerechtigkeit der Handlungssouveräne in drei großen Parabeln Jesu Mt 18,23–35, Mt 20,1–16 und Lk 15,11–32 und ihre Konsequenzen für die Eschatologie." *MThZ* 64 (2013) 232–51.

Zimmerli, Walther. *Ezekiel 1: A Commentary on the Book of the Prophet Ezekiel, Chapters 1–24*. Hermeneia 26A. Philadelphia: Fortress, 1979.

Zvi, Ehud Ben, and Christoph Levin, eds. *The Concept of Exile in Ancient Israel and Its Historical Contexts*. BZAW 404. Berlin: De Gruyter, 2010.

Author Index

Author Index

Ancient Document Index

NEW TESTAMENT